CULTURAL PROBLEMS IN
WESTERN SOCIETY

Cultural Problems
in Western Society

Sundry writings and occasional lectures

CALVIN G. SEERVELD

Edited by
John H. Kok

DORDT COLLEGE PRESS

Cover design by Willem Hart
Layout by Carla Goslinga

Dordt College Press   www.dordt.edu/dordt_press
498 Fourth Avenue NE
Sioux Center, Iowa, 51250
United States of America

ISBN: 978-1-940567-02-0

Printed in the United States of America

The Library of Congress Cataloguing-in-Publication Data is on file with the Library of Congress, Washington D.C.

Library of Congress Control Number: 2014934732

Cover: The *Nero Malt* artwork by Anselm Kiefer (©1974) puts the question to artists and cultural leaders: what are you painting and saying while cities of our world lie burning on the distant horizon, and fields nearby become blackened furrows?

Table of Contents

Abbreviations used throughout this volume:

NA   Calvin G. Seerveld, *Normative Aesthetics: Sundry writings and occasional lectures*, edited by John H. Kok. Sioux Center, IA: Dordt College Press, 2014.

RA   Calvin G. Seerveld, *Redemptive Art in Society: Sundry writings and occasional lectures*, edited by John H. Kok. Sioux Center, IA: Dordt College Press, 2014.

AH   Calvin G. Seerveld, *Art History Revisited: Sundry writings and occasional lectures*, edited by John H. Kok. Sioux Center, IA: Dordt College Press, 2014.

CE   Calvin G. Seerveld, *Cultural Education and History Writing: Sundry writings and occasional lectures*, edited by John H. Kok. Sioux Center, IA: Dordt College Press, 2014.

BSt   Calvin G. Seerveld, *Biblical Studies and Wisdom for Living: Sundry writings and occasional lectures*, edited by John H. Kok. Sioux Center, IA: Dordt College Press, 2014.

Introduction

My Sensibility is European...

Barbara Carvill

Cultural Problems in Western Society is a collection of eight papers written by Calvin Seerveld most of which were published in the proceedings of the *Symposium of Christian Artists International* (CAI). Seven of the papers Seerveld delivered in person at the symposia held in the Netherlands in Doorn. These yearly events were convened by the *Christelijke Nederlands Vakverbond* (CNV), under the leadership of Leen La Rivière, and financially supported by the European Commission and the EZA (*Europäisches Zentrum für Arbeitnehmerfragen/European Centre for Workers' Questions*). It might seem odd to Americans that performing artists and government and union delegates would gather each year for a conference around a common theme, and it might seem even stranger that a labor union would invite a Christian philosopher to be the plenary speaker at its annual conference; nevertheless, since 1991 the CAI symposia have been bringing together

> leaders from trade unions, Christian political parties and associated arts organisations to discuss topics such as European culture, the role of Christian artists and, in view of the growing unification of Europe, the possibility and desirability of a common, concerted policy and support for the arts at a European level.[1]

The idea for such annual conferences originated in 1992 with the Treaty of Maastricht in which it was first mandated that the arts and culture should play a fundamental role in the process of European integration and in the promotion of European citizenship. These conferences provided Calvin Seerveld a fitting context to share insights he thought about, taught, and published throughout his career.

In 1997, a time before the actual establishment of the Eurozone,

---

1   Quoted from Susan Snell's history of the Symposium at http://www.christianartists. org/node/118

Seerveld gave the first of his lectures in Doorn. The last he presented in 2010 just as Europe was experiencing a deep financial debt crisis, a time during which the wisdom of an economic union for Europe was seriously questioned and the Eurozone itself was facing the threat of collapse. What Calvin Seerveld presented over thirteen years in these eight papers remains pertinent for the second decade of the 21st century. Europe's thorny problems, such as the treatment and place of minorities, the problematic practice of Enlightenment tolerance, or the question of Europe's cultural identity are no less significant now than they were at the time that Seerveld first raised them in the papers he submitted to the conference at its annual events.

One might ask what Calvin Seerveld, born in the United States and now a Canadian citizen living in Toronto, could have to say about the problems of present-day Europe and its artists. The answer is simple. The author thinks of himself as European. His "sensibility is European" (46), he says, "despite my New York birth and Canadian citizenship" (133). Without a doubt, Seerveld's training in theology, art history, and philosophy during his years in Switzerland, Italy, and the Netherlands give strong backing to his claim. His vision is grounded in the Reformation and nurtured in the Kuyperian tradition first developed in the Netherlands. In addition, Calvin Seerveld has a stellar command of European languages. All these elements of his personal experience and his professional career are testimony to the fact that his European sensibilities run deep. He is an erudite son of Europe, with a remarkable bent towards Germanic scholarly *Gründlichkeit*, while embracing, as he states, both the miseries and the glories of Europe's rich heritage ("both Acropolis and Auschwitz" 133).

As the invited plenary speaker for the Symposium of Christian Artists, Calvin Seerveld was asked to address a theme selected each year by the CAI for the symposium. This theme often dovetailed with the topic of the "European Year" as designated by the European Parliament and the member states of the European Union from which financial support for the CAI conferences was being received. For instance, during the "European Year against Racism and Xenophobia" in 1997, Calvin Seerveld gave the first lecture in this volume on "Minorities and Xenophilia." In 2006, the Symposium chose as its topic "Gender Equality, Gender and Work in the Cultural Sector." In this instance the plenary paper reaches far beyond the European context to explore origins of and responses to women's issues worldwide. For the 2008 "European Year of Intercultural Dialogue," the symposium in Doorn chose as its conference theme "Social Dialogue about Cultural Diversity," which topic Seerveld addressed in his seventh lecture (129f.). 2010 was the "European Year for Combating Poverty and Social Exclusion," reformulated for the 2010 CAI symposium as "Social Dialogue about more and better Jobs in the Cultural Sector." This is the subject Seerveld explores in the last chapter of this book.

With each lecture, Calvin Seerveld spoke to the predetermined topic while at the same time deftly laying out his Christian vision. On the one hand the topics Seerveld addresses are remarkable for their broad range. Each of the eight is well documented and carefully researched, a work of scholarly expertise in its own right. In view of this it is even more remarkable that the addresses to the CAI and EZA delegates all center around a single crucial question: How can Christian artists play a faithfull redemptive role on the European stage of God's *theatrum mundi?*

Seerveld's responses to this question are nuanced and complex. With each new lecture he approaches the subject from different angles and touches on new foci. He explores the problem of minorities, of tolerance, of European cultural diversity and identity. He puts forward suggestions for revitalizing the Christian cultural heritage in Europe. In his review of the book *De Kunst van het Leven,* edited by Jan Peter Balkenende (former Prime Minister of the Netherlands), Prof. Roel Kuiper (member of the Dutch Senate), and Leen La Rivière, he calls for a "new" European Christian art "that is compassionate, troubled, healing" (40).

The formulation of the official themes designated for each year by the organization did not demand a distinctly Christian and biblically grounded treatment. The depth of insight with which Seerveld analyzes Europe's problems is a scholarly and thorough response to the call for papers. Even more remarkable than the professional expertise of his response is his prophetic courage in speaking with strong biblical convictions to a very mixed audience of Christian and post-Christian Europeans. Seerveld calls on Christian artists to "take fresh root in the biblically christian source of the rich cultural heritage of Europe" (141), to make "holy spirited art aware of sin yet bearing glimmers of hope fit for the streets, the cabaret, the theatre, hospitals, airports, mall, and art gallery . . . showing love to their neighbor" (40), and to provide "imaginative manna." With a memorable Seerveldian coinage, he calls on these artists to be a redemptive "glocal saltlick" in the "patchwork quilt of Europe" (151).

All of Calvin Seerveld's lectures contain similar elements that in each new instance he elaborates with a fresh approach to the changing themes of the annual conference. First, they all explore the unfavorable conditions in which European society and its Christian artists find themselves today. To name just a few: the erosion of the Judeo-Christian ethos with the consequent loss of a biblical horizon, the destructive effects of the supra-national commercial empire that the global market has created, and the hedonistic materialism that has commercialized all of culture so that the arts become artifacts reduced to mere market commodities.

A second element in each lecture is a condensed historical overview that Calvin Seerveld sketches for his audience. He masterfully locates current quandaries in the large time frame stretching from Ancient Greece, across the medieval period, the Renaissance, the Enlightenment, Romanticism, and 20th century isms, and leading to the present. These well-researched thumbnail accounts invite his artist and labor audiences as well as the readers of this volume to be "critically history-wise" (4). We find, for instance, historical sketches of the idea of tolerance, of Europe as a cultural entity, of the suppression of women, and of the social and economic situation of artisans and artists.

A third and most significant element of Calvin Seerveld's papers introduces normative alternatives that are biblically oriented. He posits "enduring norms anew for lives today" (140). God-ordained societal structures are fleshed out as Seerveld reminds his audience how everybody including the artist is embedded in them. He clarifies what it means to heed God's command of loving our neighbors. In the pastoral part of his papers, Seerveld draws on Kuyperian insights to describe just and proper roles as well as limits for the state, church, labor unions, and other societal associations. He then challenges artists to fulfill their calling in all of these places by offering "imaginative manna" to fellow citizens.

A fourth element of Calvin Seerveld's lectures is the inclusion of artwork mostly by 20th century or contemporary artists. Their work exemplifies the kind of redemptive, modern, Christian art Seerveld is advocating. With pithy verbal strokes he opens the eyes of his audience to encourage a deeper look into these works. The choice of pieces reveals Seerveld's "glocal" orientation. He presents the works of more or less "local" European artists from Spain, the Netherlands, the United Kingdom, and Sweden. He also includes local artists from far away corners of the globe such as South Africa or Australia.

Those upon whom Calvin Seerveld calls to illustrate his points about the role of the artist are often ones whose work does not get exposure in secular galleries or secular media. Yet for Seerveld they deserve as much attention as the work of globally renowned figures like Henry Moore, Ernst Barlach, Ossip Zadkine, Käthe Kollwitz, or Anselm Kiefer.

Seerveld asserts that the works of the lesser known artists he showcases in his lectures exemplify the calling of Christian art, to "reenchant the unimaginative neighbor to become alive to the crevices of surprises in God's world" (80), or to make "art that is interculturally fertile, not parochial, and breathes a sure spirit of winsome certainty on the abiding goodness of creation, despite the horror we humans often make of it" (50).

Cultural Problems in Western Society offers a collection of papers, but in a delightful way it reads like a coherent book of eight engaging chapters in which the author gives insight, direction, and guidance to a small group of Christian artists in Europe. Calvin Seerveld models what he preaches. Based on his translation of Isaiah 54:1–3 (35–36), the author tells artists: "enlarge the tented terrain where you cultivate things and culture the next generation; also pound the tent stakes of your dwelling more firmly deep into the ground the LORD God provides. . . know surely your identity as a faith-community, so you can be more hospitable to strangers. . . ."

Deeply rooted and staked in biblical wisdom and in Jesus Christ, Seerveld has erected a very wide and sturdy tent for European artists both present and future. It is a tent to which Christian artists, sojourners as well as strangers, believers as well as unbelievers, are welcomed to find refreshment, encouragement, and inspiration.

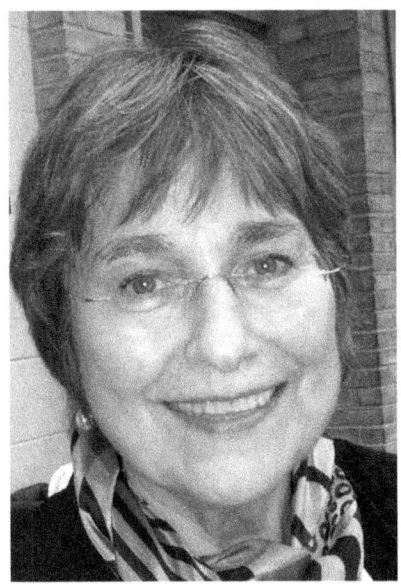

Barbara Carvill
Professor Emerita of German
Calvin College

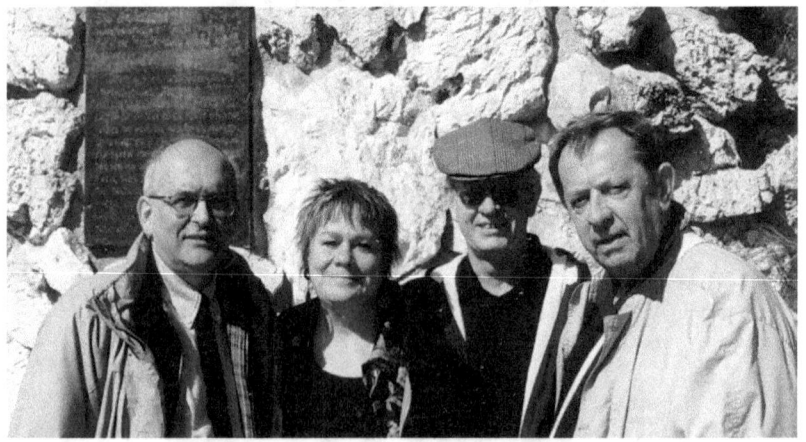

Judges for the worldwide young artists' competition organized by the Hellenic Scripture Union to accompany the Olympic Games in Athens: Peter S. Smith (UK), Britt Wikström (Netherlands), Dirk van der Berg (South Africa), Calvin Seerveld (Canada), missing from photo (Filimon Kaloterakis (Greece) in Kifissia/Athens, 2004

MINORITIES AND XENOPHILIA

Since the kinds of minorities in society are so different—disadvantaged ethnic peoples, mentally impaired or physically handicapped persons, the chronically unemployed and poor folk in many lands, those abused by militant political power mongers, and, not to forget, true disciples of Jesus Christ (they're also a minority in God's world!)—and because the snarl of problems that surround the refugees and frustrated outcasts both within European society and elsewhere on the globe is so complicated, let me first tell you a true story with a story in it.

> Once upon a time a trained lawyer stood up to put Jesus to a test and said, "Rabbi, what must I have done to inherit eternal life?"
> Jesus said to that lawyer, "What is written in the law? How do you read it?"
> The lawyer promptly answered out loud: "Love the LORD your God out of your whole heart, with your entire soul, in the whole of your strength, and with all your mind; and love your neighbor as yourself."
> Jesus said to the trained lawyer, "You have answered correctly. Go do it and you shall live."
> But the lawyer who wanted to show up as being righteous, said to Jesus, "And who is my neighbor?" [It was a controversy of the day whether Gentiles were "neighbors" to believing Jews, whether convicted criminals, heretics, habitual sinners were "neighbors"—what are the limits to "neighbors" out there?]
>
> Catching the drift of his remark Jesus answered with a story:
>
> A certain man was going from Jerusalem down to Jericho and he happened to meet up with bandits who stripped him of clothes, beat him, badly, and took off leaving the fellow behind half-dead.

Complete text of what was spoken on 21 August 1997 at the Christian Artists Symposium sponsored by the European Union, Doorn, Netherlands. A shorter version was published in Proceedings of the Seventh Symposium on the Role of the Arts in a Europe on the way to Integration (Rotterdam: International Christian Artists Seminar sponsored by the European Union, 1997), 38–43.

> It just happened that some priest or other was traveling on that road, and seeing the half-dead fellow, passed by on the other side. And—what do you now—a Levite coming to the place and seeing the half-dead fellow did the same thing, passed by on the other side.
>
> A certain Samaritan who was going on a journey came to where the half-dead fellow lay and seeing him was filled with tenderness. The Samaritan went to the fellow, bound up his wounds (τραυματα), pouring on olive oil and wine. Then the Samaritan placed the fellow on his own mule and brought him to an inn, and self took care of him.
>
> On the next day the Samaritan came up with two denarii [enough cash to cover more than a month's lodging], gave them to the innkeeper and said, "Take good care of the fellow. Whatever extra you spend, I'll reimburse you when I return."
>
> "Which of these three seems to you to have been neighbor to the one got caught in the circumstances of bandits?"
>
> The lawyer said, "The one who showed mercy to the fellow."
>
> So Jesus said to the trained lawyer, "You too go on a journey, and do likewise." (Luke 10:25–37)

By retelling this biblical true story I don't mean to imply that the Red Cross (the Red Crescent) is "the answer" to Turkish *Gastarbeiter* in Germany who cannot become German citizens or for the Vietnamese boat-people held in barbed-wire refugee camps outside rich Hong Kong. "The Good Samaritan" is not the sum of what civil society has to say to drug companies with their patents about thalidomide victims who have flippers for arms. But it's surprising how a biblical orientation can cut through mounds of analytic palaver, evasive bureaucratic maneuvers, pious alibis, and give sound direction for understanding the stubborn knots of societal injustice and neglect at hand: on your journey to wherever it be, act with tenderness, (compassionately) toward your neighbor.

I should like to try to order now our thinking through the structural, institutional problems of minorities on our hands in terms of (1) ethnic cultural realities, (2) poverty and abuse, and (3) the politically vulnerable and violated. Then I should like to show you what artists can do/have done/are called to do in responding to the plight of this confusing variety of oppressed humans and us overlords. But I do not want to do this as a trained armchair philosopher who knows all the correct answers yet lacks compassion on the journey for the outcasts who complicate my way. So before I spell out my thoughts and slides of artworks for your discussion let me briefly disclose my working presuppositions.

Working presuppositions.

(1) There is no one grand solution to the miseries "minorities" experience.

Master plans for a happy society from Plato's *Politeia* to Campanella's *Città del Sole* to Thomas More's *Utopia* to Brazil's *Brasília* have been the well-intentioned dreams of "intellectuals" but in fact have an impractical nightmarish side. Any simplified solution to complex historical problems is tyrannical. "Final solutions" are always bad because they usually are disembodied schemes, and today they come with a Pragmatistic "fixit" mentality, something you do to machines. But society is not a machine: persecuted people suffer real pain; criminality is never "fixed" by rationality; and industrialized acid rain does not go through customs at the border between the USA and Canada.

So I assume there is no single "fix" for the "have-nots" among us humans, whether it be those who have not work or have not a country, have not a living cultural tradition, or have not faith.

(2) To begin to have wrongs in society righted, the history-deep, dated location of the problem must be understood and respected. Although 1997 Africa is not 1967 North America is not 1937 Europe is not 1907 Indonesia, sins of one generation can fester on for three or four more generations.

To have European journalists not misread the 1994 uprising in Chiapas, Mexico, as a ragtag band of masked insurrectionists stupidly taking on armed government troops, they would need to know that the land reform promised the peasants and legally enacted after the 1911 revolution was never carried out in Chiapas; and without land, Ch'ol, Tzeltal, and Tzotzil Indians have to leave their villages, sever ancestral ties, lose their languages to stay alive with dislocated work that begins the process of *mestizaje* ("westernization"), *un génocide en douce.*

Aware of the malaise that deracination of Western culture is bringing to the fore, Allan Bloom (*The Closing of the American Mind*, 1981) seems not to know that Matthew Arnold's canon for civilization has historically failed the test: education does not necessarily make people better; increased secularization of our old-fashioned christianized Humanism has allowed a quick succession of horrible world wars; higher education can simply lead to more refined torture, like forcing Beethoven's *Eroica* symphony to be played as Jews are marched off in style to the gas chambers.

That is, revolution is wrong and schooling in literature is sound—as generalizations—but historical contexts bring significant differences to bear on evils, which must be recognized if corrections are not just going to introduce new oppressions. So I assume that to be critically history-wise is a prerequisite for a generation to be gingerly finding its way out of dead-ends—not forgetting to also look at history with the eyes of the defeated ones.

(3) Because we (rich Christians—you are rich in God's eyes if you have food and drink, wear clothes, and have a safe place to sleep, see 1 Timothy 6:17–19) are part of the problems connected to powerless, disadvantaged minorities, our communal task lies in responding to what is historically given by setting in process a more normative matrix for doing what is just in the limited societal sector where you have a measure of authority.

No human should try to bring in the millennium. That's God's prerogative (see Revelation 21:1–4). Our generation does not even have to get everything right—I learned that long ago from Abraham Kuyper: since God is faithful throughout the generations, our responsibility is limited, like that of a husbandman or a midwife only to till the ground and bring to birth an economic practice, a philosophical theory, artistic fruits of one's womb, political deeds—whatever—that shall give a more redemptive lease on cultural life, God willing, to the next generation than what we historically inherited and began with.

Sometimes one needs to take a judicious step in faith—I learned this from Bob Goudzwaard—and then God opens up new possibilities for shalom you couldn't see before you took the first step. For example, right now nobody is able to get out of the mess of "third-world" countries' impossible debt load; but if somebody could get key financiers of the World Bank simply to recognize that their very bank policies are part of the problem, who knows what might not possibly happen for good?

We are not to be *bricoleurs*, doing helter-skelter patchwork from grab-bags of discarded ideas. I just assume that the results from any faithful little steps we take will be modest, also thanks more to God's holy spirited blessing than to our own grubby efforts.

Working definition of minority

By "minority" I understand a group of people whose identity is challenged by those who are stronger; the "minority" experiences great difficulty or inability freely to make their own different way in society at large.

Jehovah's Witnesses and covens of Wicca witches are faith minorities in most countries. Single mothers in Detroit furnace-basement apartments and Mexican "wet-back" migrant farm laborers in Texas are economic minorities there. The many, many Vietnamese fugitives and refugees from South American countries in Canada are political minorities who have had to flee their country on pain of death. Japanese sushi bars, Italian pasta meals, French wine cuisine, Indonesian *rijsttafel,* exemplify ethnic cultural minorities' foods outside their home base.

On this definition hemophiliacs, lesbians, intellectuals, and women are minorities, of quite different sorts, in many societies around the world. And it is important, I think, to distinguish the kinds of minorities there be, which actually are usually co-present and superimposed, because people are not above demanding political minority status to gain economic advantage, or use cultural minority difference to gain power in affairs of an exclusivist faith. Fudging minority boundaries brings trouble over and above the ordeal of interacting with minorities themselves whose diversity from what is dominant seems to unsettle lives.

Experience of ethnic cultural minority color
It is ethnic minorities that seem to me to be the most malleable among minority kinds and open to sharing with one another their different cultural gifts. Chinese folklore, Grimm's *Märchen,* aboriginal Northwest Canadian coastal Indian drum music, traditional British breakfasts, Schwytzer tüütsch conversational language, Yoruban ceremonial masks, Australian accents, an Inuit sweat lodge, the custom of parentally arranged marriage in India, do not seem so threatening to those for whom such practices are strange because your ethnic coloring does not need to adopt such cultural modes, although you may pick and choose to synthesize certain new features into your own ethnic repertoire. Here is a carnival opportunity for humans to bewonder and joy in the rainbow diversity of our visible ethnic minority riches.

Unfortunately the ethnic minority well of fresh waters has been historically poisoned in the last fifteen generations by colonizing, mainly European, empire-building powers.

The Spanish conquistadors not only plundered Inca gold but annihilated the militarist Aztec culture in South America as Spanish priests annexed the worship of the indigenous peoples. Belgium and French mercantilist conquest of the Congo and Mid-Western Africa territories, mixed with medical missionaries throughout the continent, always combined exploitation of natural resources and, wittingly or not (along with charitably combatting disease), terrible dislocation of tribal cultures. Nigerian Chinua Achebe's novels (e.g., *Things Fall Apart,* 1958, *No Longer at Ease,* 1960) movingly lament this inevitable overpowering of the local "heathen" ways of being human by the mechanized, efficient white man's "standard of living." Frantz Fanon's *Les Damnés de la Terre* (1961), however, curses the imprint of subjugated inferiority on native black African cultures, and counseled a return to violence in order to eradicate the stigma and be able to flower as a people in their own civilized cultural right.

When you think about it, how British explorers brought back potatoes and tobacco leaves and "noble savages" from the New World to show off at the court of his Majesty George III in England, like living wax museum exhibits, the imperial gall of it all seems striking, no matter how benevolently it was intended. Of course, we tourists with camera often carry on similarly, in diluted fashion, by exoticizing natives of Thailand or "doing Tibet" to gain wisdom. How can we who command technology and money ever be humble enough to realize we *kabluna* (the Inuit word for us "whitened faces") are ourselves strange to other cultures and not necessarily the norm? To have to eat with clumsy metal forks and knives seems almost "savage" to those who delicately pick up morsels of food with slips of wood or ivory.

The current debate on "post-colonial" *modi vivendi* and an almost ideological affirmation of multiculturalism skews the problem of interfacing ethnic minorities a different, decentering way: since the historical Christian and also Marxist premillennial meta-narratives are now generally suspect in educated circles, and the dominant Western cultural mold perhaps no longer holds, it is every migratory ethnic culture for itself.

The acclaimed Kenyan novelist Ngũgĩ wa Thiong'o decided in his jail cell in 1977 henceforth to write novels only in the Gĩkũyũ language. In 1986 he also wrote his last English essay, *Decolonising the Mind*, "From now on it is Gikuyu and Kiswahili all the way" (xiv) to service his people's deep-structural need for a self-respecting cultural identity and, along with world literature in translation, try to decenter from the Kenyan literary educational program stalwart pillars in the schools like Matthew Arnold, T.S. Eliot, and F.R. Leavis (90, 98–101).

Or suppose you are faced with this: "Who are you Canadian medical males to tell us Somalian women we may not perform clitoridectomies or infibulation [the drastic "Pharonic" circumcision that cuts off virtually all the external female genitalia] of our pubescent girls! This is an important traditional custom of our Somali people. You don't outlaw Jewish male circumcision, do you?"

That is, the glory of ethnicity can become touchy and ugly as ethnocentricity, where cultural relativity is absolute, untouchable, and the anodyne cliché of "We should all be multicultural" faces its échec in a common society.

A further difficulty is that within every ethnic minority there are micro-minorities, just as within the Dutch language there are dialects— Gronings, Zeeuws, Jordaans, even the paired language of Fries. Who is the spokesperson for the Dutch Language? For the large ethnic Somali community in Ontario?

The key point I want to make here is that a person's ethnic cultural minority colorfulness does not define you as a human. One's ethnic cultural inheritance, significantly embodied in one's mother tongue you might say, is a valuable feature of your hybrid identity. But for someone to say, "There goes a Dutchie," "That's a Somalian woman for you," "It's a dead white male," as if that simple ethnic minority designation gets at the crux of somebody's being there is merely to stereotype another person from a distance. Such stereotyping is a hateful act of hasty prejudice that tends to wall in the parochial judgmental person with ghetto mentality and perpetuate cultural ignorance and war.

What our society needs instead is for ethnic peoplehoods to feel secure enough to share their cultural gifts without fear or insistence they be adapted. Maybe Europeans could join the exercise and give evidence of repentant deed for past, repressive cultural measures by learning a non-Western language or non-Western artform—just a suggestion—precisely of an ethnic culture you have disparaged, since a strange language carries a whole different way of looking at things that one's own language may overlook, and to learn a different language is an act of love. Offended ethnicities throughout the world could perhaps forego anathemas and reach out to us Western ethnics who are ashamed of our deteriorated culture so replete with *Face/Off* rapacity and triviality and teach us the strengths of "Oriental" friendship or "African" tenderness.

There are great riches waiting to be mutually discovered, like the astonishing surprise I experienced less than a year ago in an expensive Greek nightclub in Thessaloniki around 1:00 AM on a Saturday night/ Sunday morning, when a second-generation gypsy balladeer Alexandros Chatzés did a hard rock rap number with 1 Corinthians 13 as text! I didn't get all the Greek, but I heard *agape*-love celebrated with a terrible, passionate biblical authenticity I'll never forget: it was a gutty, angry, selfless, hurt tough love shouted-sung hammer blow after hammer blow—

Love is patient! Love is kind! Love is not rude!
Love does not insist! Is not resentful!

Agape bears all things! believes all things!
hopes all things! endures all things!

It was a battered, homeless, truly gypsy cry of offended love that would go gently to the death for a friend, so help you, the grace of God!

I could sum up my point on this first kind of minority with the old nursery song you may know too:

Jesus loves the ethnic stranger,
all the cultures of the world;
red and yellow, black, gypsy, and white,
they are precious in God's sight.
Jesus loves your ethnic neighbor in the world.

My leading idea is that if we could determinedly act out cross-cultural, inter-ethnic surprises at the level of language, artistry, and domestic practices, exchange gifts of food and song, tears and hopes, then there might be an improved world climate for our grappling with the harder, different minority problems of intractable poverty and a veritable murderous political racism. Since I want to have time to show you with images how talking over the fence does not erase boundaries but can encourage minorities to be themselves together, my remarks on the following two minorities shall be more brief than they deserve.

Plight of the minority poor, impaired, diseased, or abused

Carlyle tells the story of a rich man in an industrial town who would offer no help to a poor widow who lived on the other side of the town's tracks, "I have nothing to do with her." That widow contacted typhoid fever that spread back over the tracks into the town and killed the rich man in his mansion. It appears that they did belong together in the human race.

When Jesus told his ungenerous disciples, "The poor you will always have with you," it was an accusation, not a statement of fact (John 12:1–8), because the Older Testament Law taught God's people that there would be no poor among them if those who had enough opened their hand to the needy in the land (Deuteronomy 15:1–11).

Peculiar about the minority of needy people in society, no matter the reason for their destitution, and whether it be a minority grouped by ill health or lack of sustenance to stay alive: peculiar about this minority of the weak is that they cannot shift for themselves. That's why Liberalist democracies are embarrassed, since their programs normally operate on the assumption that self-sufficient adults are available to pursue life, liberty, and prosperity. There's no place for children, who have been abused, long-term invalids who were not "workmen" (able to receive industry-insured accident compensation). The best a secularist society can do for anonymous alcoholics, drug addicted persons, mentally disabled or homeless people, is to run humanitarian programs with United Front drives and Kiwanis or Rotary Club involvement, and think of it all as the domain of tax-deductible charity, something churches and synagogues still do well.

And it is good to have people who will volunteer to visit the sick, clothe the naked in disaster relief, feed the hungry, and correct ignorance on hygiene, since we have God's word for it, the handicapped and destitute are not so much a social headache as an opportunity to meet Christ in person! (Matthew 25:31–46).

When it comes not to sickness but to idleness, chronic unemployment—no work available for willing hands—the ensuing despair in many countries of the unsuspecting "new poor," and even famine from central Africa to North Korea (while grain is being stockpiled in North America), the systemic evil in our powerful monopolistic capitalist economic setup shows through. It's almost as if we rich economies practice the kiss of Midas: to whichever poor economy we give massive bank development loans in American dollars, Deutsche mark or Japanese yen, the weak economic receivers become worse off in quality of life with depleted natural resources, surplus high-tech machinery inappropriate to local labor-intensive needs, a few profiteering company officials, and the rest stymied by products they covet but cannot buy.

Even among "Western" economies, when McDonalds, Microsoft, or Starbucks comes to town, non-chain food servers, even the Macintosh Apple computer company, mom-and-pop coffee shops wobble and tend to close down. The survival-of-the-fittest sting in the gospel of Democratic Competition we preach is precisely why the Russian people since 1992, euphoric about their imminent good fortune to be free from a totalitarian tyranny, are so depressed, because Free Market reform does not let everybody live happily ever after. Instead, the shadow economy grows (which is organized stealing or bartering self-defense, depending on your income point-of-view).

One's job does not define your humanity any more than does your ethnicity, but the laboring poor—menial service jobs in cities, artists who are not superstars, pick-up/layoff agricultural harvesting help—as well as the "new poor" and drifters who lack the basics of food and habitat are pinned down to the economic survival of their lives, much as cancer (when it's got you) reduces your whole life to a vomiting, hairless, radiated survival.

What normative steps could one take to shift the burden of survival off the backs of the minority poor?

There needs to come a change in the consciousness of the rich. (Remember, everybody with food, drink, clothes, and a safe place to sleep is rich, I said, and if you have a credit card, including an outstanding debt due, you are very rich.) We need to be converted from the omnivorous principality of Consumption. Television advertisements, like TB bacilli, make a person consumptive: one is driven always to want more; never is enough enough. This worldwide Consumerist epidemic is tied to the greedy policy that profit is the top line of a business, as well, as the bottom line.

I know a professor who told his university he was paid too much; he wanted only a half-salary and a university commitment to pay his travel costs occasionally to hard-up foreign universities where he would teach short courses for free. Maybe certain mega-corporation CEO's and lawyers could follow suit. It might start a snowball effect so that transnational corporations, instead of pushing governments around, might even forgive! foreign distributors in shaky economies some of their debt—banks I'm told know how to write down their "bad" debts all the time. . . .

A christian labor union like the one in Canada translates its concern for a just wage (in tandem with inflation) rather than a philosophy of "Gimmie more" into having an open-shop policy. When the Christian Labour Association of Canada unionizes a given company's labor force it will bargain co-determiningly rather than adversarially for a just wage for all the workers whether or not a worker joins the CLAC and pays dues— a labor union is a voluntary communal organization and has no right to exclude anybody skilled to work from doing the job. So the CLAC is hated both by coercive (closed shop) secular unions and by union-unfriendly employers; but the CLAC has broken the neck of greed and works with principles of thrift and generosity.

A few people I know who arrange meals, find jobs, talk with the police in the name of Christ as an arm of the church among the current generation of hapless First Nations Indians of Canada off the reserves took the drastic normative step some time ago of ending handouts and the victim-dependency cycle. It took some of the natives a shocked long time to realize they were being asked to volunteer their services at the communal drop-in center and that only a few with skills (secretaries, instructors) would be on a payroll; but the change in communal spirit and self-respect at the center became exhilarating. Oftentimes, it is my experience, showing genuine deference to those who are down-and-out and providing a few means for the weak to make themselves useful: such a move restores a sense of humanity much more than to dispense cold-blooded money.

As for the ill: my wife has the uncommon patience to visit and listen to the same decrepit elderly persons a couple afternoons practically every week for more than four years, to read stories to a fellow bed-ridden with MS, simply to hear a woman with Alzheimer's disease chat disconnect-edly as she packs and unpacks her belongings in cardboard boxes as if she has to go somewhere—

I know how the DDR (Deutsche Demokratische Republik) edu-cational policy affected vocational orientation when Russian was made the first required second language (only after you took Russian in East-German schools could you study English or French). I wonder what kind of difference it would make for the minority of the ill in society if at least "christian" schools generally promoted as vocation not com-puter technology (where the money is) but nursing, teaching, social-care giving as occupations where you would daily meet Jesus in the faces of AIDS patients, truculent ignorance, disoriented helplessness. It would be quite a shock for youth raised in our sanctimonious Darwinian society to suppose that Jesus was not a successful entrepreneur who "gets things done" and then presents a double tithe in church on Sunday (see Luke 18:10–14); but such an imaginative shock of recognizing who the poor are might be a Good Samaritan move.

Minorities confronting racist and religion-persecuting hatred
Any minority athwart political governance is in special trouble, because nation states police conformance to their law by exercising "the power of the sword" as it has been called. If you are found to be at odds with Cuban or Chinese official platforms, you could be imprisoned or possi-bly executed. Simply by being a confessing Christian in the Sudan, Iran, Saudi Arabia, or Pakistan, before a Fundamentalist Muslim reading of Shari'a law you are liable to death—a form of "faith cleansing" you might say (Marshall, 15–39).

As the past dominant worldview of christianized Humanism be-comes more and more secularized to a version of hedonistic Materialism (which always foments fragmentation of culture and any order), and as our world shrinks into a global high-rise (McLuhan's "global village" is out of date), there will be more and more political and faith refugees fleeing to Europe and North America claiming asylum under Article 13 of the Geneva Convention regarding the Status of Refugees. Resentment of the inundated nationals toward these strangers who it is thought tend to depreciate our standard of living becomes palpable in "America First!" and repressive European country regulations for acquiring immigrant citizenship. This growing minority of refugees fleeing intolerable intimidation and atrocities, who are caught in the cracks between countries, exacerbates old hostilities and enflames new ones, as the merciless horrors of Orthodox Serbs, Bosnian Muslims, and Croats in the desolated, former Yugoslavia remind us daily.

I would prefer to put my hand over my mouth here lest I play the trained lawyer who wanted to appear to be righteous to the crowd attending Jesus. But let me dare say the following, stammering a little: the Enlightenment cosmopolitan idea (John Locke, Montesquieu, philosophe Voltaire) that a nation is a consensus of rational individuals who for common good decide to be citizens of a parliamentary government over a specific territory is the major European and North American inheritance on what the "state" means. There is also a "Romantic" Idealist conception of nation promoted by Herder among others of a Folk, like an extended blood-related family speaking the same language, that has a shrouded mythical past and future destiny to be freely a great and superior people.

When a political minority (whether refugees, natives to the land territory, or a relatively independent entity) has the Folk idea of peoplehood and senses it is being absorbed by the majority practice with the "common denominator" and "equal rights" idea of a nation-state—one man or woman one vote—you have a recipe for permanent trouble, especially if all the parties are armed with weapons. Some folks do not want to be assimilated into a nondescript legalized union where you have to abide by the tyranny of a nondescript majority.

It does not help anybody out of the trouble to call the Romantic Nationalists and their opponents racist, and refer to Shi'ite Muslim Fundamentalists as Fascist fanatics, or Israel's Zionist policies toward Palestinians on the Arab land of Palestine as both—though the judgments, I think, are correct: it were better if we could appreciate the purist fear of peoples to be absorbed by the Secularist power hidden within the Western commercialistic/Pragmatistic Neocolonialism that is blanketing the earth. Many Americans are often uncritical of the fact that their melting pot creed of *e pluribus unum* bespeaks hegemony because *unum* covertly means "American," and not everybody in the world wants to be "Americanized." And not everybody or every people can accept the condition of political Secularism that expects a person to admit that one's ultimate faith-commitment to Allah or Jesus Christ is only a private opinion and such a faith stance should not be at work in the public arena shaping political transactions.

Is the only alternative to such pseudo-tolerant Democratism, however, acts like Iran's Ayatollah Khomeini's issuing a worldwide Muslin *fatwah* that anybody anywhere may kill with impunity the apostate author Salman Rushdie? Are there no primordial human rights like safety of life, absence of torture, due process of law (and all the items spelled out in the *Universal Declaration of Human Rights* adopted by the General Assembly of the United Nations, 10 December 1948) that must hold even for those who are undemocratic or even deny the existence of sin?

Yes. But human terrorists act otherwise, and political demagogues with guns abrogate fundamental human rights and life, and different nations draw different lines on which important human liberties can be suspended when and how. Also, political interests often overrun justice, so with a show of righteousness Reagan's government blockaded Nicaraguan ports with mines and gunboats for an embargo (1983–85), or you begin building houses anyhow at Har Homa. And there are many legitimate hard calls: Quebec Bill 101 forbids francophone families and new immigrants from sending their children to English-language schools but allows Anglophones to do so, yet all commercial signs in businesses in Montréal may only be in the French language; the Newfoundland provincial government of Canada has been busy (1997) wresting schools away from "church control" and turning them into institutions for state dictation (replaying backwards the old Dutch *schoolstrijd*), forgetting that Article 26 of the *United Nations' Declaration of Human Rights* says "Parents have a prior right to choose the kind of education that shall be given to their children." So the struggles of multiple minorities within a single political body go on and on. Also, if a government in power be corrupt, it becomes very messy indeed to sort out legal political action from criminal deeds.

I offer two thoughts: (1) Sovereign state power structurally also has limitations (Revelation 13 follows Romans 13); so it would seem wise to me always to work toward restraining the power that persons in political office have the authority to exercise. Internal to political government that means what Leen La Rivière and others refer to as the principle of subsidiarity: "higher levels of government should only do that which cannot be done by the citizens of lower levels of government" (69–72, 169–74). As for the power a nation readies to use toward those external to its boundaries: one should maintain only defensive forces, this non-militarist says, and not build up a weapons capability to attack others. It is normative, as I understand it, that the Swiss are trained to protect only the terrain of their resident canton in that country.

I realize nobody can be authorized to enforce such a matter, but I am trying to formulate a norm. A political policy aimed at "defensive power only" would support continued disarmament of nuclear weapons, which are invented to cause indiscriminate mass destruction, and would give top priority to stopping the massive export trade in heavy weapons, which Western countries quietly perpetrate and Eastern European countries do because it is the best way to get "hard currency." If the most powerful nation states could somehow curtail this madness, it seems to me it would be a small positive step toward having nations gain other nations' wary trust.

Movement toward a politically confederated European Community of member states—not NATO alliance and beyond an economic Common Market—would also be in line with an attempt to limit military strength to defense rather than aggrandizement. But having read a little about how difficult it was for Norway and Sweden to separate peacefully as nations, I have no illusions about how incredibly complicated it will be to unite politically the historic, different nations of Europe into a peaceable realm. If the (Canadian) mosaic pattern of *unitas in pluribus*, rather than the melting pot dynamic, could be the guideline, maybe then there would be political hope also for just-doing toward the multiple minorities among us.

(2) The peculiar glory and scandal of biblically christian just-doing among minorities in the political sphere will be its firm gentleness and spirit of going the extra mile, also for those who may be enemies! (Matthew 5:38–48).

I am not talking appeasement of injustice, but I do propose a political just-doing that has a different quality than the "justice" that demands, "I want my pound of flesh!" "Reverse discrimination," which would give expropriated indigenous peoples punitive damages as well as market value for land that was stolen from them centuries ago, leaving them enslaved to poverty for generations, would be "christian" just-doing.

The unprecedented provisions of the South African "Truth and Reconciliation Commission" set up to deal with apartheid atrocities and counter-apartheid wrongs that can never be made right is an incredible attempt suffused by an appeal to the christian reality of forgiveness and the communal African orientation of *ubuntu*, compassion for the neighbor's vulnerable humanity: it is a redemptive attempt to do restorative justice, an opened-up reconciliatory justice that gives personal amnesty in turn for detailed public confession of the evil one did in the throes of the apartheid days 1960–1993.

Christian just-doing, which does not "throw the book at you" as minority—white or black, Turk or Vietnamese, Muslim or secularist—and also does not play antinomian law with an *Ausnahme Ethik*: such just-doing by a judge who fallibly bestows God's tender justice to all comers is exactly what John Calvin in my confessional tradition said was the highest calling a human could fill in God's world (*Institutiones Christianae Religionis*, IV:xx). Biblical just-doing is forbearing, able to be talked to, un-hypocritical—what the Newer Testament calls "wise" (James 3:17–18)—and heals divisions.

When the disciples of Jesus Christ are the cornered minority faced with the hatred of murderous political persecution, God forbid—it is everywhere today and largely unreported by the secular press—one undergoes martyrdom, God helping you, as a witness whose life hid securely in Jesus Christ is laid down without heroics, preferably on behalf of a fellow believer (1 John 3:13–18).[1]

Do you remember? Christ's disciples once complained to him, "Why couldn't we get the disturbing spirit out of the boy?"

Jesus answered: "You can only get certain demons out of people if you prepare yourself for the exorcism with periods of intense prayer and fasting" (Mark 9:14–29).

Who in the world will do that to exorcize the neglect and hatred for the various minorities in society?

---

1 In the lecture-presentation I showed a glimpse of how artists can practice and prepare labor officials and politicians, church leaders and journalists, the general public and even bullies, if they had eyes to see, for the simple, basic gritty gift disciples of Jesus Christ are enjoined to share with minorities: *philoxenia*, kindness to strangers, deep hospitality, an unjudgmental giving of yourself, your time, your goods to a stranger whom you accept for the time being, and who just might be—you never know, smiles the Bible—one of God's angel messengers (Hebrews 13:1–6)!

Examples came from black and white South African artists, Swiss, Canadian, and Brazilian-born artists, and also Britt Wikström's installation of five poles and figures for an Amnesty International artistic invitational, entitled *Cathedral of Suffering* (see *RA* #6, 31, 33-35), which was temporarily installed on the grounds of this Seventh Christian Artists Seminar in Doorn, Netherlands.

Bibliography

Ash, Timothy Garton. "True Confessions," *New York Review of Books* 44:12 (17 July 1997): 33–38.

Confronting Insecurity in Eastern Europe: Challenges for the European Community. Falk Bomsdorf, Cesare Merlini, et al. (London: Royal Institute of International Affairs, 1992).

Dallmayr, Fred. *Beyond Orientalism: Essays on cross-cultural encounter* (Albany: State University of New York Press, 1996).

Devine, Philip E. *Human Diversity and the Culture Wars: A philosophical perspective on contemporary cultural conflict* (Westport: Praeger, 1996).

Engelstad, Diane and John Bird, eds. *Nation to Nation: Aboriginal sovereignty and the future of Canada* (Concord: House of Anansi, 1992).

Goudzwaard, Bob. *Aid for the Overdeveloped West* (Toronto: Wedge, 1975).

———. *Idols of our Time* (Downers Grove: InterVarsity, 1981).

Guttmann, Amy, ed. *Multiculturalism: Examining the politics of recognition* (Princeton University Press, 1994).

Hawley, John C., ed. *Cross-Addressing: Resistance literature and cultural borders* (Albany: State University of New York Press, 1996).

Huber, Max. *The Good Samaritan: Reflections on the Gospel and work in the Red Cross* (London: Victor Gollancz, 1945).

Inagaki, Hisakazu. "Challenge of Religious Pluralism to Christian Philosophy," Seminar paper at Fifth International Symposium, Association for Reformational Philosophy, Hoeven, Netherlands, August 1994.

Jacobs, Jane. *Canadian Cities and Sovereignty Association* (Toronto: Canadian Broadcasting Corporation, 1980).

Kahn, Joel S. *Culture, Multiculture, Postculture* (London: Sage, 1995).

Kessler, Michael and Jürgen Wertheimer, eds. *Multi-Kulturalität: Tendenzen, Probleme, Perspektiven* (Tübingen: Stauffenburg Verlag, 1995).

Marshall, Paul. *Their Blood Cries Out* (Dallas: Word, 1997).

Ngugi wa Thiong'o, *Decolonising the Mind: The politics of language in African literature* (Nairobi: Heinemann Kenya, 1986).

La Rivière, Leen. *The Kingdom in Deed* and *The Kingdom of Righteousness* (Rotterdam: Christian Artists, 1996).

Seerveld, C. "Dooyeweerd's Idea of 'Historical Development': Christian respect or cultural diversity," *Westminster Theological Journal* 58 (1996): 41–61 {see *CE*: 199–209}.

Strauss, Gideon "Footprints in the Dust: Can neo-calvinist theory be credible in post-colonial Africa?" *Acta Academica* 28:2 (1996): 1–35.

Van der Walt, B. J. *Afrocentric or Eurocentric? Our task in a multicultural South Africa* (Potchefstroom: Institute for Reformational Studies, 1997).

BEYOND TOLERANCE TO TOUGH LOVE

What "tolerance" and "intolerance" mean depends upon where you are coming from. What your most fundamental standpoint is—Allah, Jesus Christ, Reason, or the Euro—gives a context and carries a Spirit that gives shape to the matter, since "tolerance" is a weasel word like "equality" and "pluralism." A mass of people can be "for equality," but before you know it, some are more equal than others. Almost everybody is "for pluralism," but it is rather important whether it be a recognition of the structural plurality in society of a state institution next to faith communities along with a commercial sector next to families, for example, as irreducibly diverse though interconnected institutional groupings, or whether you mean truth is basically plural, truth never declares other affairs to be false or lies.

If "tolerance" means the practice of deliberately putting up with what one disapproves of, and one could rightfully prevent it, such as allowing persons to harm themselves by indulging in addictive drugs, different questions arise: (1) How do you determine limits to what is tolerated? (2) Is a society still humane if it tolerates the sacrifice of human children? (Child slave labor in Nike˙ sports shoe-making plants in Indonesia could be seen as a contemporary variant of burning babies in the ancient fiery furnace of the Canaanite idol Moloch.) That is, toleration can be as repressive to those who are its victims, as Enlightenment Rationalism would have us believe is the bigoted cruelty of intolerance.

Muslim, Jewish, Christian, and Secularist zealots can inflict horrible atrocities in the name of their God or No-god, and this makes tolerance seem saintly. Even if being tolerated as a minor evil in society, not yet

---

Spoken at a Symposium held by the Christian Artists International union, on the topic of "Toleration, and the Role of the Arts in a Europe on the way to Integration" on 19 August 1999, Doorn, Netherlands. A shorter version was published in Proceedings of the Ninth Symposium on the Role of the Arts in a Europe on the Way to Integration (Rotterdam: International Christian Artists Seminar sponsored by the European Union, 2000), 39–43.

having authorities with power **respect** your human identity, toleration of what is considered subversive is more normative and embodies historical patience, I believe, than would be outright, ruthless annihilation of what doesn't fit and is considered malignant and condemnable.

But tolerance, I think, is a contaminated guideline because it tends to make compromise with evil a principle rather than an expedient practice for the nonce. Again, depending on what it means exactly, "tolerance" does not seem adequate to me—for describing how church authorities shall work with the power of excommunication, and political authorities with the legitimate power of imprisonment, and commercial authorities with the power to declare others bankrupt. Toleration is a weak-kneed idea for guiding societal life toward shalom, toward a fullness of prospering in God's world. Punishment in the various sectors of society should indeed be tempered by "the quality of mercy [that] is not strain'd. / It droppeth as the gentle rain from heaven" (Portia in Shakespeare's *Merchant of Venice*, IV, 1). The guiding biblical idea for leadership in political, social, economic, and faith-confessional affairs, however, would complement its forbearance (τὸ ἐπιεικὲς) with one's neighbors by the action I will call "tough love" (ἀγάπη), appropriate to the societal sphere where one is officiating as leader or participating as follower.

So the thesis of my remarks is: **our human calling as citizens, workers, family-members, faithful believers, and neighbors is to go beyond tolerance to tough love**. Since I would prefer not to be an armchair strategist, even though I am a theorist by trade, and because I know that we must beware of an oversimplified understanding of the complex matters before us so our leading ideas do not become platitudes, let me try to rehearse briefly the problematics on our hands and then dare to be specific on what a biblically contoured direction might be for us to take in the coming generation as the "European Union" struggles with our complicated, embattled human societal life.

Historiographic setting

The history of tolerance nuances blanket judgments and is still relevant for understanding our so-called "post" or "ultra-modern" climate. So to get at the **societal** import of tolerance, which goes beyond the working definition of being "a break on an individual person's intolerance," first a brief story of (in)tolerance in Europe.

Roman Emperor Constantine came officially to tolerate Christians in 313 AD. As the established state church, ecclesiastic officials then used the power of the sword to get rid of those who were judged to be not orthodox. Since religious faith was a public matter—hard for us in the West to grasp today—the heterodox were considered revolutionary insurrectionists who aimed to subvert the rightful order and stability of society. The Roman catholic medieval Church tolerated Jews and Muslims (stuck in their ignorance) but executed heretics, since heresy was considered conscious, malicious opposition to God's legitimate Rule on earth. It was the English John Wycliffe and Czech John Hus (who was burned at the stake for his faith, in Constance, 1415) who initiated the Anabaptist call for total separation of church from state to foreclose such evil, since one's particular faith or not in God, they argued, is not a matter that can be coerced.

Anti-clerical, secularizing Renaissance thinkers like Michel de Montaigne (1533–92) promoted a more naturalistic toleration of differences, and tried to sidestep the power politics entwined with the struggles of the Latin papacy with Reformed Martin Luther (1483–1546) and the Germanic princes. Luther defended a person's freedom of conscience, but still maintained the dictum of *cuius regio ejus religio* (whatever the ruler's confessional allegiance be, that becomes the faith of the populace)—a Lutheran prince, Lutheran subjects, a Calvinist ruler, Calvinist believers, Roman catholic leaders, a Roman catholic country. Needless to say this left the Anabaptists scrambling, because Reformers Luther, theocratic Ulrich Zwingli, and John Calvin were not tolerant of the non-conformist *Schwärmerei* they considered sectarian. Creedal and political matters were still generally confused in the 1500s, and this fusion invited persecution by the intolerant majority.

The learned Humanist Desiderius Erasmus (1466?–1536) had looked for undogmatic truths common to humankind so Muslims, Jews, Hindus, Roman catholic and Reformation Christians—everybody— could unite peaceably: *summa nostrae religionis pax est et unanimitas*. Although different Lutheran leaders and Roman catholic bishops with an irenic Erasmian spirit tried by colloquia to dialogue to resolve differences on doctrines like "justification by faith alone, or by faith and works" and on practices like penance and indulgences, tolerant discussion and reduction of core dogmata to as few disputes as possible—*in necessariis unitas, in non necessariis libertas, in omnibus caritas*—faith-allegiances apparently go so deep in human nature that persecution and martyrdom are preferred at times to live-and-let-live.

So despite voices for civil tolerance from many quarters,[1] the so-

---

1   The Confederation at Warsaw, 1573, had Lutherans, Calvinists, Bohemian Brethren, and Roman catholics agree to not shed the blood or to exile *dissidentes de religione*.

called "religious wars" ravaged the landmass of Europe for several generations, until the Peace of Westphalia (1648) recognized three faiths as lawful—Roman catholic, Calvinian, Lutheran, along with liberty of conscience. A short time later Oliver Cromwell (1599–1658), as Lord Protector of England (1654), proclaimed liberty of conscience to be a natural right under the constitution. In the American colonies Puritan Roger Williams (1603–83) founded the province of Rhode Island with liberty of religion as a natural right for all races and faiths—heresy does not exist! And Quaker William Penn (1644–1718) set up Pennsylvania rule defending liberty of conscience to mean everyone has the right to public worship of one's faith. As those who had been disenfranchised as citizens because of their faith-commitment came into political power, there were moves to honor civil rights as more basic than demands for conformity in belief.

Gradually in Western Protestant European lands, toleration of most faith-dissidents became standard policy (if not always political praxis). Jew Baruch Spinoza (1632–77) in free-trading, prosperous, cosmopolitan Amsterdam epitomized the universal toleration of faiths, picking up earlier themes from the Bohemian educator John Comenius (1592–1670) and jurist Hugo Grotius (1593–1645), who rejected penalties for heresy on grounds of Jesus' parable in Matthew 13:24–30, 36–43, admonishing Christ's disciples to let the weeds and wheat grow together until the Final judgment takes place. And John Locke's (1632–1704) *Letters concerning Toleration* (1689, 1690, 1693) at this time probably articulated best what the working conception of tolerance still is for many today.

Tolerance, said Locke, means freedom of the individual's conscience is an immutable principle of Reason; civil government has no business making laws for souls; the Church, a voluntary association in society to worship God, is true to its nature only if it tolerates confessional disagreements since one's human knowledge is not infallible, so others may not be permanently wrong. Huguenot Pierre Bayle (1647–1706), who lost his job in France only to become professor of philosophy in Rotterdam, and Gottfried Ephraim Lessing (1729–81), in his drama *Nathan der Weise*, both emphasized this last Enlightenment tenet of Locke: don't be so certain you have the absolute truth, O Roman catholic priest, O Protestant prophet, O Muslim mullah; it is immoral to persecute and kill those who serve a different god. Let Reason be the calming influence; to tolerate all kinds of sects in one state is better than to ferment civil strife with winner-take-all. "There is no one truth," **believes** Cas Mudde; this is the core of Lockean individualistic democracy.

Countries where the hierarchical Roman catholic Church is dominant have less easily followed this latitudinarian wink to be less sure in proclaiming what must be believed as true. French King Henry of Navarre's Edict of Nantes (1598) gave Protestants minority rights in that Catholic state, but those provisions were gradually invalidated and finally revoked by the Edict of Fontainebleau (1685), leading to the Huguenot exodus from France. As late as 1832 Pope Gregory XVI issued an encyclical that labels "freedom of conscience" to be an erroneous proposition, better, *deliramentum*.[2] In 1870 the Vatican Council under Pope Pius IX promulgated the infallibility of the Roman Pontificate when he speaks *ex cathedra* on faith doctrines and morals, and those pronouncements are "**unreformable**."[3] So there is little flexibility in such a setup to be "tolerant" of other doctrinal/moral judgments. Only in *Pacem in terris* (1963) by Pope John XXIII and the II Vatican Council (1962–65) are the fundamental rights of a human to profess religion both in private and in public recognized by the Roman catholic church.

But no brand of the (christian) faith is innocent of intolerance; we all have blood of Ulster Protestants, Orthodox Serbs, Afghanistanian Taliban, the Mexican Catholics on our hands. . . .

Systematic reflection

So how does this sketchy review help us come to grips with the problematics of tolerance and intolerance in our day, as the European nation states with this history consider the myriad conundrums on our hands: political power formation of new peoplehoods wanting the right to determine their own way; the enigma of growing economic prosperity for us few at the expense of the stifling, hopeless poverty for the many in the world; the continuing degradation of women and children despite the woman's movement, UNESCO, and many emergency shelter programs; the burning hatred of different ethné for one another—groupings with almost tribal, racist, religious gut fervor in their cultural markings.

---

2   ". . . illa fluit ac erronea sententia seu potius deliramentum, asserendam esse ac vindicandam cuilibet libertatem conscientiae" (Denzinger, *Enchiridion symbolorum*, #1613).

3   "Romanum Pontificem, cum ex cathedra loquitur, id est, cum omnium Christianorum pastoris et doctoris munere fungens pro suprema sua Apostolica auctoritate doctrinam de fide vel moribus ab universa Ecclesia tenendam definit, per assistentiam divinam ipsi in beato Petro promissam, ea infallibilitate pollere, qua divinus Redemptor Ecclesiam suam in definienda doctrina de fide vel moribus instructam esse voluit; ideoque eiusmodi Romani Pontificis definitiones ex sese, non autem ex consensu Ecclesiae, irreformabiles esse" (Denzinger, *Enchiridion symbolorum* #1839).

For all this mayhem, we use a term like "Tolerance"? It sounds like wishful thinking by a fairy godmother whose magic wand is worn out and threadbare from over-use.

Perhaps the affluent Western Church has even forfeited its right to be heard. Given our history of the Crusades against the Muslims; the past internecine struggles between Lutherans, Calvinists, Roman catholics, Anabaptists; and the fact that Christians have often sided with tyrannical power—colonialist and otherwise—while certain secularized intellectuals have bravely stood up for redress against majority wrong: why should the troubled ones of the world expect anything redemptive from followers of the Christ?—are we without guile, and wise?

One thing worth noting is the erosion of the Judeo-Christian ethos in society. We no longer have Sabbath or Sunday rest, but "weekends." And if church is a voluntary association like a club, as Locke argued was rational, and faith is the private matter of one's own individual conscience, why get all heated up in society about heresy? There are more taxing problems to take our attention, like the layout of cities and access to good drinking water. After all, everybody would be better off if the Jews assimilated into secular society—they can still have their *seders* at home if they want to, even invite *goiim* to share in such a quaint good meal.

That is, with the loss of biblical horizons that assume we people inhabit the LORD God's world where who you believe the Messiah is has everlasting consequences: in the secularist mentality bred by Locke's brief for rational toleration, there is general agreement that truth/falsehood and right/wrong are decided by rational argument, and values are subjective decisions ("opinions") by good-willed people of whom each one should be tolerant. We humans create our own world together; so let's get on with it rather than act like fanatics ("fans") persecuting others for God's sake!

It is no wonder that US department officials with this secularist, do-gooding perspective simply **cannot** understand the intransient militancy of Fundamentalist Shi'ite Muslims in Iran and can hardly plumb the **religious** depth to the opposition fervor on land governance between Israeli Zionists and a displaced Palestinian people. Such wretched hostility seems to Western career diplomats like a throwback to pre-Enlightenment times.

Two comments about justifying toleration before I try to advance the guideline of tough love: (1) A flaw in the Enlightenment banner of Tolerance is its hidden push toward unanimity. If Tolerance succeeds in society, you move towards uniformity in political and confessional matters. Whether it be a lowest common denominator in creed or opposing political parties that become practically indistinguishable in their election platforms, Enlightenment tolerance has the covert prejudice that everyone tolerating diversity for now in order to achieve general agreement later will eventually realize that we are all quite alike in our rational autonomous individuality, providing humanity in the end with its life, liberty, and happiness. In the tolerant democratic system you can never say, "This is the truth and not the lie."

John Stuart Mill took this position in his essay *On Liberty* and wanted to extend the utility of tolerance to mores, morals, and gender. The fault in its positive program is the assumption that consensus provides truth and that tolerance is the way to end error and evil. Enlightenment tolerance is not self-critical of its deep **religious** bias that rational discussion by good-natured men results in peace, and all humankind can enjoy *fraternité*, sisterhood, or at least friendship. But, as Sander Griffioen notes (218), there is no universal ethical conscience, even though Thomas Aquinas, natural law theorists, and C. S. Lewis think so. And to pretend that truth by nature is complementary rather than exclusive is to make an enormous (false) assumption, because men do not live by reason alone any more than humans live by bread alone. Truth cuts through rationalized deceit too, and what is right **cannot be united** with what is wrong, can it? At least, if Tolerance is your guiding Rule, then one should admit that you are dealing in ends as well as means. The laissez-faire nature of tolerance held as a creed often results in lukewarm agreement bordering on indifference, or in a sunny-side-up despotism of the stronger, the better debater, those who know the managerial ropes best, wreathed in smiles.

(2) What gives the lie to Enlightenment tolerance is also the fact that one's neighbors sometimes are predominantly bad, violent, evil, and are committed in their hearts to intolerance. What has Tolerance to say to rape, abuse, torture, and cruelty but to itself become intolerant of such **human** acts or to show its bankruptcy as a societal principle for us to live by. Everybody picks their intolerancies[4] because humans, as Luther argued with Erasmus, are less a pleasant free-will debating society than they are jackasses being ridden by God or/and the devil jockeying for control.[5] Because humans are built to be wholeheartedly committed to God, to an Ideal, to their native country, or to self-satisfying *über alles*, tolerance can

---

4   Plato and Locke both have no place for atheists to stand in society.
5   Cf. Martin Luther, *De servo arbitrio* (1525), 635W. *Luthers Werke in Auswahl*, ed. Otto Clemen (Bonn: Marcus und Weber, 1913), 3:126.

be viewed as simply an ingenious device to give the greatest gain to those who are committed to the least.

A particular wrinkle in our day shows how old-fashioned and toothless the Enlightenment principle of Tolerance has become, because it misses the faith-gut and Spirit-driven character of human nature: a virulent Pragmatistic cultural dynamic has no compunction against using tolerance and democratic liberties to promote its own ideological preparations to seize power legally, half-legally, or illegally and then, as Goebbels and Stalin did,[6] ruthlessly be intolerant and impose authoritarian rule, forcing people to choose between undesirable alternatives. Bullies tolerate restrictions only until they can bulldoze through their agenda, destroying not only whatever would respectfully differ or demur, but even annihilate the very societal fabric at large and permit holocaustic savagery.[7]

Support survival of the weakest

Faced with, I think, the self-destructing impotence of Tolerance as a directive for our day—diplomatic immunity is disappearing, issuance of a worldwide *fatwa* against a novelist is possible, utter disrespect in war zones for old age, women pregnant with life, starving children—is there a biblical christian alternative direction to take instead of just repeating old saws, finding a **personal** way out, and trying to reconstruct christian signposts of sanity that became secularized in the Enlightenment and are now knocked over? (Matthew 7:12 turned into "the Golden Rule": Do good to others as you selfishly wish would be done to you.)

I think there is an alternative, but you will not like to hear it any more than I do: **In whatever capacity of authority a person holds power, support the survival of the weakest.**

I purposely formulate it as a thesis that Darwinian Friedrich Nietzsche and Pragmatist John Dewey fulminated against in order to point up the biblical radicality of such a direction. I pose this policy of tough love—**see to it that the weak flourish in your limited jurisdiction**—so that it not remain a general philanthropic kind of neighborly love ("Love your neighbor as you do yourself": cf. Leviticus 19:18, Matthew 22:34–40, Romans 13:8–10, Galatians 5:13–15), and also so that the injunction not absolve us "individual persons" and be a directive solely for

---

6   Mieczyslaw, (190–91): "Freedom should not be abused and transformed into a tool for hurting, humiliating, and degrading people."

7   And I do not think Cas Mudde's correct apologetic for the "right" of the Belgian Vlaams Blok to speak its extremism has the horizon of wisdom to discern the "duties" of the Vlaams Blok in a democracy where just-doing should prevail.

institutional leaders. Everybody has certain authority over others—parents and children toward one another, teachers with students, employers with workers, sellers and buyers, rulers and voting subjects, friend toward friend: so, **get those to whom you are related, especially if you have power over them, to sparkle like the grass does when the sun shines on it after a rain** (cf. 2 Samuel 23:3b–4). This biblical christian directive of tough love stretches out all the way to enemies. The God known in Jesus Christ says we should **love** our enemies (Matthew 5:43–48), not **tolerate** enemies, not **know** our enemies, but **do good to our enemies** (Proverbs 25:21–22, Romans 12:14–21)!

It all sounds preposterous: a policy that would lead to certain defeat of whatever is good, true, and beautiful in history as well as to your own demise. Rather than promote the excellencies/virtues (*aretai*) and skills of the best, we have to care for the least capable in our society? What in God's world would that mean for the European Union countries amid their troubles with monetary policy, the plight of migrants and refugees who want to achieve new national citizenship, the prosecution of war criminals, or administration of government grants to artists? Could "tough love" lead to more normative resolutions of problems with promise to bear long-range good fruit instead of the makeshift, fix-it-for-now compromises tolerant leaders tend to settle for?

Let me try out just a few ideas-in-progress that assume, along with the dynamic of tough love, that we inhabit a society where a plurality of institutional tasks are extant, necessarily interrelated but distinct, differentiated, and limited in their field of normed service. Also, contrary to the regnant ideology derivative, let's say, from Pico della Mirandola and Johann Gottlieb Fichte, that we humans create the only world we know, I would posit that **there are realities objective to us** humans, like an atmosphere and biosphere of plants and animals we need to respond to with care. And that there are **creational ordinances**, for cities, for trade and manufacture of resources, tribal and family connections, the governance of peoples, that impinge in common on aboriginal animists, Hasidic Jews, evangelical Christians, Muslims of all varieties, European Humanist, post-christian nihilists; and that the ordinances for social, political, and economic order the Creator God set are discoverable, depending on one's 20–20 or skewed vision.

One cautionary note: every historical period and geographic location has its own physiognomy, and nobody ever enters a scene with a clean slate. Citizens of a nation, labor officers, neighborhood leaders, and graphic/sculptural/musical artists always take initiatives in a contested setting, often not of their own making. It is somewhat like what King David experienced when he angered God by counting up his military potential, and God said, "OK, pick one of these three alternatives for the punishment of your pride: three years of famine, three months of being bombed in your territory, or three days of a cancer plague among the population" (cf. 2 Samuel 24). We novices need to be aware that leaders in the countries of the budding European Union often face similar unpleasant choices because of our history of ungodly disobedience and years and years of gratuitous cultural vanity.

Social, political, and economic steps to take
One nest of problems I see facing the European Union is the confused fusion of **socio-ethnic peoples** and **national political citizen responsibilities** and **economic employment** to furnish sustenance for one's extended family. The confusion and disarray is exacerbated by the fact that the **social identity of ethnic peoples** is an undifferentiated mix of language, mores, blood-relations, faith, and cultural history, while the **nation states** of Europe have allowed their national political status to become almost creedally sacrosanct because of warfare history, while the economic generator of our current envied, moneyed prosperity is virtually a supra-national **international commercial empire** beyond national political power to control and call to justice. In such an overlapping societal turmoil fueled by distrust between ethnic peoples, eroding national sovereignties fighting to keep their particular identity—France has Euro-Disney!—and the steam-rollering business/bank corporations that find willing converts in the most unlikely places to join McWorld, how can one take any steps of tough love?

(1) **Nation states need to honor ethnic peoples within their territorial borders with cultural room—language, schools, customs, creed, art—so that ethnic communities will honor the different, representative nature of a political union and not force the racist definition of a state as an ethnic right.** Ethnic communities are rightly social neighborhoods who need places to be good neighbors, to care for orphans and the homeless like an extended family, to provide for kin who are uprooted by war or extreme poverty. Once ethnic communities are hated and persecuted, it is no wonder nationalism is born, and the Jewish people believe they need political power as Zionists to survive as a people, even if it be on the Palestinian people's territory. When ethnic Serb and Kosovar, ethnic Hutu and Tutsi demonize the other, they destroy the possibility of inhabiting a joint political commonwealth or union for doing

justice to all.

Tough love says ethnicity is not grounds for a nation state. But that means that the Turkish **state**, as I understand it, must provide room for the Kurdish **people** to flourish, not as a sovereign state but as an ethnic **social community** with a legitimate identity, even if recognizing that peoplehood comes at Turkish **people's** expense. Tough love also says reluctantly (if my information is correct) that somebody needs to stop "ethnic cleansing" in the former fragmenting Yugoslavia, since no nation may perpetrate genocide in God's world with impunity (and this does not mean NATO was right to bomb civilians antiseptically in murderous technological warfare fashion, or that the USA should play world cop).

(2) **To help national citizenship transmute into European Union citizenship, the just rights and responsibilities of citizens of the various lands and regions need to be strongly affirmed and kept differentiated as bona fide *political* privileges and duties**. Nation states in Europe evolved quite differently—England, Spain, Holland, Belgium, France, Germany, Italy, Norway—and no amount of **economic** homogenization begun by the Maastricht Treaty (1995), no internal custom border control, or the invention of the Euro, will effect **political** integration. And a European political formation is necessary, I think, to preclude the burgeoning neurosis of national**isms**. European **political** consolidation needs to transfer the power located in the Council of Ministers and bureaucratic inter-governmental meetings to the elected Commissioners of the European Parliament, provided the Parliament functions as a body with political power held accountable to the citizens, so the commissioners be the ones who set the agenda for a unified system of just-doing that will honor national concerns but **fashion a common legal standard for all the nations to adhere to**.

Tough love says that rallying public opinion behind a political European Union is crucial, making clear (this is especially where the media and the arts come in) that **political standardization** does not entail socio-ethnic dissolution or the American functionalistic assimilation ethic based on sheer individualism. It is fair to ask displaced **peoples** to take time to meet criteria before they assume **citizenship** in a political entity, since responsibilities and duties ensue with rights. Tough love also says that a priority for the **political** European Union would be to **preserve public space** (jural space) where citizen minorities can receive justice and to stop the investing privatization of common concourse places (postal system, shopping centers, roads, parks, waste disposal), abdicating civil responsibilities, so that *unitas in pluribus* (unity in plurality) be the European state pledge, and not the swallowing-up formula of *e pluribus unum*. Citizenship needs to be prized and legally empowered by a European Union—and that will take nation states' sacrificing their sacrosanct status—to offset the current gap where international tribunals adjudicate rights and punishments to persons and peoples although such authority is supposedly vested in national states. Only if the European Union comes to furnish citizenship with legitimate political clout, I think, will its promises materialize.

(3) To curtail the unbridled, destructive global power of multinational corporations and world financial currency markets that exist nowhere but internet virtually everywhere seems almost impossible, an insurmountable force, a principality of ruthless evil posing as an angel of light (cf. 2 Corinthians 11:12–15), because Money is blind to political, ethical, and creedal tenets even as it destroys socio-ethnic treasures and perverts cultural realities like artistry—this is what Elaine Storkey is calling "Consumerism." Mammon is a protean, seductive despoiler of life. The World Bank (1947) and World Trade Organization (1995) need to realize that they are part of the problem rather than part of the solution to the globalization of desperate poverty, serious environmental pollution, and destabilizing of nations and countries struggling with preindustrial economical setups in a wired world of monopolies in markets and the distribution of goods and resources. Even the International Monetary Fund (IMF, 1944) forced debt-ridden countries in Africa, Asia, and South America to trade more, grow export crops at cut-rate prices, instead of allowing them to grow food for the local people. The World Bank forces poor young governments to don Saul's industrial armor, and then takes up cudgels in debt crises for creditor nations.

Tough love is ashamed to be part of the West's recolonialization of the world under the subterfuge of "economic reconstruction," and proposes the orientation of jubilee for CEO's instead of riches, stock options, and fringe benefits. Let workers be paid in hours of leisure for overtime work rather than in more money; let medical aid accrue to part-time laborers and the unemployed sick; let the *Polder Overleg Model Holland* (the consultational model of employer organizations, labor unions, with government officials) show European Union countries that employment is improved when partisan interest is replaced by cooperative taking responsibility for undergirding work in society, so crucial to human self-respect and peace in the workplace. The international NGO project of "Jubilee 2000" should be taken seriously by national governments—one small step to undo their complicity in strangling debt through the world, and for changing the economic hopelessness of so many victims of corruption. Tough love would expose the lie in corporate double-speak like "downsizing" (=You people have lost your livelihood), "structural adjustment" (=Get rid of family farm subsidies or we banks declare your country bankrupt), and sees the evil perpetrated on Eastern Europe countries who are told to privatize, commercialize, and trust free markets to bring democracy, when such a rote capitalistic program only incites mafiaocracy. **International regulatory bodies need to organize regional decentralization of economies rather than encourage nations to make slaves of their women and children to compete in a monolithic world market.**

Artistic contribution

To reinforce the thesis that we **not** "tolerate" difference and what is other than our accustomed patterns or even what we consider wrong, but that we go the second mile, as it were, or better, take the new track of "tough love," I will share images of artistic work that illuminates the topic under consideration for persons concerned that the European Union proceed with "integration" mindful of the fact that our Western civilization is breaking down and that we need to find imaginative ways to redeem normal life by taking little steps of restoration in social, political, economic, and cultural affairs that will give hope of shalom to the world and its burgeoning inhabitants.

Anselm Kiefer's momentous constructions like *Zweistromland* [#1] or *The High Priestess* (1985-89) and *Lot's Wife* (1989) [see *RA* #138]

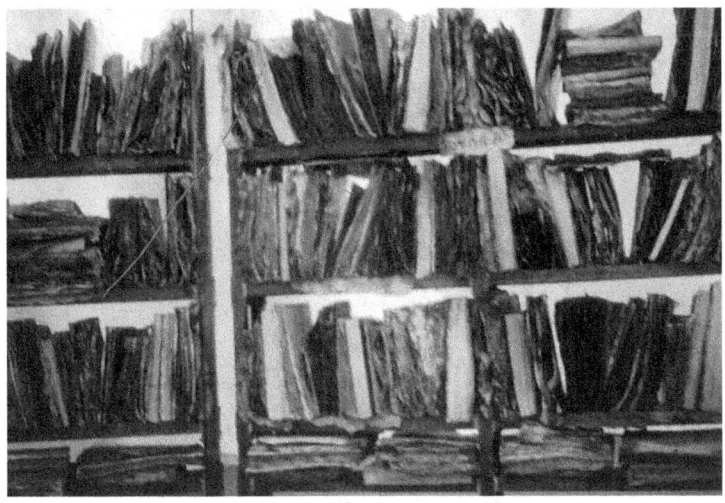

[#1] Anselm Kiefer, *Zweistromland*, 1985-1989

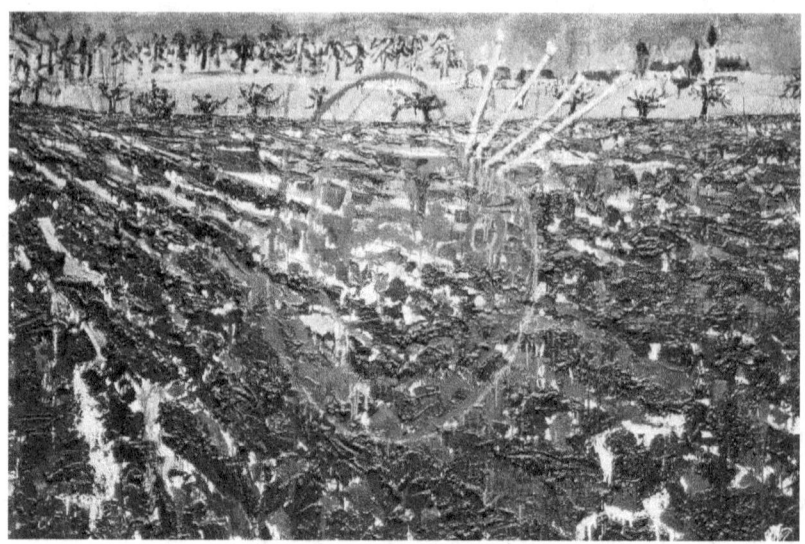

[#2] Anselm Kiefer, *Nero malt*, 1974

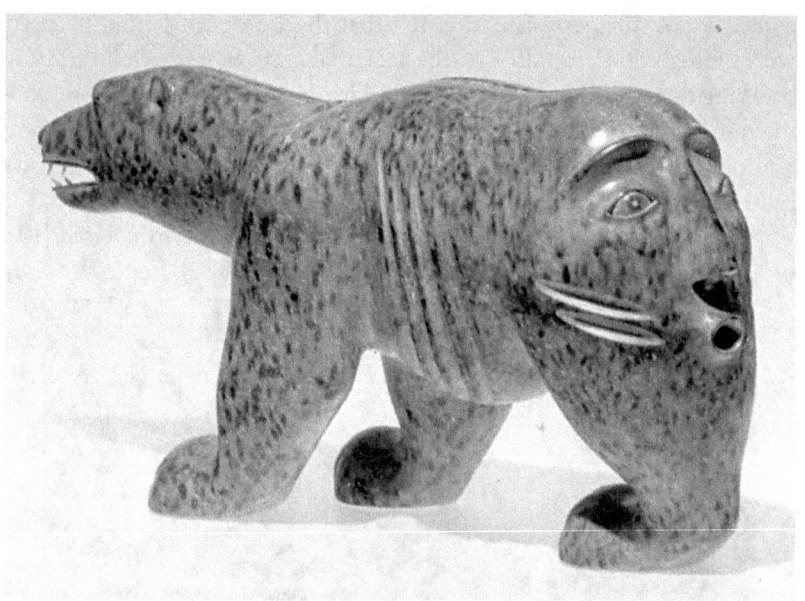

[#3] Piqtoukun, *Death of a Tradition*, 1992

show the rubble Europe's "world wars" in this century have made of God's good creation. Kiefer's *Nero Malt* [#2] (1974) asks the passionate question: Is the art we are producing historically aware of what time it is societally, and are we giving away tough love in our artistry to one's disbelieving neighbor?

Ernst Barlach's memorial [*RA* #120] for the (Protestant Evangelical) Magdeburg cathedral, commemorating the German soldiers who fought, lost, and died in 1914–1918 (1929), and Ossip Zadkine's *De Verwoeste Stad* (1951) [*NA* #30], commemorating the Nazi saturation bombing of Rotterdam in May 1940, hint that maybe our monument art that would honor **justice** should remember the victims of war rather than the so-called victors.

Consider also how Inuit Canadian artists [#3] have been given the Midas kiss by the North American economy since the 1960s, and how Inuit artists, with their history of being exploited, struggle to this very

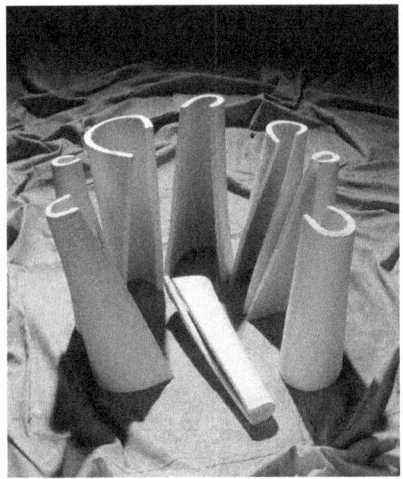

[#4] Henny van Hartingsveldt, *Mourning*, 1992

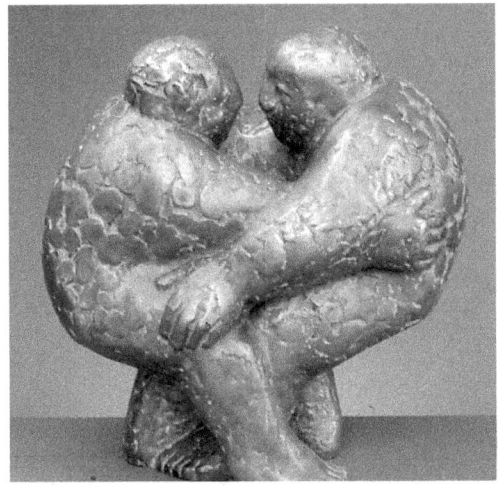

[#5] Britt Wikström, *Jacob and the Angel*, 1996

day to find a voice, as it were, in cultural exile.

Henny van Hartingsveldt's ceramic *Mourning* (1992) [#4] and Britt Wikström's bronze *Jacob and the Angel* (1996) [#5] show tough love in action, the kind of God-obedient love that may bring struggle and sorrow to us humans in our adversarial society, but is tough enough to expect the relief and fruit of the resurrection still to come.

Finally, consider an Afro-American style blues rendering of Psalm 92 played and sung as requiem/doxology. The early rural Afro-American blues intone the bittersweet candor of a christian tough love that should permeate our societal endeavors to be normative in God's world gone awry. *Blues 92* complements the philosophical analysis of my remarks

Blues 92

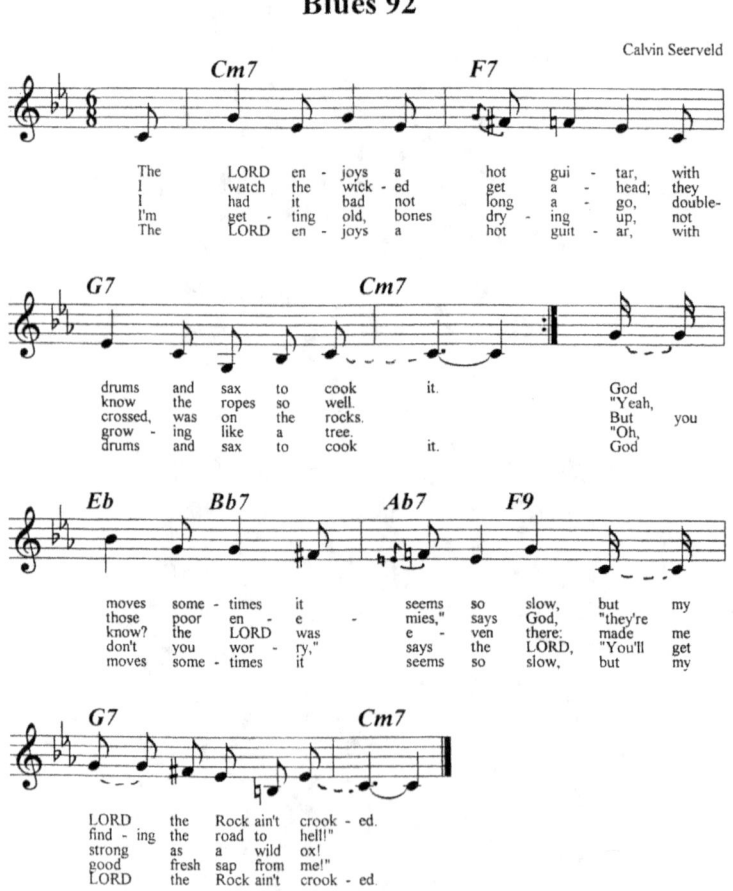

Calvin Seerveld

and gives them the intuitive artistic color they need. While we struggle to find redemptive ways to counter hatred, greed, loneliness, and waste, we are called to work with an authentic trust that the LORD knows our personal and societal troubles, and promises to come through for those who remain faithful servants with holy spirited wisdom. "God moves sometimes it seems so slow, but my Lord the Rock ain't crooked."

Bibliography

Anderson, Benedict. *Imagined Communities: Reflection on the origin and spread of nationalism* (New York: Verso, 1983/1991, revised edition).

Arendt, Hannah. "The Crisis in Culture: Its social and its political significance," in *Between Past and Future: Six exercises in political thought* (New York: Viking Press, 1961), 197–226, 240–41.

_____. "Truth and Politics," in *Philosophy, Politics and Society*, eds. Peter Laslett and W.G. Runciman (Oxford: Basil Blackwell, 1978).

Barber, Benjamin. "A Place for Us," CBC radio program *Ideas*, 28 July 1999.

Breton, Philippe. *L'utopie de la communication: Le mythe du village planétaire* (Paris: La Découverte, 1997).

Canovan, Margaret. "Friendship, Truth, and Politics: Hannah Arendt and toleration," in *Justifying Toleration: Conceptual and historical perspectives*, ed. Susan Mendus (Cambridge University Press, 1988), 177–98.

Favell, Adrian. *Philosophies of Integration: Immigration and the idea of citizenship in France and Britain* (University of Warwick Centre for Research in Ethnic Relations, 1998).

Goudzwaard, Bob and Harry de Lange, *Beyond Poverty and Affluence: Toward an economy of care, with a twelve-step program for economic recovery*, translated Mark Vander Vennen (Geneva: World Council of Churches, 1995).

Goudzwaard, Bob. "Towards a European Economy of Care," in *Towards an Economy of Care and Compassion*. Occasional Paper no. 3, ed. Alastair Hulbert (Brussels: Ecumenical Association for Church and Society, 1996), 5–12.

Griffioen, Sander. "Kleine typologie van pluraliteit," *Pluralisme, Cultuur-filosofische beschouwingen*, eds. Theo de Boer and Sander Griffioen (Amsterdam: Boom, 1995), 204–26, 235–36.

Grotius, Hugo. *Prolegomena to the Law of War and Peace*, translated by Francis W. Kelsey (New York: Liberal Arts Press, 1925/1957).

Kamen, Henry. *The Rise of Toleration* (London: World University Library, 1967).

Locke, John. *A Letter concerning Toleration* (William Popple's translation from the Latin, 1689) (New York: Liberal Arts Press, 1950).

Mieczyslaw, Maneli. *Freedom and Tolerance* (New York: Octagon Books, 1984).

Roper, Duncan. "Aristotle and the State of the Nation-State: A critical look at some aspects of political theory in the light of history and the gospel," in *Humans Being. Essays dedicated to Stuart Fowler*, ed. Doug Blomberg (Melbourne: Association for Christian Scholarship, & Sydney: National Institute for Christian Education, 1996), 225–74.

Rushdie, Salman. "Forgiving Kosovan Serbs may Prove to be Impossible," in Commentary, Toronto *Globe and Mail* (Friday, 6 August 1999), A11.

Soysal, Yasemin Nuhoglu. "Changing Citizenship in Europe: Remarks on post-national membership and the national state," in *Citizenship, Nationality and Migration in Europe*, eds. David Cesarani and Mary Fulbrook (London: Routledge, 1996), 17–29.

Suzuki, David. "Globalization Blues," CBC radio program *Ideas*, 24 May 1999.

Tolerance. Based on an original idea by Dominique Roger and Clandine and André Parinand. (Paris: Cultures of Peace, UNESCO Publishing, 1996).

Van Empel, Frank. *Model Holland: de kracht van overleg* (Amsterdam: Stichting van de Arbeid, 1997).

Conversations with Euwil Beukes, Bob Goudzwaard, Sander Griffioen, John Hiemstra, Harry Schat.

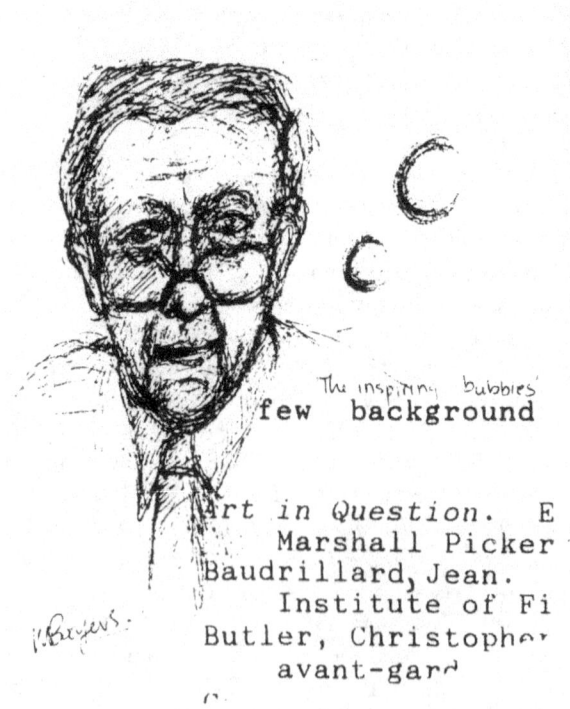

The inspiring bubbles
few background

rt in Question. E
Marshall Picker
Baudrillard, Jean.
Institute of Fi
Butler, Christopher
avant-gard

Doodles by a graphic artist at Christian Artists International conference, supported by the European Union, Doorn, Netherlands, 2003

DOES THE WORLD ASK EUROPE
TO SACRIFICE ITS BEAUTIFUL ART?

This good book, *De Kunst van het Leven*[1] (*The Art of Living*) embodies, in my judgment, a certain Reformation Dutch grit, a European tradition of educated, humane reflection, and grapples with complex problems facing human creatures everywhere today in God's world. Leen la Rivière asks us to determine what of it is true, what holds water, offers good direction for our society to take. And, is the vision astigmatic? are there blind spots in some of the contributions we, from a little different viewpoint, could shed light on?

I have been asked as a Christian from Canada to set us up for discussion on the section dealing with "culture and church." Since today is Sunday, when one normally celebrates living out of the power and certain hope of the resurrection of Jesus Christ, let me start off my remarks with the upbeat passage found in Isaiah 54:1–3, spoken to a body of believers who were wondering how to comport themselves culturally in forbidding societal circumstances.

> Shout joyfully! [you] barren one who gave no birth—
> Whoop it up! I said; sing and laugh! you who suffered no childbirth
>   pains,
> for the lonely one knowing no intercourse
> has more children than the married one, says the LORD.
> Spread out the area covered by your tent, and
> stretch out further all the tent canvas covering where you eat and
>   sleep—
> don't hold back hemmed in!—

---

1   *De Kunst van het Leven: De cultuuruitdaging van de 21e eeuw*, eds. Jan Peter Balkenende, Roel Kuiper, and Leen La Rivière. Rotterdam: CNV-Kunstverbond, 2000. [=KL]

First published in *The Art of Living*, eds. Jan Peter Balkenende, Roel Kuiper, Leen La Rivière (Rotterdam: CNV- Kunstenbond/Europäisches Zentrum für Arbeitnehmerfragen, 2001), 13–17. Used with special permission of Continental Sound/Christian Artists, Rotterdam, Holland.

Lengthen your ropes and hammer down more firmly your tent stakes!
Left and right you will expand!
Your children's children shall inherit [the spoil of] nations
and populate whole cities left empty....

The prophetic (not "imperialistic") biblical Word of the LORD for the people of God is this: enlarge the tented terrain where you cultivate things and culture the next generation; also pound the tent stakes of your dwelling more firmly deep into the ground the LORD God provides. Or, I could translate the Scriptural message this way: know surely your identity as a faith-community, so you can be more hospitable to strangers, outcasts, unbelievers, even middle class people or bankers (Isaiah 58:6–7, John 4:1–22, Matthew 25:31–46, Acts 10, James 2:14–17), as you freely struggle together, with the tent flaps blowing in the gusty wind, to do your art, make music, negotiate labor contracts, find just political solutions, teach, conduct funerals or whatever, in a way that lets God smile.

Christians do not have to save the world. The Holy Spirit will complete that work Christ accomplished (Revelation 1:8, 2 Corinthians 5:19, John 14:1–16:15, 19:28–30). The adopted children of God in history only need gratefully to prepare the Way of the returning Lord who will bring the refined cultural treasure of the nations (τὰ ἔθνη), "the ethnics," says Scripture, finally into the holy city when Immanuel again lives on the new earth (Isaiah 60, Revelation 21:1–4, 22–27).

So, I have three points: (1) a systematic look at the identity of God's people in a society where institutions like church, state, commerce, media, the artworld, and more coexist; 2) an historical judgment on what time it is culturally in the world; and (3) a few philosophical thoughts and artistic examples of faithful cultural responses busy redemptively in God's world—always keeping in mind and referring to the writing of Birtwistle, Bronswijk, van Setten, Eschbach, and Veenhuizen.

Identity of a people of God
Roel Kuiper's judgments are apt: Secularization in Western civilization has privatized faith and left the church mostly a ceremonial ornament; spirituality within Eastern cachet ("New Age") and Muslim Fundamentalism have filled the vacuum of effete Christianity (KL, 9). Also, rampant Individualism has left institutional groupings like marriage, family, church, unions, even certain nations, on tenterhooks, up for grabs, while globalization makes cultural activities in the public domain vaguely anonymous, they are not located anywhere specific (KL, 10).

In such a floating smorgasbord culture Veenhuizen recommends that churches provide a kind of intimate home base for face-to-face communion, where small circles of people can converse, question and answer about how the Bible tells us to live, so we know God's presence more surely (KL, 219-220). You need a community of faith around for your own personal faith to grow, says Veenhuizen (KL, 217).

I agree, especially for artists, political and labor powerbrokers, and academics, who can live insulated lives. But very important to me for getting our tent stakes firmly in place is the crucial distinction, supported by Scripture, relating the body of Christ (*corpus Christi*), the city of God (βασιλεία τοῦ θεοῦ), and the worshipping church institution (ἐκκλησία). These three manifestations of God's Spirit at work in humans—body of Christ, city of God, institutional church—are linked together but discrete, just as what the Older Testament of the Bible describes when it reports on Jerusalem's becoming the city of God (because the LORD would insure that justice would be done among its inhabitants); and in the city a temple was built around the ark of God, where priests in the line of Aaron mediated the sacrifices and prayers of God's repenting, sinful people—city, temple, ark.

Since Pentecost, as I understand it, God's temple on earth is no longer a building constructed with stones in Palestine but is the communion of two or three saints, the Spirit-filled body of Christ at large, in which every faithful disciple of Jesus Christ is self a royal priest in the order of Melchizedek (Psalm 110, Matthew 18:19–20, Hebrews 7:1–10:18, 1 Peter 2:5–10). Zion, the city of God, for Newer Testament followers of the Christ, is not the real estate contested by the Palestinian people and the Israeli's, but is there wherever God's will is done in faith: wherever on earth—in the arts, education, commerce, for example, or in the political sphere of action—the Messiah's redemptive Rule takes place, there is a manifestation of the holy city of God's ordening. As for the crucial Older Testament ark of the covenantal LORD God: its rough, post-resurrection, biblical equivalent is found in the official, organized center of congregational or parish liturgical worship presided over by ordained elders, deacons, bishops, pastors, or charismatics.

Although it may be too difficult for me to initiate precision on the slippery term "church" in our discussion, what I am proposing could reorder our thinking more clearly: Christian Artists International is not a church; its board are not clergy; it is not the sacraments that are offered to you participants. But Christian Artists International is the body of Christ, a union—communion—of sinful saints who confess that Jesus is Lord of their artistry, their commercial contractual obligations and responsibilities, their life at large. And if I do not misunderstand it, what Leen and Ria, Britt Wikström, An Knaeps, and the other leaders have been after for twenty years in Christian Artists International, is to bring a measure of the Lord's shalom upon a younger generation's engagement in the arts; not in an ivory tower, but in the muddy terrain of European labor and political unification, so that the members of Christ's body gathered here for a few days may return to their distant places of work to spill Mary Magdalene's perfume (cf. Mark 14:3–9) over the feet of their neighbors— a redemptive sign of the coming of the city of God, the compassionate Rule of the Lord. But Christian Artists International as labor union is not a "church," in my book.

The institutional church is the heart of the body of Christ, and the heart is central to the body, but the heart is not the whole body. All those who make up the body of Christ, who are temples of the Holy Spirit (1 Corinthians 3:16–17, 6:17–20), every such one is anointed in one's bodily task as eye or ear, mouth or hand, dancing foot or therapeutic liver (1 Corinthians 12, Romans 12:3–21), to be yourself a prophet, priest, wise man, or wise woman in training, an ambassador of Christ (2 Corinthians 5:16–21) in one's bodily task—at least this is the legacy of the historic Reformation. That is, a church worshipping congregation is crucial as invigorating source and pastoral encouragement for those on a bodily artistic, political, or commercial mission; the church is the setting where the cultural "missionaries" return for rest, directional blessing, and prayer. But the church is not the boss, who keeps its members dependent upon the ecclesiastical nod for approval. Christian statesmen, media pundits, business women, Christian artists, in their institutional diversity, communally are directly responsible to God for their deeds, each after its own kind of service, and each is asked by the Lord to wash the other feet with the special gifts God has given each institution of them: then you have the heartbeat of the church and the multi-membered body of Christ working in concert as they stretch out their diaconal services to provide shelter and community for anyone in need . . . in the city.

If one carefully conceives the identity of God's people in this overlapping systematic way, certain radical things can be faced. (1) The church does not have to reform the culture industry. The institutional church does not have a monopolistic authority over christian leadership in society. From a biblical viewpoint, it is the task of a union of christian artists— practitioners, critics, theorists, patrons—for example, to configure the artworld into a more normative place of imaginative meaning than its current hard-nosed regimen of superstars and also-rans. From a biblical viewpoint, it is the task, for example, of christian labor leaders and management to codetermine policies that promote employment at just wages for worthwhile products people need instead of a ruthless competitive drive to corner markets in luxury items.

Yes, the church will hold the hand of christian artists and officials in the world of commerce, and intercede for statesmen and women struggling to enact just deeds, but the church serves the frontline body-of-Christ culture-workers best, I believe, when the church minds its limited task of being a retreat, R & R, for battle-fatigued mature sons and daughters of the church exercising their competencies in society, and as an emergency room for those who have lost their way in society and must be cared for. The church is supposed to get the biblical writings oral so you hear God talking to you in a colloquial voice, fellow, handing over a cup of cool water, God talking to you in love poetry and sometimes in four-letter words, so you know without a doubt the Lord of life and death is facing you and wants despicable-you to join the eucharistic feast of those who are thankful to God (Matthew 22:1–10, Veenhuizen, KL, 218).

(2) Christ's body is not a collection of devout, loose individuals. Christ's body is composed of persons who belong to a variety of confessional churches, a rainbow of language groupings and ethnic idiosyncrasies, a diversity of occupations, geographic mix of neighborhoods around the world, who are members of fractured families, warring tribes, different levels of education. This variegated constituency of Christ's body, both the natural and the organized unions of Christ's disciples busy cultivating the world, was present from the beginning, so to speak, even before the differentiated butterflies of races, professions, and specially gifted groups matured from the cocoon of the early church.

There were Jews and Greeks, slaves, poor, women and children, rulers, men (Galatians 3:27–28), eunuchs (Acts 8:26–40), and intellectuals (Acts 22:3–16, 2 Peter 3:14–16), all being unified in their differences to show what the love of Christ might mean for turning the world society upside-down. The fact that Christ's body can show up in political circles (CJL, Canada; CPJ, USA), in the economic sector (CLAC, Canada; CNV, Netherlands), as art organizations (CIVA/CITA, USA; SECK, Greece) is a good development in its plurality for the witness of God's presence in history. It would be a mistake, I think, to try to take a romanticized view of "the New Testament church" as a model for Christ's diversified body today (Eschbach, KL, 210) (as if the New Testament church had no headstrong leaders, no Ananias and Sapphira, no synodical debates about kosher food and schisms on circumcision [Acts 4:32–5:11, 15:1–35, Galatians 2]). That would be like asking the butterflies to revert to their caterpillar stage. We do not need an undifferentiated body of Christ acting as if it be simply a church.

(3) Christian artistry is not synonymous with art for the church. We need art with redeeming quality proper for the liturgical, ecclesiastical setting of worship too, but holy spirited art aware of sin yet bearing glimmers of hope fit for the streets, the cabaret, and theatre, hospitals, airports, mall, and art gallery, is critical for artists' showing love to their neighbor. You don't make art "christian" by popping in "Jesus words" or making a verbal testimony between musical sets in a gig, any more than you become a liberating labor union by having "Christian" in the name and opening certain meetings with a formal prayer. "Christian" art, outside or inside the church doors, as I understand it, does not have to advertise its allegiance to the Lord, but simply proffers imaginative insight and understanding that is compassionate, troubled, healing.

Young Australian Julian Di Stefano's egg tempera on wood (*Ornamental Hope*, 1966) [#6] has a pristine churchly art character that by lively white, black, and color brings a resurrection brightness into the crucifixion emblem. (It reminds me of how Mondrian began to break out of *De Stijl* with his *Broadway Boogie Woogie*, 1942–43.) Di Stefano's oil on canvas (*Community of the Saints*, 1998) [#7] also quietly balances the circle of saints around the Word or altar, almost a paradigm of the completing communion and welcoming safety authentic church worship promises.

Henk (Senggih) Krijger's gouache on board (*Estranged*, 1963) [#8] is not church art, but is deeply christian: the woman, being sent away by the black male figure with triangular arm upraised as if in adieu or a withheld blow, is heavily pregnant; her arms have no hands—you can't hold on to anything! —and the child spread-eagled in her womb is unhappily cursed, only one eye. Yet the yellow, green, and blue colors and gentle rose petals floating nearby seem to caress the sad pair, whose vertical body lines are just a-kilter to one another, pleading that maybe something good could still come after this *End of an Affair.* . . .

James Ensor's huge oil on canvas (c. 2.5 x 4.3 meters) Bronswijk mentions (KL,186), which shows *Christ's [triumphal] entry into Bruxelles* (1888) [#9] as a kind of *Fasnacht* parade, would have offended far fewer people if they had realized that a normative painting on a biblical theme

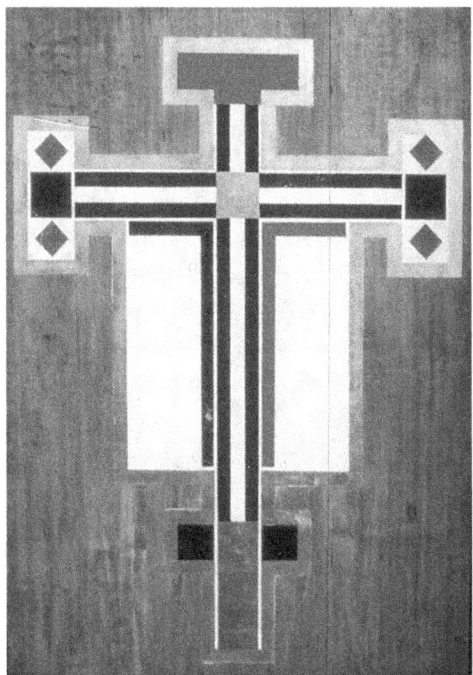

[#6] Julian Di Stefano, *Ornamental Hope*, 1966

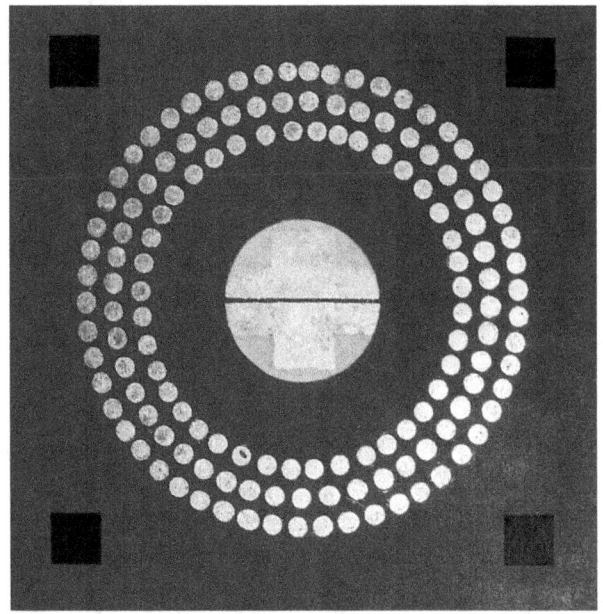

[#7] Julian Di Stefano, *Community of Saints*, 1998

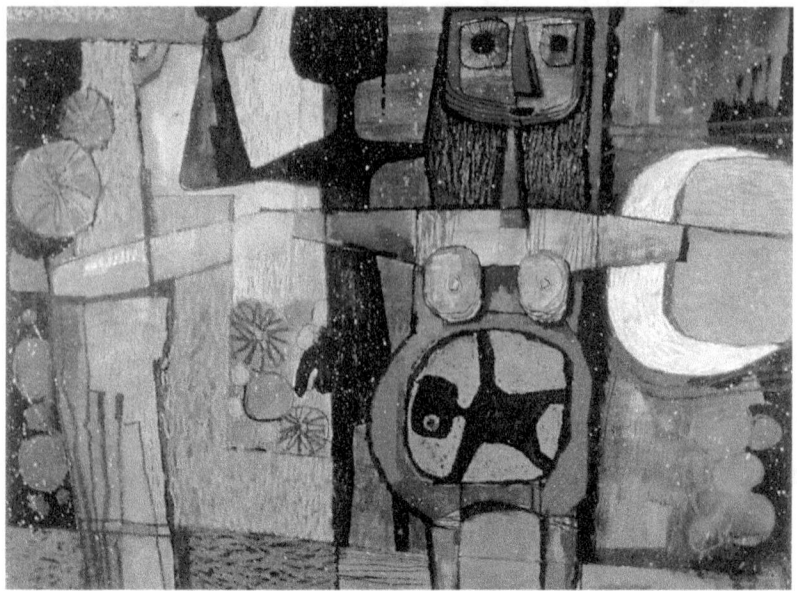

[#8] Henk (Senggih) Krijger, *Estranged*, 1963

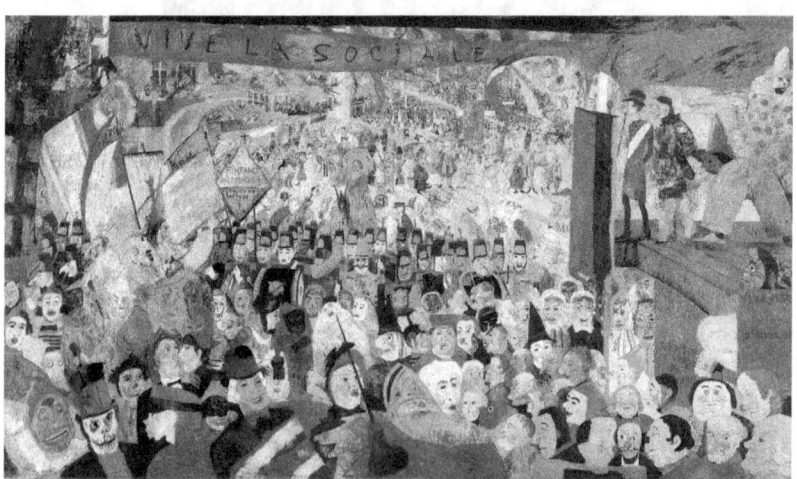

[#9] James Ensor, *Christ's Entry into Brussels in 1889*, 1888

does not have to be art for church, churchly art. Ensor's panorama, *Vive la sociale! Vive Jesus, roi de Bruxelles!* catches the riot of the crowd excitement, which dwarfs the Messiah on the lowly ass. Many in the tumult wear masks of stupidity, vulgarity, and greed because—no wonder—as the Gospel narrates it, they who shout in the happening today, "Blessed is the king who comes in the Name of the Lord!" shall change face in a very few days to become the rabble screaming, "We want Barabbas!" (Luke 19:28–44, 23:1–25). Such penetrating painterly critique of our human fickleness is a choice gift everybody, it seems to me, should take to heart as a signpost for the good of your own worldly city, whether it be Bruxelles, Paris, Djakarta, Tokyo, or Rio de Janeiro.

What time is it culturally in the world?

The thrust of the whole book on *The Art of Living* is that we live world-wide today in a technocratically compressed society—my term would be "global high-rise" (not "village")—where the commercialization of human nature is so pervasive (Kuiper, KL, 10–11) that it becomes natural for everybody—poor Asian as well as rich American—to live out passionately the creed, "Me First!" Goudzwaard (KL, 88–89), de Knijff (KL, 110–111), Veenhuizen (KL, 220), and Van Setten (KL, 199) all posit how the universal drive to live for the consumption of goods superficializes relationships, acts like acid on "local" cultures, and is a mark of immaturity, of losing or lost faith-identity. And such individualistic, subjectivistic Mammon is the major export of Euro-American culture to the world. "Individualism," in ordinary language, is philosophical masturbation, solely self-preoccupation. "Subjectivism," in ordinary language, is the pragmatist dictum, "ME is GOD!" The combination of subjectivistic, individualistic greed is pandemic, I think, and is even worse in the world than AIDS is in Africa, because the SIG virus (Subjectivistic Individualistic Greed) lets its dead . . . to God walk around as if they know "the art of living."

Eschbach thinks the Western church has drowned itself in trying to rescue our floundering, secularized civilization (KL, 209). Bronswijk says the church has not really understood our sophisticated, ironic culture, which amuses itself to death with erotic violence (cf. also Knijff, KL, 108) and thrives on experimentalism; so the church has tended to censor the arts and to revert to a more old-fashioned idealism (KL, 186). Since I belong to "the church" too, I find it very difficult to generalize in judgment, about whether our sins of chiliastic world-flight, three centuries of military Crusades, fellow-travelling with Colonialist exploitation, our church's constant foot-dragging in being martyred for resisting political tyrannies: have our churchly sins finally caught up with us?

I do know, remembering Jacques Ellul's 1981 exaggerated warning in *La parole humiliée*, that I feel very uncomfortable with Eschbach's remark that the church "fearfully preserves the word-preaching-culture when the world has long since switched over to an image-culture" (KL,

209). And when he says, "too long have congregations searched for a 'theologian' instead of a shepherd and teacher for the congregation"— (KL, 213; to me a false, anti-Intellectual option), all the while promoting the Willow Creek (near Chicago) Community Church praxis of using "creative" professional theatrical sitcom vignettes and comic relief scenes to spearhead "seeker services" (KL, 208)—then your church grows in numbers!—that vision strikes me as so Americanic: Growth and a trend-setting avant-garde Jesus church (KL, 211–212).

For me Christ's church is not a volunteer organization you coax people to join, like the "Y." Christ's church is God's handpicked adopted children who have heard the Word of salvation and been branded for life by God's Spirit (Galatians 4:4–7, 1 Peter 2:9–10) to undergo persecution for living according to what our Lord says to do in the Bible, and it is often sore steadiness under pressure than dramatic breakthroughs (Romans 8:12–17, Philippians 1:27–30). It's true, we church are often more like a confusing smokescreen between God and unbelievers than the winsome midwife of shalom.

You are impressed at the roar of sound a block away from the building where a Korean church prayer meeting is in progress, since the hundreds of people are unashamed to pray hard out loud simultaneously to the Lord. During a Sunday service congregations a thousand strong will cheerfully sing with Korean words the old sentimental pietist hymns of the nineteenth century the U.S. Presbyterian missionaries taught them. I wondered, does "Blessed assurance" (1873)—one of the better songs—sound fresh and pertinent for daily life or is the tune more pleasantly other-worldly if any Buddhist ears should hear the singing, which are accustomed to the brusque cell phones on the urban streets of Seoul and Pusan?

I walked to the church service held outdoors in the village square of Alikalia, inland up-country of Sierra Leone, in the cool of the early morning, called "storytelling," so the Muslims would come too. During the worship service the children song was taught, "Be careful, little eyes what you see; be careful, little eyes what you see; for the Father up above is looking down in love, be careful, little eyes what you see." I don't understand much of the Kuranko language, but I'm certain the following stanzas dealt with the "ears, what you hear," and "fingers, what you touch." It made me disconsolate, and I cried inside, thinking, "The christian faith is supposed to break taboos, not perpetuate them! Is this tinny melody the best the church of Jesus Christ can do to give animists a sense of the LORD's glorious mystery?!" Better that those African children taught us to drum and dance in the spirit of Psalm 150. [Today some of those children of God I met in 1983 are grown up, and their hands have been chopped off by marauding rebel troops, so they cannot touch anything at all— I pray that maybe they can still dance.]

Sometimes when I am discouraged, I think I should do what Blaise Pascal (1623–1662) did. A few days after his death, they found a piece of parchment sewn into the lining of his cloak with a handwritten poem on it which began:

Feu.
Dieu d'Abraham, Dieu d'Isaac, Dieu de Jacob,
non des philosophs et des savants....

After I go join the cloud of witnesses, maybe they will find in the lining of my rain coat an updated version (cf. Hebrews 12:14–29):

FIRE!
The God of Hannah, the God of David, the God of Isaiah,
The LORD of unemployed fishermen, handicapped youth, wise from the
    East, and outcast women,
not the God of TV evangelists, armchair Christians and cheap song. . .[2]

I will need to add a postscript to my poem recalling Philippians 1:15–18, where the imprisoned apostle Paul says, "Remember, Seerveld, with all your rhetoric: whether it was for show or for real, if Christ was preached, still be glad."

One other matter I must broach on what time it is culturally in the world, before I go to my last point, is this: despite various keen analyses and helpful encouragements for the church to take art seriously (KL, 189), I found the Bronswijk chapter unfortunately Eurocentric, maybe because he cites with approval Pope John Paul II's letter to artists dated at the Vatican state, Easter 1999. I don't relish being controversial, but the Pope's well-intentioned letter last year to artists is, in my judgment, utterly Eurocentric and thoroughly out-of-date, because, let me dare say it, our age is post-christian!

I do not mean there are no Christians: the church will be here, promises Scripture, until the Lord returns (Revelation 21); and there are clusters of the faithful around the inhabited world today still serving food, offering wisdom and protection, giving blood to their neighbors

---

2   Although I may disagree with Van Setten that music can never point to the demonic (KL, 195), I found his analysis of "feel-good" music, which induces listeners to become stroked "observers" rather than knowledgeable hearers, most insightful. Van Setten's judgment that church "praise and worship" music is also tempted to degrade itself into a commercialistic mannerism that borders on "vertical kitsch," an attempt to escape "this vale of tears," I find true; "*vermaaksmuziek*" of Babylon, inside the church walls too, lacks *tikwah*, genuine hope (KL, 198).

in Christ's name. By calling our age post-christian (not "postmodern") I mean that the grand synthesis of Egyptian-Greco-Roman culture with Constantine Christianity that has characterized for two millennia the dominant Western civilization in the world is disintegrating (Bronswijk details this too, KL, 184–185). Secularization has gone so deep for so many generations that the residual biblical idiom in the mix can no longer be taken for granted in "the art of living." "The Church" has forfeited (pace John Paul II) credibility in ending wars and doing what is just. The Hindu philosophical poet Rabindranath Tagore (1861–1941) said it already two generations ago (1933):

> It has become increasingly plain that, beyond the bounds of Europe the torch of its civilization was not meant to give light but to start fires. (349)

We do not need to stop being European—I am from Canada but my sensibility is European—yet we must find ways to be biblically christian without being Eurocentric. For example, talk about "third world" disables those who are not citizens of "G8"nations who met in Okinawa recently and decided they would give the poor of the earth digital technology: such "third world" countries, if they were "first" for a change, could say, "We need pure water wells, supplies of grain and good seed to plant before we will look at your hi-tech instruments." That is, we Europeans need to humble ourselves in terminology, in taking vantage point, in making assumptions. Not all those who speak first and are saying, "Lord, Lord," are genuinely serving the neighbor (Matthew 7:15–23).

Bronswijk posits, if I understand him well, what I think is an error, that art itself (following Regamy, Couturier, Tillich) is a symbolical epiphany of "the Spirit," of "supernatural reality," as well as telltale of where the artist stands in what kind of societal milieu (KL, 190–192). John Paul II's letter to artists is even more decisive on this point, stating that artists, thanks to their special "divine spark" (sect. 3), are natural mediators of "religious experience" (sect. 10) of "the Absolute who is utterly beyond" (sect. 15), if the artist, as Plato says, serves "Beauty" (sect. 3). The "sacred art" of Gothic splendor, Michelangelo, Raffaello, Bernini (sect. 8–9), epitomizes, says the Pope, "that true beauty, which, as a glimmer of the Spirit of God, will transfigure matter, opening the human soul to the sense of the eternal." "Artists of the world, may your many different paths all lead to that infinite Ocean of beauty[3] where wonder becomes awe, exhilaration, unspeakable joy" (sect. 16).

I question whether such Beauty theology, and the covert imperial-

---

3 This is a precise quote from the ecstatic Diotima of Mantineia speech in Plato's *Symposium* (210c6-e1), although the papal document does not footnote the source.

ism of christening by dogma all artists of the world as naturally "inspired," is what the world needs today. In fact, if I may be so bold, I think it is time for Europe to sacrifice its "beautiful art" if we should ever want to make earnest with becoming genuinely christian in our culture. I do not mean we go iconoclastic or burn lovely paintings as Botticelli did after he was self-convicted of vanity by the preaching of Savonarola in Florence (mid 1490s). I do mean that we stop thinking that the magnificent ("Christian") Humanist art of cinquecento Europe is the norm for artistry, and maybe consider too whether such "Beauty" does not betray unchecked power, luxury, the pomp and circumstance of which easily accommodates vanity. Even Michelangelo changed his style from the heroics of the Sistine chapel after he started assiduously reading the Bible near the end of his life with Vittoria Colonna, so that his late (Rondanini, c. 1552–53) *Pietà* has no bravado [see *RA* #111], but is a sagging marble lump of sorrow, a depleted, exhausted Christ figure.

The non-European world is suffering woe that staggers our well-fed ability to take it in. The world at large is asking us European Christians to retrain our eyes and expectations away from appreciating the grandeur of Rome and the faded Victorian *Light of the World* (Holman Hunt, 1853) into thanking God for an artwork like Australian Warren Breninger's *Gates of Prayer* [#10]. Imagine using this series of 44 "praying mouths"

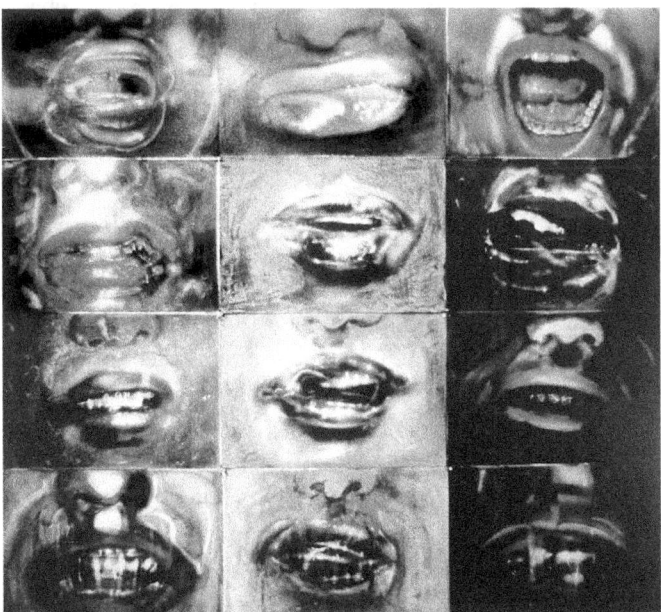

[#10] Warren Breninger, example of *Gates of Prayer*, 1993-2008 [detail]

with pursed lips, clenched teeth in anguish, pleading with God to answer, as Job did: use it in church as backdrop for your "Good" Friday message on the text, "My God, my God! Why have you forsaken me!" (Psalm 22, Mark 15:33–39). Do you see what it could mean for an artist to deny yourself in our European culture, take up Christ's cross, and follow the Lord as a living sacrifice (Romans 12:1–2) by bringing imaginative nuances of compassionate meaning to those who are weeping in God's world, not only in the atrocious massacres of Christians by Jihad warriors in East Timor and the Sudan, but believer or unbeliever who may feel on occasion like damaged goods in this very room?

Faithful artistic snake-and-dove responses in God's world
As God's people in a post-christian historical period, pummeled by the principalities of technocratic Pragmatism and a powerful cultural elite gone quite deliberately, urbanely profane, our calling is to giveaway the Lord's gifts indiscriminately, and do it as worldliwise as snakes while remaining as innocent as doves (Matthew 10:16). Most persons have quite mottled ethnic identities, but I believe a person should thrive in being who you culturally are—whether it be Dutch, European, sub-Saharan African, mainland Chinese—so long as you know what time it is globally and do not practice insularity, on pain of obsolescence. Also, everybody in their dated location should giveaway to their neighbor what is truly needed rather than just whatever the giver has in surplus, lest the receivers resent the gifts. What does this mean for making art in the coming generation?

Let me tersely fill out Birtwistle's careful prognosis on "new" art. In the Bible "new" does not moan "novel"; a "new" song (Psalm 33:1–3, 40:1–3, 96:1–6) refers to a melody that will not wear out, does not go out of date. I think the criterion we need for deciding what art is "new," that is, what past art is worth remembering (to avoid the helter-skelter pastiche Birtwistle correctly finds rampant [KL, 182–183]), and to judge what contemporary artistic activity deserves our attention at present (Is video installation more engrossing than other art forms? [KL, 181–182]) is this: does the art-making and the artistry made build up imaginative human abilities and proffer allusively for attentive neighbors sorrowful wisdom and good cheer for "the art of living" in God's troubled world? Then it will be genuinely "new" art that endures.

For example, I think Nicolas Poussin's (1594–1665) masterful, complicated, finely tuned art like *The Exposition of Moses* (1654) [#11] is as dated today as ordering in classical Latin a hamburger at McDonalds.

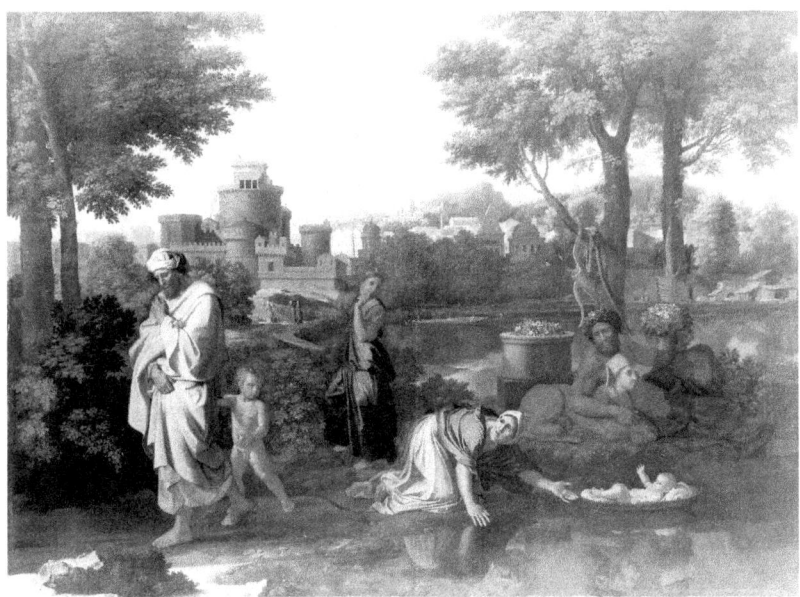

[#11] Poussin, *The Exposition of Moses*, 1654

I could exegete the painting for you: Poussin's architectural amalgam here, the usual Roman fort complex with Egyptian pyramids and Greek temples, has its cosmopolitan commentary curiously heightened by a river god holding a sphinx creature behind which hang an assortment of Pan pipes, Bacchus cymbals, and Diana's bow and quiver of arrows—an unusual decor indeed to accompany Moses' mother and family leaving him adrift, while sister Miriam cautions silence and points to the middle ground shadows where Pharaoh's daughter and retinue approach. Poussin's homogenization of classical mythical, historical, and ordinary biblical events to stage such a tableau tries to endow the story with timeless significance: we people should live as if gods attend our vicissitudes. But such art and its "European" thesis is artificial today, played out.

The art of Poussin's contemporary, however, Johannes Vermeer (1632–1675) is still new, in my judgment, even though it takes some doing to learn the casual painterly intricacies. *Woman Holding a Balance* (c. 1662–64) [#12] quietly allows light in the darkened room to fall softly on the woman's stately (pregnant) bearing and bathe her tilted face, bare arms and fingers; the right arm holds the scale with sure poise and the left hand touches the solid wood tabletop just to assure her balanced sense of reality. Indistinct on the back wall is a baroquish painting of "The Final Judgment," where Christ is blessing the saints rising in the air to be with him while the naked sinners below fearfully shriek for the mountains to

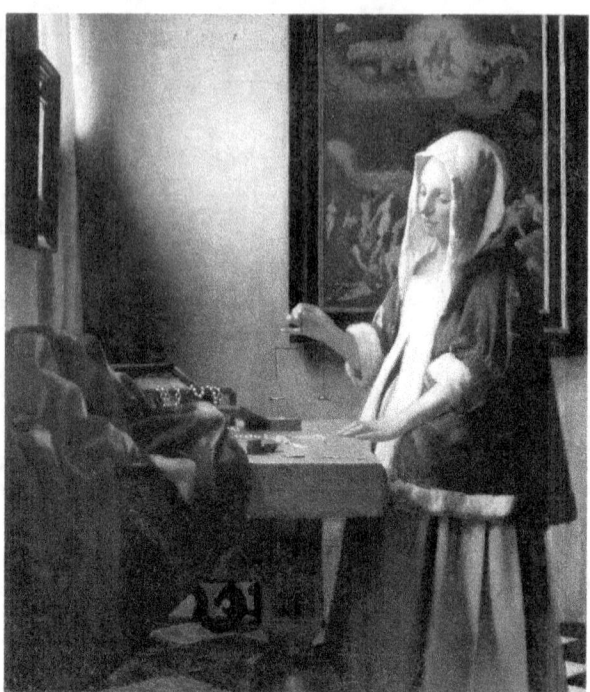

[#12] Johannes Vermeer, *Woman Holding a Balance*, 1664

cover them, a subtle commentary in counterpoint to the woman's serene testing the truth of the balance. The unhurried equanimity and judicious judgment featured in her whole demeanor assure anyone that lifetime and human decisions, as well as pearls, are precious. And anyone who knows Vermeer's oeuvre also knows how women almost always hold key importance in his paintings, not as objects of male desire, not as Dutch *huisvrouwen*, but as bearers of enigmatic, resourceful glory close to the encomium of Proverbs 31:10-31. Such an "old" sturdy portrayal of womanhood is good news today too.

As for finding contemporary art that is interculturally fertile, not parochial, and breathes a sure spirit of winsome certainty on the abiding goodness of creation, despite the horror we humans often make of it, I'll show just one modest example. Catalan ceramicist Joan Cots (1927–2004) seems to take the wonderful plasticity of clay and fashion figures, plates, plaques, hangings, that are not Eurocentric but African Mediterranean in shape and feel, which take root somehow in neither the Greco-Roman nor Italian Renaissance Beauty traditions [#13]. Cots' stele have the enigmatic presence of objects consecrated to something mysterious. The Miro-like markings remind one of faces that are both intimate and

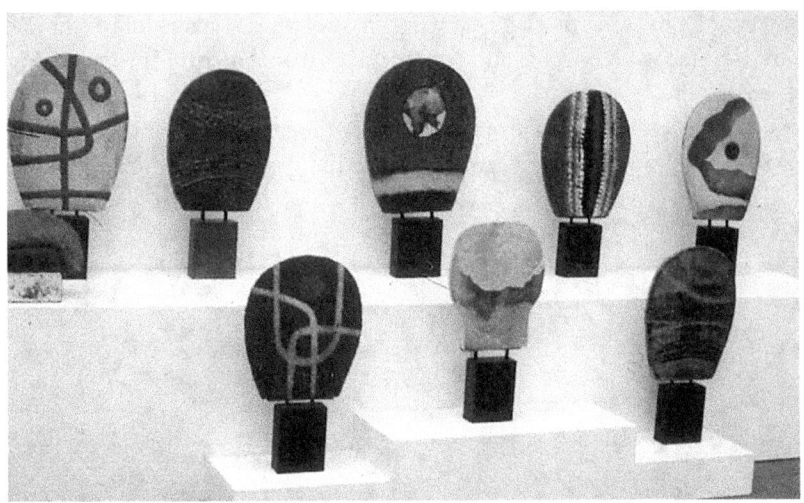

[#13] Joan Cots, *Stele*, (1995)

strong, with an uncanny personality, weather-beaten, firmly aristocratic. There is a glow of warm desert sands to some of these "signposts," which look both severe and delicate. When you see a whole family of Cots' stele you think of a reunion of very different persons who somehow still belong to one another: they have idiosyncratic quirks, these creatures, whether human or not does not matter.

It is simply "christian" (=what God wants), I think, to explore the protean tactile glory of clay material, to shape and bake mud into sturdy breakable objects like these, as unexpectedly arresting as brilliant flowers are from bone-dry cacti. Stele were used by the Older Testament people of God to commemorate important events (Genesis 28:16–22, Joshua 4:1–9, 1 Samuel 7:9–12), and were used by the migratory Canadian Inuit to give direction to the younger generation on the hunt. Cots' stele have that same sturdy, forthright, friendly character, to my eye, a quiet inviting nobility that welcomes you to say "hello," and be assured of acceptance in your wonderful peculiarity.

No matter what is societally in store for the earthly culture of your generation, Isaiah's Word of God about firm tent stakes and a stretching out canopy is reliable: let God's people as a faith-community, spread out in ethnic diversity around the world, cohere their cultural offerings into living imaginative sacrifices; discover the forgotten host of artistic witnesses from the past, and forge a minority culture, God willing—not "counter-culture"[4]—a minority culture of well-staked shalom in this de-

---

4 Bronswijk seems to miss my meaning on this fine point (KL, 189). The Christian community of artists are thetical; they make art, song, poetry, and literature out of

racinated post-christian age blowing in the wind, a winsome minority culture that will conceive and consecrate diaconal artistry for deepening everyday life.

Joyce Recker's collage of ripped paper called *Shadows Crossing* (1992) [#14] as a simple greeting card shows up the general superficiality of the

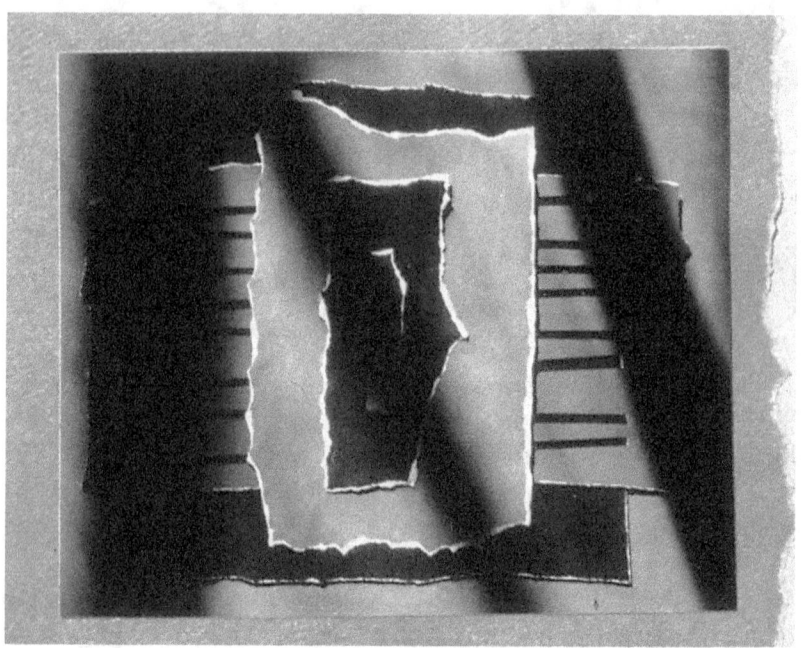

[#14] Joyce Recker, *Shadows Crossing*, 1992

Hallmark Card industry, without a word. The burnished golden space around the inner black long center is quieting and steady, and the large rectangular frame on the brown background does not show ripped edges; so the black shadows crossing this field of subdued color are indeed crossing, passing, going to move on, as the superimposed pieces stand their torn ground. Dear friend, your dark shadows are passing through. . . .

Because Christ's body lives out its faith in public, normally Christian artisans will tend not to privatize their artistry either. Britt Wik-

---

their own faith guts and perspective spired by the biblical revelation. The fact that the reigning secular culture is opposed to the culture of shalom sets up an opposition and the christians' minority status, out of joint with the post-christian age. But artists in Christ's body do not want to assume a 1960s counter-cultural, subversive stance, since there is a long nurturing history of redemptive art that serves as tap root for artists who would be redeeming the time today. Cf. my *A Christian Critique of Art and Literature* (Toronto Tuppence Press, 1995), 8 n.4, 143–144; also *Rainbows for the Fallen World* (1980/2005), 195–201.

ström's memorial stone for a saint's taking leave [#15] speaks with quiet friendship to anybody wandering into its vicinity: the bird bath incised in its granite top lets the birds of heaven come wash their feet and drink the gift of rain from the artistic basin here shaped like hands open in prayer receive a blessing. Maybe even one of Noah's doves will bring a sprig of olive leaves to hint of new life beyond the grave.

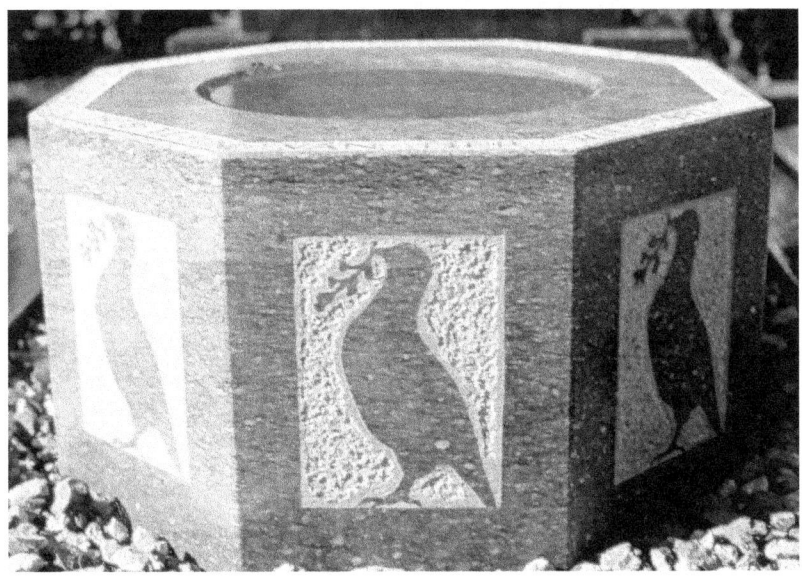

[#15] Britt Wikström, *Wim de Mol* gravestone, chiseled granite, 1983, Essenhof Cemetery, Dordrecht, The Netherlands

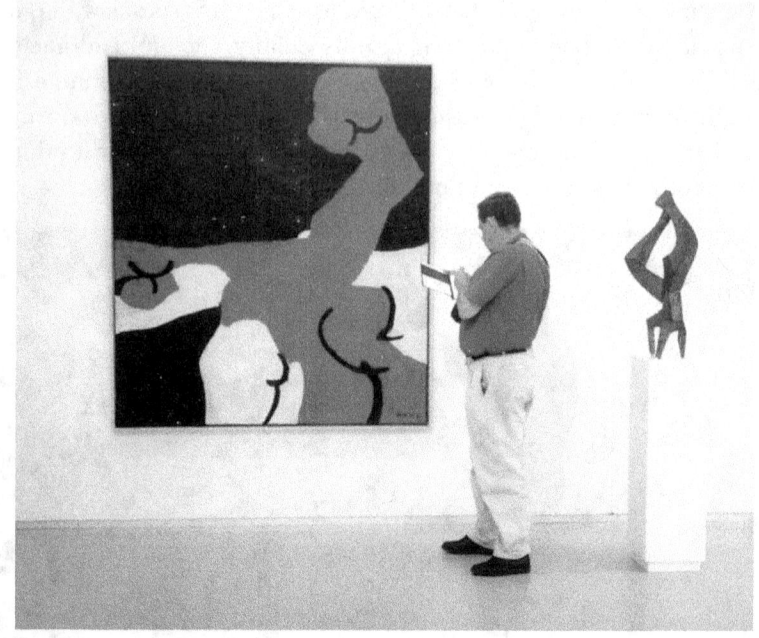

Seerveld at work on location in the Cobra museum outside
Amsterdam, Netherlands, 1996 (photo by William David Romanowski)

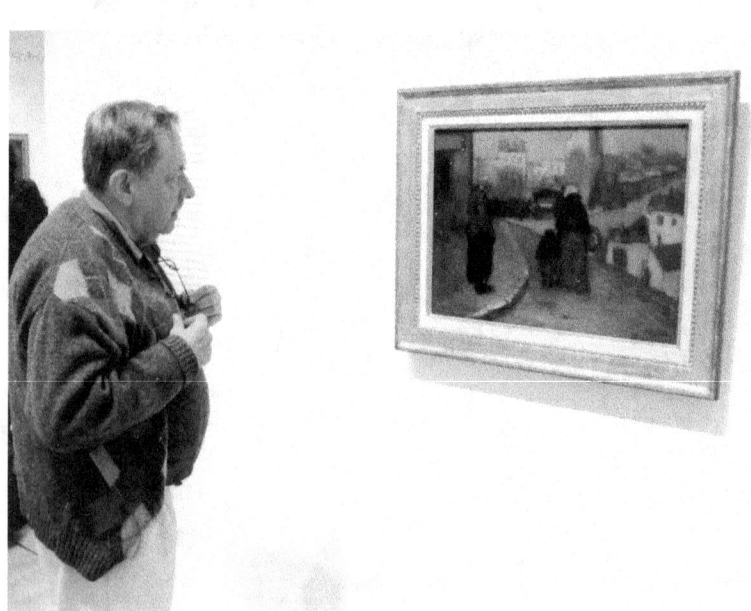

Scrutinizing an early Picasso,
San Francisco Art Museum, 2011 (photo by Jan Seerveld)

Imaginative Reenchantment of Society in God's World: a redemptive artistic task in the European Union

While it is true you can only finally resolve problems of war, poverty, racism, and mindless cultural violence at large if people like us here at heart be convicted that the Jew Jesus was the Christ, the Son of God, who saves us and our neighbor from the wages of sin, which is death, whose Spirit can drive us humans to follow the Lord's Rule of shalom to forgive, to put the neighbor first, to give away your gifts: while that is true, it would be an historical cop-out for Christians only to preach the gospel as evangelists, because then you would have to wait for the end of the world before you tended to the societal evil all around. I think I am saying precisely what Christian Artists International has stood for and for what *The Art of Living* book is a sturdy signpost.[1]

From my Christian stance in the faith tradition of the French-Swiss-German-Dutch biblical Reformation, I believe that if human leaders, and followers, can institute normative policies in society—programs that follow how the God of the universe wills things to be done—if one can take discerning small steps to initiate, sustain, and carry through in cities, in transportation and commerce, nation-states, media, friendship networks, church-synagogue-mosque, a direction good for the commonweal, then God will bless those efforts despite evil forces remaining at work among us, despite foot-dragging churchgoers or fake good people who serve their household idols.

We have heard several gifted speakers describe in practical detail the societal status of authors and artists in different European countries, as well as noon-hour meditations on peace. My conclusion for these meetings

---

1   *The Art of Living: The Cultural Challenge of the 21ˢᵗ Century*, eds. Jan Peter Balkenende, Roel Kuiper, Leen La Rivière (Rotterdam: CNV-Kunstenbond, 2001).

Spoken in 2001. First published in *Art AD 2001: The social and cultural challenge of Europe. Reflections on the treaty of Maastricht (1991)* (Rotterdam: Christian Arts International Proceedings [11], 2002), 81–89.

tries to focus on certain structural societal matters that have been opera-
tive in Europe's history so far and is the legacy behind the last ten years
of problems and endeavors that affect the place and task of artistry in
the European Union being formed. In the thrash of geopolitics, global
corporate economics, burgeoning cities, and displaced people greedy for
normal living conditions, amid extension of the American Empire and
the commercialization of culture, it would be wise not to be idealistic,
but to be committed visionaries with our feet responsibly on the ground
in judging what could be redemptive steps to take.

The "artworld" of artists, art critics and theorists, patrons, art managers and promoters, as well as art performers, has, I believe, an integral
role in our civilizational turmoil, namely, to reenchant the imagination
of society in God's world. The communion of professional and artistic
saints has a joyful task to bring cheer indiscriminately to people that
bears hope, rather than to let each one simply drift along as best one can
in the global gulfstream of events spelling disaster. So my conclusion is
similar to those of ten years of conferences: **revitalize the christian cultural heritage of Europe; bring about a reformation of the artworld
so that it serves the ache of poor and rich alike to have an imagina-
tively awakened, redemptive conscience in our weal and woe.**

The International Association of Christian Artists is right to voice the
concern that artists be able to put bread and wine on the family table in
laboring at the gifts God created us to have to give away to others. But
we need to understand why it is and has been so difficult for artists to
do their proper imaginative service for fellow citizens and neighbors in
the last several generations. That means we need to keep revisiting the
basics in a fresh way so newcomers are able to get on board and so we
individuals who tend to go off on tangents of our own keep a common
focus as Christian Artists International continues to be a rallying point
for thoughtful makers and performers of art.

The complex creational structure of society

So much changes in human life in ten years or in a generation that it
could be beneficial to realize that certain things remain structurally the
same in world society.

Everybody has a parent, even if you disown them or because of
some atrocity you become a motherless child or orphan. Normally you
are born or adopted into a group of caring people bonded by blood ties
we call a clan or family.

Persons usually inhabit a locality. Even nomads frequent roughly the same territory. Many are so mobile or displaced today it is hard to be at home anywhere; but cities, where people settle down in neighborhoods have been around since the days of Cain (Genesis 4:17).

Children are always taught as they grow up, by doing menial chores in the household, learning on the streets in the school of hard knocks, or getting educated in an academic institution. People usually find themselves a community of faith of sorts. Whether it be orthodox Jewry, Sunni Muslim, church of Jesus Christ, Masonic lodge, the Moonies, a gang of Hell's Angels, or a makeshift arrangement of trust under a self-appointed guru: people seem to seek out a communion where they can fellowship and celebrate rituals of initiation, union, and burial.

Everybody also belongs to a country where you have some kind of a paper or promise to protect you from criminal acts. A chief of your tribe and tribal council or the Legislature and rulers of your nation state have covenanted to defend you from harm and count you as a responsible, loyal member of the body politic. Sooner or later humans barter goods, trade services, engage in commerce.

Men and women have always kept records inscribed in stone, inked in papyrus, and sent signals by smoke or messages by pigeons until radio and telephone joined the newspaper, to mediate communications native to human society.

And from the beginning of time there have been tillers of the soil, weavers of clothes, bards and storytellers, craftsmen and women who made utensils with their hands and built structures to live in. . . .

That is, I am pointing out that amid all the myriad changes since the day God made the first fur coats (Genesis 3:21) until viruses spoil websites on the internet, society is a complex archipelago of various enduring human groupings all of us are meant to be members of. Families, neighborhoods, training centers, communities of trust, government with rulers, businesses, media, hand laborers—no matter how differently they are fleshed out—God has instituted such possible structural unions of humans to prompt what is good for us creatures. How we embody a family, set up a school, plan a city, run a government, or demolish such responsibility is quite varied. But society, as a matter of created fact, imbricates you and me throughout the ages with certain hugs of God we delineate as institutional structures.

I know, some thinkers hate institutions and deny that society is an interlocking mesh of multiple communities. They see only loose individuals confronted by an organized bloc of oppressive power. Maybe because they experienced a dysfunctional family, a hard-nosed church, a corrupt government, they decide to be individualists (although they inadvertently try to turn friends into a pick-up family, may start their own cult, and have to play the citizen parasite—it's very hard to practice individualistic ideology when you need currency to pay for a train ticket or taxi).

Such a Kierkegaardian (or Lockean) atomistic approach to society cannot help but misconceive and oversimplify the place of artists in a European Union. It is not just artist me and the impersonal state, which holds the bags of taxed money I want grants from. It is not just artist me and the Church hierarchy. Public taxed citizens live in countries where there are hundreds of vital and comatose congregations, but we artists are also always inflected by our habitations, past mentors, (un)employment, what we do or do not read, hear, and ponder in our heart. So *I emphasize the wonderful complicated nature of society* and its process and flow, lest we be tempted to think there can be one easy solution to the problems of artists in society in Europe, or anywhere in the world.

Changing historical integrators of society in Europe

What is the historical track record of artistry in European society? I do not presume in the next few pages to rehearse the history of this peopled land mass as it became Europe, but we need a running start to help assess where we are today, ten years after the Maastricht Treaty (1992) amended the "European Economic Community" (1958) to make it the "European Community."

Europe as a cultural entity

When the conquering people who followed the prophet Mohammed with the *Qu'ran* in the later 600s AD brought an Islamic unity of law, language, and way-of-life to Palestine, Syria, Egypt, and North Africa, the Muslim civilization set off at a distance what was becoming the geography of "Europe" from the old Roman Empire spottily Christianized by Constantine (ruled 306–337 AD). You could say that the hybrid of the christian Church—its Roman catholic, Carolingian, or Byzantine Orthodox version—grafted onto the Hellenistic Greco-Roman civilization is the background inheritance to why Italian, Irish, Dutch, Bulgarian, Germanic, Russian cultures have had a certain European commonality that has distinguished their *mentalité* from lands served by quite different ancient sources like the Taoist-Confucian Asiatic Chinese, or the animist African Ghanian civilizations. The cultural identity of Europe may be variegated, even conflicted, and is constantly changing, but seen globally,

I dare say, **Europe's specific particularity for a couple millennia exists thanks to the fermenting yeast of the christian Church.**

As the so-called Holy Roman Empire after Frankish Charlemagne (emperor 800–814) struggled to rule unruly regions from its roving Carolingian court, bishops of the Church, and later mendicant orders of the Church, became major patrons with their cloisters and cathedrals for manual laborers, which included artisans and musicians and literate readers and writers. In sync with the loose feudal localized setup of vassal lords and serfs, the Church paternally employed painters, carpenters, sculptors, manuscript calligraphers, jewelers, embroiderers, singers; and the guilds saw to it that the artisan journeymen and apprentices made a living, until a plague drove you elsewhere for safety and a new cathedral jobsite opened up. It is interesting that although greed was considered a mortal sin, if you donated riches for sumptuous artistry in the Church, it counted toward your salvation.

Wealthy trading families in circles like Sienna, Venezia—the renowned Medici bankers in Firenze (1200–1500s)—became *maecenas* (munificent benefactor),[2] patrons of art who by their exceptional artwork were to bring dignity and fame to their donor's name and city. The cinquecento papacy of Julius II (1503–13) and Leo X (1513–17) aimed to bring monumental grandeur to Vatican Rome that would impress the world with the splendor of a new Jerusalem; so they commissioned spectacular artwork from superstars like Michelangelo, Gianlorenzo Bernini, and Raphael, and treated them like princes, while ordinary art makers, it must be said, labored hard at guild hall wages just to put bread on the table.

A wealthy Flemish city like Brugge in the 1400s not only had a court of Burgundy royalty to contract for expensive artworks, but also a flourishing commercial class of cosmopolitan bourgeoisie who supported a regular international import-export trade in raw materials for artists and attended outdoor fairs where Memling and lesser known artists sold their wares in the marketplace, despite certain restrictions imposed by the Image-Makers Guild-union. The Dutch too, caught up in the entrepreneurial mercantilist spirit of the times bought and sold art pieces on the open market; art dealers began to come into the transactions.

Different European countries developed varied societies

As wars between nation-states forming in Europe firmed up quite dis-

---

2 Maecenas was the benefactor and patron who gave a lifelong salary to the poets Virgil and Horace (c. 65–8 bc).

tinct cultural traditions in the jostling countries, and as artists gradually professionalized themselves independently, agents of what they produced, different patterns emerged in various jurisdictions on how artists functioned in society.

The French monarchy of Louis XIV centralized control of the arts under the French Academy in Paris, and the state's monopoly on art schools' figure-drawing(!) and theatre/opera companies continued past the revolution into Napoleon's code of control. Non-sanctioned troupes were harassed by the police, although puppetry, pantomime, and shows not in competition with the approved arts were allowed to happen on the streets.

Principalities and kingdoms in Austria and Germanic dukedom initiated, recruited, and supported their own regional *Bildungstheater*, literati, musicians, and graphic artists; later on *freie Genossenschaften* (unattached societies for the arts), with princely patronage, continued to shore up arts meant to improve the morals of the citizenry, while commerce was left to regulate the poorer taste of the non-elite who existed outside the brilliant tiny cultural centers like Weimar.

In England, where it had been illegal to import foreign paintings until the 1680s, there was a struggle as to whether an indigenous guild, farm system of experiential apprenticeship on the job should provide the artists for the country, or would it be an intellectual academic formation from a royal approved institution? Sir Joshua Reynold's inclinations prevailed over Hogarth's plans with the inauguration of the British Royal Academy (1769), and doing full-length portraits of English gentry with domesticated footnotes of "history paintings" in the Franco-Italian manner became *de rigueur* for artists who wanted to be accepted in the fashionable circuit as professionals.

Over in Holland, without a Vatican papacy or a French monarchy, it was long conventional for manual artists to live from a mix of market sales, commissions if you could get one, and a second job—Jan Steen owned a tavern, Hobbema was a wine taster, Vermeer and Rembrandt were art dealers—since you set a price on a painting depending on its size, hours of labor, and the strength of the artist's CV. Ordinary people owned small paintings on a devotional theme, a landscape, or of everyday objects—no big deal.

What I am suggesting is that in Western Europe there is a substantial history of how artists have been interwoven with European society, which at various stages in different places was dominated if not mainly integrated by one or another of the normal institutions in society. The

Roman catholic Church held Vatican Italy together; the centralized state in Paris ruled France; cities in Flanders gave cultural leadership; the market energized Holland; *maecenae* led the arts in England and German territory. Whether you were a superstar or a run-of-the-mill artist, you had a relatively respected or decorative regular place in the society of the country according to its major integrating institution. The same held true, with variation, for Scandinavian and Slavic European life too. But such—not always comfortable—integration of artists in society changed.

Artists in France (*l'art pour l'art*), Holland (*de Tachtigers*) England (aestheticism of the 1890s), Germany (*Jugendstil*), declared with brazen security that they would be beholden to no church, no state, no moneyed interests, no morals, nobody in heaven or on earth, but only to art itself. This stand was taken by important artists in Europe in the aftermath of industrialization, which helped certain individual financiers amass fortunes at the expense of laborers, at the peak of colonialist policies in which European nations were exploiting countries for resources around the world, and at the time when many churches were turning pietistic, formalistic, or declaring themselves to be infallible on doctrine and morals.

Prices on art were going up because the *nouveaux riches* were bidding through dealers at art auctions against other plutocrats to buy prestige, and museums were removing "masterpieces" from the open market. And then the Americans entered the European equation! A Croesus of Pierpont Morgan who had unlimited money, and could buy up whatever art he could get his hands on. "No thank you," said the purists, "we don't intend to sell our burning gem-like soul to be hung up like a 'collectable' in somebody's private mansion; we'd rather shock their pants off!"

A consequence of this stand-off has been a stream of successive art movements with manifestoes in the last century, with many artists resolutely "free" from (= bereft of!) church and state connections, a local municipal supportive milieu, benefactors, or a normal task that does not need to create a sensation to be taken seriously. As graphic art became explicitly more esoteric, professional orchestras more expensive, and national theatre troupes giving less bang for the buck than a national film board, modem democratic states were reluctant to expend so easily the largesse of a Louis XIV or Catherine the Great of Russia for highfalutin art. It's better for a government to use the lion's share of its official cultural money, as do France, Italy, and Greece, for the conservation of its artistic heritage; and let the current performing arts like entertaining pop song take commercial care of itself.

An American wrinkle

Before I draw this thumbnail history of artists in European society to the point of our current circumstances and you think there is not so much new under the sum, let me interject just one relevant contrasting matter from the American scene.

Coming from a deep anti-royalty bias, and out of a Puritan/Quaker church tradition that was not "catholic" and frowned on theatre and sensuous art, American democracy—farmers paid the bulk of the taxes early-on—had no reason to suppose church or state should support the arts. Besides, somebody like P.T. Barnum's farraginous mixture of songbird Jenny Lind and grotesque freaks under the same big top took care of people with their God-given need for "art" and circuses. Further, after the American War between the States (1861–65) when boom times from building railroads, mining, banking, communications, led to unparalleled prosperity amid a great increase in population through immigration: what happened minted the American approach to artists in society. The rough-and-ready immigrant laborers as a mass took political power away, for example, from the coterie of Brahmins in Boston—there were 400 millionaires in the city of Boston before 1900—who then organized a nonprofit Museum of Fine Arts (chartered 1870) and the Boston Symphony Orchestra (1881) with the profits of their business ventures. The result was that these nonprofit cultural institutions, which this closely knit social class set up independently, governed, patronized, and staffed themselves, could function without the interference of any politically run governments. The museum and symphony orchestra were instituted partly for their own highbrow benefit, but also to educate the rising middleclass on what was truly "fine" art. This development unfortunately canonized the divide between "high art" for the urban elite and "pop art" and "folk art" consumed by the masses, but inadvertently, something societally correct was implemented: art museums and civic orchestras are, and are to be, I believe, not-for-profit organizations.

Root problems to the rich European identity and cultural diversity

Depending upon where your home base was for practicing art in European society between what is called World War I and World War II, you had to fend for yourself, live off your output, your copyright, lock into a municipally funded organization, or find a private sponsor for your projects. (A *maecenas* like Peggy Guggenheimn, advised by Herbert Read, practically established unknown surrealists and later Jackson Pollock as the reigning lords of avant garde art.) But after the war in Europe, national governments began, with prosperous '60s money, to subsidize artistry liberally. The dependency of artists on such protectorate grants soon underwent the vagaries of the '70s focus on disadvantaged groups, the decentralizing trend of the '80s, and the cutback shortage of public tax monies for cultural institutions taking place in the '90s. Today there is uncertainty about who should, or can, pay for what art, and why, since there are so many pressing needs worldwide—health care, literacy, safety for the weak and poor, while wars and atrocities persist. There seems to be a gridlock of interests that stymie any clear, specific sense of how the budding European Union should now deal with the arts.

Let me try, on the strength of the history I sketched, to get underneath the myriad surface difficulties and pinpoint a couple of root problems of our impasse, before I end with a few firm suggestions.

1.   If historical "Europe" is the non-Muslim spiritual amalgam of christianity and Greco-Roman civilization, is that "Europe" chipping to pieces like dried out glue in the fingers of your generation? In our secularized, homogenized day, who cares for or is even aware of what the "common cultural heritage" of "Europe" is (Treaty of Amsterdam, 1995, art. 151)? Once upon a time Jewish intellectuals consciously "assimilated," it was called, becoming leading Europeans. Will Muslims do the same, or remain a *Fremdkörper* in the community of Europe? **Is there enough European cultural cohesion to make respecting "national and regional diversity" meaningful?** Or is the European Union, just crying to patch up the iron and clay feet of the enormous golden, silver, bronze, iron image of Nebuchadnezzar's imperial dream once upon a time (Daniel 2)? Is "Europe" still viable?

2.   What societal institution, if any, calls the shots in the European Union? If I am not mistaken, it is Money, as the initial telltale designation "EEC" reveals, European Economic Community. The European Community's creed is "open market economy with free competition" (art. 3a), which entails compliance by the member nation-states to follow the guiding principles of "stable prices, sound public finances and monetary conditions and a sustainable balance of payments" (art. 3a). So we have the anomaly of trying to unify different political entities (which talk in the European Parliament) by compelling an economic uniformity (to a capitalistically ordered society). This trust in market forces to integrate a quality society is mistaken, I think, because it forces states to act like businesses and treat their rightful citizens more like paying custom-

ers, and compels cities, for example, to downplay their task to be centers for civic cultural identity, public sociality, and neighborhood artistry, and drives cities rather to compete with other cities for the *ad hoc* festivals that attract the global tourist dollar.

Fortunately Rotterdam resisted this tendency when it was chosen as Cultural Capital of Europe 2001, and conceived programs to deepen the "ten" cities Rotterdam infrastructurally is.

The ideology of "free market competition" pushes "privatization" upon states, to sell public utilities and public cultural features to private companies on the false grounds of efficiency, and then leaves only a bricolage of uprooted, destabilized services that had unobtrusively provided solid local community. Effects of such commercialistic tyranny, where financial management strategies assume the quasi-monopolistic control of a state, can be found troubling Eastern Europe today. To switch from communist party-state control of culture to the religion of free enterprise without time to construct a social infrastructure, a middle class sense of proprietary openings and responsibilities, legal checks on cultural quality, is to invite cultural annihilation and corruption. Hungarian cinema production by four companies, using state-controlled facilities and an official distribution system from 1948–1987, when "privatized" as needed to join the Union, led to American Hollywood high-tech, action movies capturing 90 percent of the entertainment market by 1989. The American companies took their profits out of the country and had no inclination to support the Hungarian film industry.

Money is not the root of all evil, but when powerful corporate Money institutions usurp away from political governance the role of chief integrator of society, you are asking, I think, for uniform desire rather than a union of diversity.

3. Which cultural diversity in Europe does the European Union want to honor and develop? The national legacies, and leave it at that? Will amateur artists or only professionals receive grants? The Dutch today have a sliding scale of criteria to accommodate this problem; Ireland has its Asadana (1983), which is an elite Academy of about only 200 artists who are subsidized. To each country its own cultural policy? Does the European Community want blockbuster exhibitions of painter treasures in major capital cities, or also see the value of showing local schools of artists in poorer outlying districts of Sicily or Portugal? Should the European Community encourage artistry that fits a general-denominator taste, or include serious partisan gay/lesbian, anarchist, evangelical chris-

tian artistic efforts in our "diversity"? How should the European Union weigh funds for public civic art and conserving old frescoes in churches next to having stellar performing artists entertain lots of people?

The euro has brought an end to money-changers at the borders within the European Community, but the euro will not eliminate the problem of deciding priorities on which artistic diversity to support. Do we artists simply agitate for a bigger slice of the European or only the national financial pie? This Christian Artist international conference was partially paid for by the European Union, not by a national government. Are you artists "European" enough for that? Or have all artists who are in the groove of "doing your own thing" forfeited any claim to be a participant in the "Culture" entitlement article of the Maastricht Treaty?

Multiple normative institutional responses still needed

Let me conclude with remarks about the root problems I have mentioned of "Europe," a Money-run society, and artists scattered on a thousand hills.

1. I am grateful to God that I became European and soberly accept the challenge to be repentant about European history in the world by acting as restoratively normative as possible with my training and gifts in this day and age. If you are serious about being European—our context is the European Community—I recommend we reaffirm the Reformation and medieval christian strain to "Europe," not to its Renaissance Humanist version of Roman antiquity (converting to secular Americanism) with its imperialistic virus.

I do not mean one should become Calvinist or Lutheran and start a "religious war," or go on an old-fashioned crusade to Talibanic Afghanistan. I mean Europeans should gratefully reinvigorate the genius of the historic Reformation, which is to realize that the world is a theatre of God, as John Calvin says (*Institutio Christianae Religionis*, I, vi, 2), and is to be worn like a garment that clothes us humans colorfully rather than be taken as a brute object for our disposal. The whole world is God's household garden (Genesis 2:8–15, Psalm 24:1–2, Ephesians 1:9–10) to be cultivated into a joyful city of God, as Saint Augustine said; **so culture becomes the wrapped gifts of us human cultivators for God and neighbors, to make them glad**. The Reformation held that the biblical word gives trustworthy direction for "the art of living"—a scandalous thing to say today—and every person is called to treat other people as neighbors, even if enemies (Proverbs 25:21–22, Romans 12:9–21, 13:8–

10), and not as unwelcome competitors.

The spirit of inner biblical Reformation, which is historically integral to "Europe," Vatican II brought into practice 1962–65 (although today's John Paul II, it seems to me, has backslid from its Reformational thrust). Europeans should certainly know that the gospel of Jesus Christ is global, so Christians should not demonize technology, government, or markets, says Goudzwaard, just because the idolatrous Darwinian globalization dictated by anonymous MONEY we have on our hands is devastating the poor of the earth. In fact, poor counties need low-priced European capital to fund businesses and employment of workers to produce food for their local needs—economic realities to which ideologues of Capitalism are terribly blind.[3]

Europeans may need to redefine their identity, which has gone somewhat missing, if we want a truly "European" community. But self-conscious identity does not demand omphaloskeptic Eurocentricity, closed to the cries of the world at war! When you have no deep faith identity as a community, no committed pivot to your gyroscopic activity, then is the time when you drift like a jellyfish to be your brother and sister's keeper (see Genesis 4:1–9).

2.   What can pull people together more than dialogue is for them to work together at resolving a problem that is disturbing everybody. One such problem is that there seem to be too many head cooks in the European kitchen, and Money is the manager making the kitchen assignments.

To correct something gone wrong historically you have to virtually reconstruct an earlier less-refined embodiment of the problematic setup, so you can channel the development anew into a more normative constellation. To help correct children abused in a family you have to find a surrogate foster family to redo gingerly, as it were, a relationship of trustworthy parents. To help connect a society fragmented by the tyranny of well-spoken cut-throat Economics, one needs at least to hold up an alternative model for reordering societal institutions more respectfully so a church is not judged on its quantitative growth, a marriage is not tested on whether its double-income can afford yuppy vacations, a hospital is not reprimanded if it does not make a profit, and artists are not judged useless because their CDs are not marketed by a major record company.

As I understand it, the task of a national/regional/local city state

---

3   See Bob Goudzwaard, *Globalization and the Kingdom of God* (Washington, DC: Center for Public Justice, 2001), 21–27.

government is to ensure justice be done in society and to promote the commonweal of those inhabiting its territory by giving legal room for nonpolitical communities in society freely to fulfill responsibly their proper tasks, whether they be families, schools, businesses, hospitals, transit, or artworld. In some circles that idea is called the principle of "subsidiarity"—a principle of Roman catholic social teaching. "Subsidiarity" in the European Community forbids the European Union to do what the national member states can do themselves unless the European Community as a whole could better achieve the goal (art. 3b).

The basic idea of subsidiarity for societal interaction, as I understand it,[4] is that each community within society provides its own original fundamental task as an indispensable auxiliary function for the other communities within society. The state, business, school, media, the performing arts center, each gives of its limited gift to the other institutional groupings to which we belong as persons.

The awesome task of government, with the power to tax and protect its inhabitants, surrounds business and the artworld, to mention only these two nonpolitical communities in society. Governments are not meant to be epiphenomena withering away (as, curiously, both Marx and right-wing Conservatists politicians promote), but are instituted by God for rulers to exercise their limited legal prerogative to be the final arbiter in society on whether different communities and persons infringe their respective rights and are enabled to perform their respective responsibilities. (If the government is constitutionally elected, the representatives chosen for that term devalue their office of rulers under God, I think, if they do nothing but reflect the changing whims of the polled populace.)

A normative business enterprise engages in commerce on the basis of capital to supply good resources that fulfill people's needs. A business profit margin is necessary in order to furnish for satisfying thrifty continuation of such generous service. A government does right to legislate

---

4   The principle of "subsidiarity" started in the 1931 Pius XI encyclical *Quadragesimo Anno* (par. 78–79) is correct, I think, in meaning that (Chaplin reading) "the state ought not to assume tasks which other communities can perform for themselves." There is, however, a somewhat paternal, fixed hierarchical cast to the papal wisdom that prescribes that the "lesser" organizations must be allowed to do their job until the "higher" authorities need to take over.

I should like to modify the concept of "subsidiarity" with Abraham Kuyper's teaching on "sphere sovereignty" and "sphere universality" as regards to the societal groupings of persons (see his *Soevereiniteit in eigen kring*, 1880). Jonathan Chaplin has a lucid formulation of the matter in "Subsidiarity as a Public Norm," *Political Theory and Christian Vision* (Lanham: University Press of America, 1994), especially pages 83–86.

rules for honest description of commercial products and content, and to curb by taxes the selling of luxuries, in order to keep attention on the welfare of the needy. But when a business, like a bank, corporation, or international finance institution, tells a government how to rule for its citizens' commonweal, you have societal insubordination. Commercial institutions may not act like the police, but are to mind their business sector within society—supplying goods and services for people's needs— while the government decides what is due justice. (If a government is corrupt, bottom-line business efficiency in a given country is little help for the citizens.)

3. When it comes to the artworld, the orbit of cultural products, like books, sculptures, songs, and cultural institutions like concerts and museums: are they to stand or fall like commercial businesses in society, or do they fulfill a different role for which the government should give special consideration? Artists like school teachers, lawyers, clergy, and doctors have to pay their bills and order their priorities, but the artistic profession is not strictly a business; although one hopes to gain one's livelihood by practicing art. And museums are not exactly McDonalds. Museums like libraries hold the collective memory of a people in its treasuries and are, although they naturally need financing, by nature nonprofitmaking institutions that provide a public service of enlarging and deepening the imaginative knowledge of successive generations.

Because of fewer tax-cut dollars there is increasing pressure on cultural institutions to be turned over into commercially viable ventures— no longer free entrance to the art gallery, the museum gift shop becomes an expensive store, decisions are made to de-access stored artwork to sell to overcome deficits. However, the 1992 Maastricht Treaty asks governments to support "non-commercial cultural exchange" (art. 128, 2, become 151.2 in the 1995 Treaty of Amsterdam) and is willing, I think, to advance NPOs (nonprofit organizations)[5] for sponsoring and even

---

5   "Nonprofit organizations" like foundations and cooperative associations for a cultural purpose are referred to often as "Third Sector" organizations in European discourse: neither private nor public, but private with a public purpose.

The French term "désétatisation" better describes the intent of NPOs than the English term "privatization." "Privatization" talk often assumes the simplisitic framework of a tension between the only two possibilities of "public" versus "private." "Désétatisation" aims rather to demonopolize cultural institutions from under state control but still maintain a respectful linkage.

NPOs are an attempt to disestablish *gemeinnützige* cultural/artistic services *d'utilité publique* from bureaucratic state managing control but keep the government in a supportive, at-arm's-length-, overseeing position. See Cas Smithuijsen, "De-monopoliz-

managing cultural/artistic endeavors and to charter such NPO art foundations for patronage loosely under the principle of subsidiarity. That is, the European Union supports political governments who give tax help indirectly and encourage, at arms-length, nongovernment patronage to rally the artworld to take its public place in society.

Governments will be practicing the principle of subsidiarity when the governments allow NPO art foundations to receive tax-free status, since they do good for the artistic commonweal. In England the government allows "Friends" of the British Birmingham orchestra to take a charitable deduction by way of a "Deed of Covenant" to support the city orchestra. In France the *Fonds national d'art contemporain* (founded 1875!) buys artworks directly from living artists to be displayed in different public places. In the Netherlands, since the 1990s, cultural entrepreneurs have organized independent theatre groups that nevertheless perform in venues rented from the state, which maintains the buildings, since theatre, says the Dutch government, is good for poorer taxpaying people to experience.

This is a good development; but emphasis could be put upon having the richer states share such imaginative gifts with the poorer countries. Or do we stop being our brother and sister's keeper when it comes to their producing culture?

There are many difficulties and sometimes dangers in these joint subsidiary undertakings: certain nations use lotteries—a most uneconomical way to circulate money—to bolster artistic efforts; corporate sponsors may support art like sports events just to refurbish their image and get their logo seen in the right places. But attempts to honor the nonprofit professional nature of artistic products and performances and art's important contribution to the commonweal, the role of art in public life distinct from commercial enterprises geared to a mass-market dynamics is, in my judgment, a mark of societal sanity.

Redemptive artistic task: re-enchant the imagination of society
What kind of subsidiary policies and art should christian artists giveaway in European society, reaching out to the whole world?

First of all, **I believe artists must grow a vivid, humbled, consciousness of their proper artistic task: providing imaginative manna for their neighbor, especially those who neglect to notice the subtle surprises God has put in creatures**. Paul Klee's *Dancing Girl* (1940)

---

ing Culture: Privatization and culture in 23 European countries", in *Privatization and Culture*, eds. P.B. Boorsma et al. (Dordrecht: Kluwer, 1988), 82–91.

[see *NA* #70] catches the innocent joy of a young girl in simply rhythmically moving her bodily limbs. Awkwardly elegant, happily carefree: such unpretentious, exuberant fun makes you glad dancing exists in God's world. Barlach's wood sculpture *Das Wiedersehen* (1926) [#16] of exquisite tenderness tells you that sadness can be consoled. You don't have to know the piece depicts Thomas seeing the risen Christ again to sense that the curved back, the sagging figure is being held up by the taller one who is accepting brokenness gently. Klee and Barlach exemplify for me the rich vein of humanity (I did not say "humanism") in Europe artistry sensitive to the christian genes in our cultural make-up.

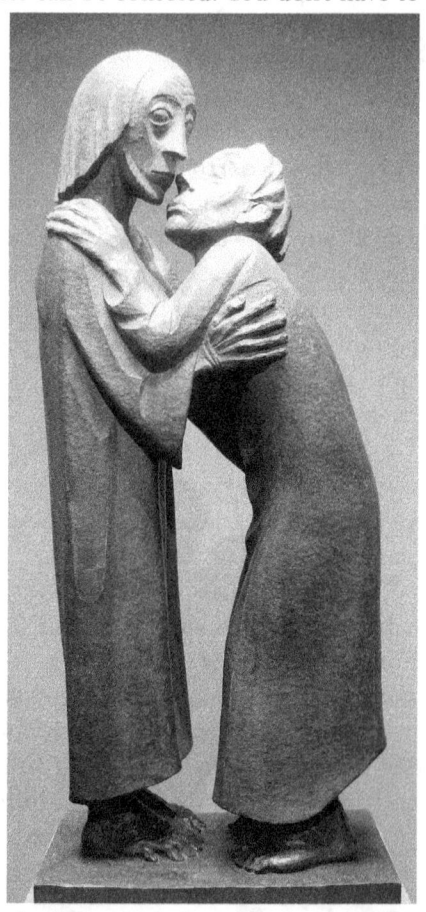

The current artworld in Europe is rejecting the christian humanism European Rodin epitomizes. *Le Baiser* (1901–04) [*NA* #55] was a daring secular move at the height of Victorian mores in England, where private matters were kept perversely hidden. But Rodin clothes the erotic sexual encounter with a Romantic Idealism in cold white marble that creates a safer distance for the viewer. Jeff Koons ruthlessly mocks what has become a museum icon by posing a naked woman and a naked man on boxes to

[#16] Ernst Barlach, *Das Wiedersehen*, 1926

be photographed in a similar position to *The Kiss*, the man's spread-fingered hand on the woman's willing thigh. Koons' piece is typical of the "post-modern"—in my terminology, "post-christian"—spirit infecting the artworld today, which is intent upon throwing out the European baby with the dirty bathwater, and deconstruct our genteel hypocrisy.

Yes, but the would-be *novo* artwork promulgated by the wealthy, most influential British Saatchi Gallery since 1987: its recent exhibition now on world tour called *Sensation* shows off art like *Au naturel* (1994)

by Sarah Lucas, which has an aggressive, self-certain intimidating cachet—smart-ass art, I might dare call it—with a brazen, mean streak to it
(pornography always reduces humans to body parts) that dirties what is
delicate. *Bullethole* by Mat Collisham (1988-91) in the same collection is
brilliant, fascinating, a cibachrome photo mounted on fifteen light boxes,
which is as invasive and brutal as the act itself. Saatchi's stable of artists
has a conquistador mission to domesticate taboos.[6] *Kranke Kunst* (1975)
[#17], says Anselm Kiefer with this watercolor painting: the beautiful
European landscape is plagued with pink sores of pus, diseased perhaps,
polluted by all its ambitious sophistication blowing in the wind, which is
something world society certainly does not need.

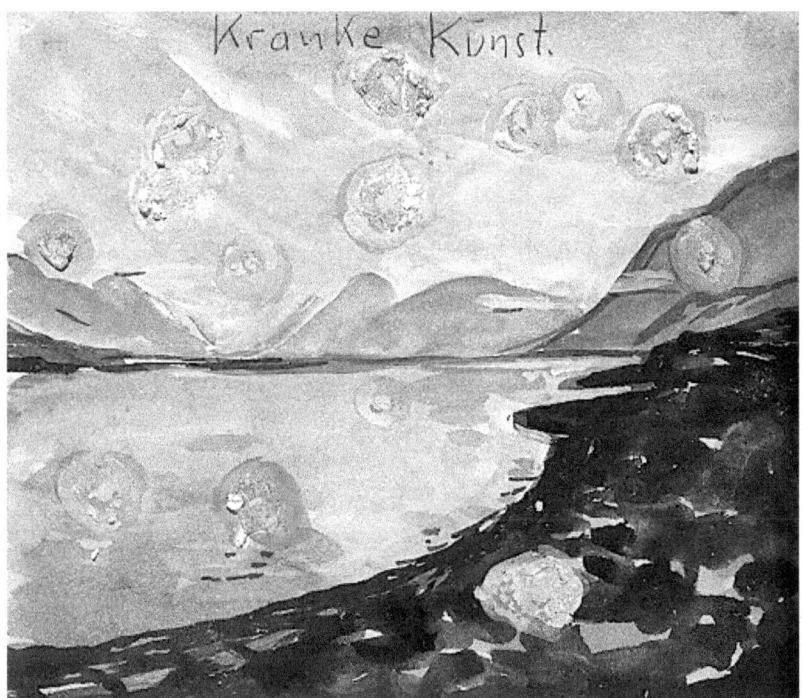

[#17] Anselm Kiefer, *Kranke Kunst*, 1974

Rembrandt's *Jewish Bride* [RA #82] (after 1665) gives us a great
European view of erotic intimacy colored gloriously by respectful passion, deeper than Rodin. This is the spirit, I believe, that artists should

---

6   See Norman Rosenthal's article, "The Blood Must Continue to Flow," in *SENSATION:
    Young British artists from the Saatchi collection*, catalogue for London exhibition at the
    Royal Academy of Art, 18 September–28 December 1997 (New York: Thames &
    Hudson, 1998), 10–11.

breathe in their artwork: normality, abundance, enchantment, shalom. You can do that even if you are not a Rembrandt. Klee's *Le Savant* (1933) [*NA* #43] is a wonderful portrait of this incredibly intent, fragile creature whose severely contracted eyebrows press down on his pale blue eyes above the nose and one line of a mouth grimace. You can see the web of the canvas through the wash of the brown paint, as if Klee wants to bring us compassionately close to this autistic, timid, frightened intelligence. Rein Pol in *Uitzicht* [*RA* #90] (1985–86) treats a dying grandmother with scrupulous care. The useless glasses, the empty chair, the softly colored bedclothes and propped up pillows leave the woman in still relief. Despite the sad immobility of the scene, the panel of light streaming into the room is alive with *Uitzicht*, the prospects of triumphant faith. Peter Smith's wood engraving, *Working Late* (1988) [#18], graces my study where I can look up from my desk and know that the monastic solitude I taste in my cell barred from disturbances by the outer world is a safe place where the fatigue is tempered by the gentle order of quietness upon faithful labor.

I do not mean that the christian artist should be *un flâneur* in the arcade of society, only the peaceful observer. Christian artists may certainly be critical of the society they inhabit. Although critique can be cheap if nothing wholesome is offered, to replace what is self-indulgent and evil; artistry worth its salt will be aware of what is going on in society and not look the other way, not champion escape or serve oneself, but try, like the jester who speaks truth with humor before the rich and powerful, to present metaphor manna that may startle with its unusual taste but eventually bring hope.

The fresh retelling of the bible story early Emil Nolde offered to give the church with *Heilige Nacht* (1912) [#19] radiates joy with its color. Maria is not made German, but looks like a migrant worker from the East, the happy handmaiden of the Lord. As usual, Joseph looks on attentively, but the horse is cleaning the manger; and the shepherds are coming over a green hillside—it is not winter. *Verlorenes Paradies* (1921) by Nolde [#20] was harder to take: the human pair are utterly forlorn, separated by the snake. Eve stares out unseeing next to the memento of a lovely red flower; Adam looks grim, darkly wondering what to do next. The church refused to put this pictorial translation of Genesis 3 anywhere near the altar, where sins are forgiven, and the rejected Nolde was deeply hurt.

Nolde was trying to reenchant believers with the gospel. Here is

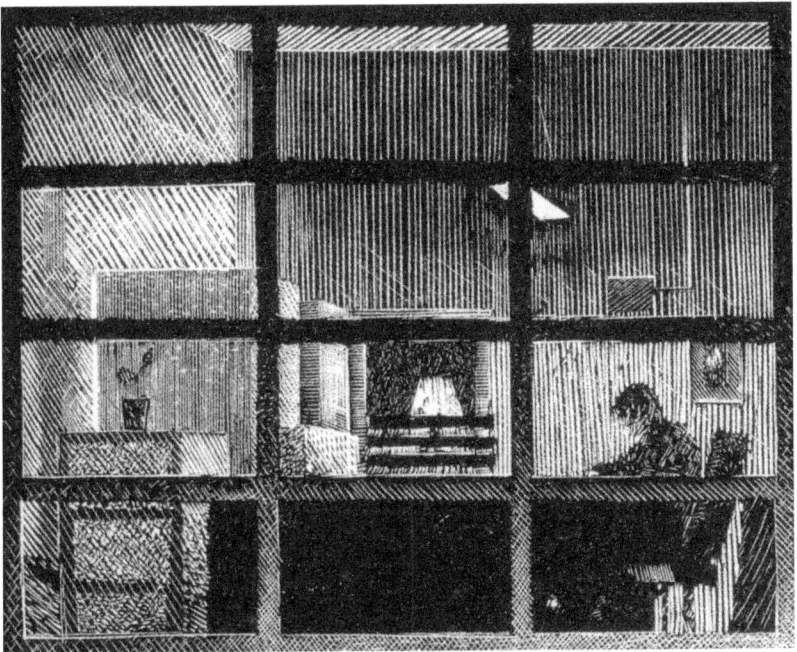

[#18] Peter Smith, *Working Late*, 1986

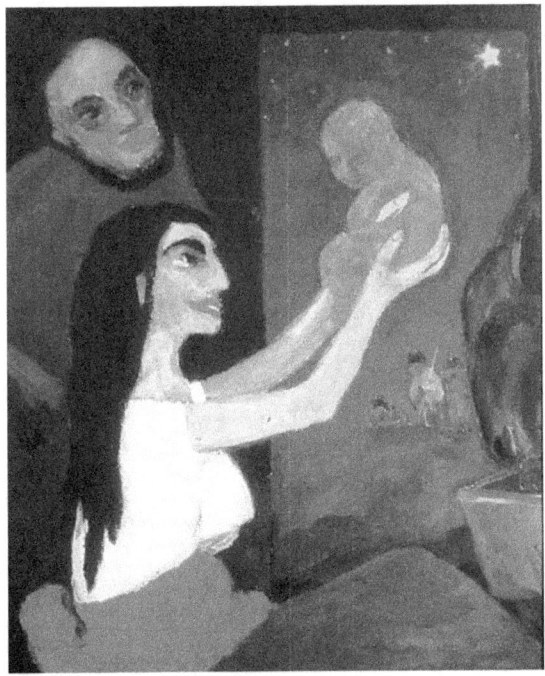

[#19] Emile Nolde, *Heilige Nacht*, 1912

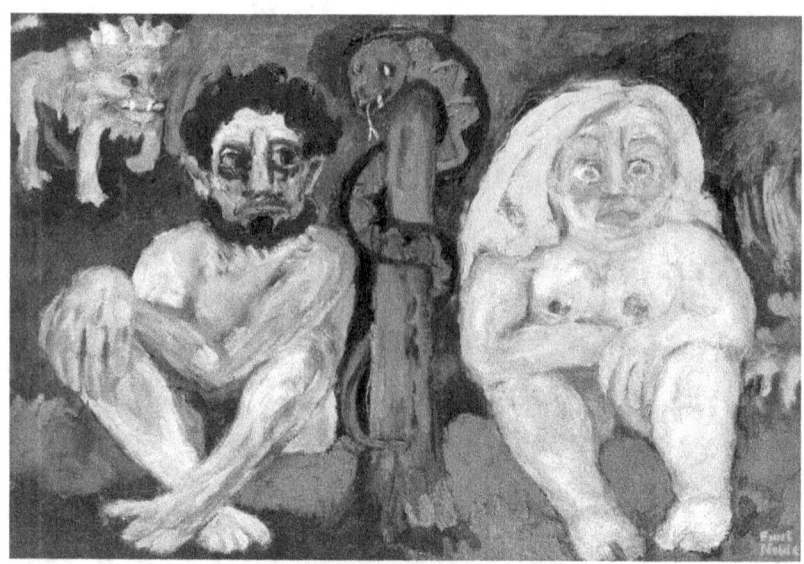

[#20] Emile Nolde, *Verlorenes Paradies*, 1921

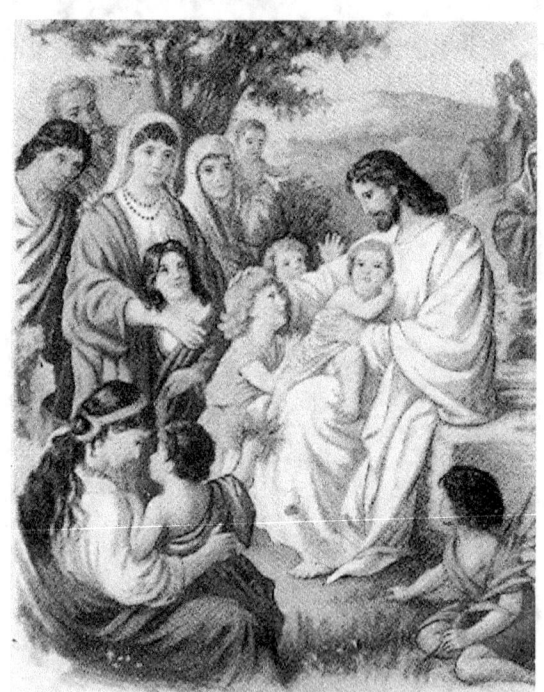

JESUS AND THE CHILDREN

Lesson Material: Mark 10: 13-16

[#21] Sunday School card for memorizing texts, 1930s

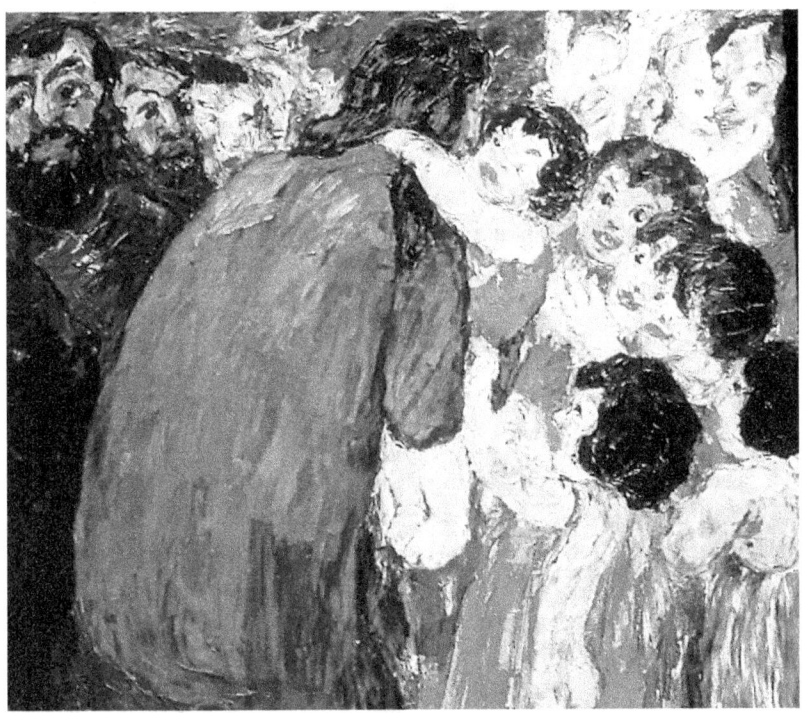

[#22] Emile Nolde, *Christus und die Kinder*, 1910

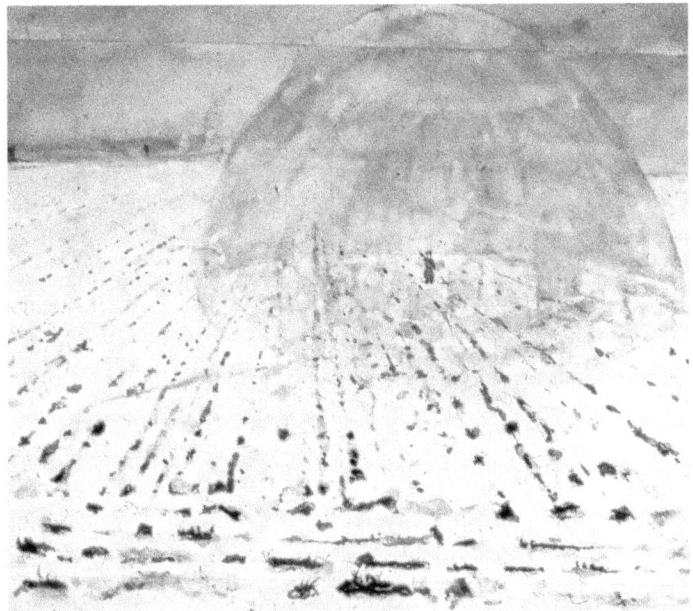

[#23] Anselm Kiefer, *Jeder Mensch steht unter seiner Himmelskugel*, 1970

a Sunday school card I received [#21] as a rural American child in the 1930s on "Jesus and the Children," where the cozy sweetness and light of the day kills Jesus with kindness and makes Him a gentleman. Nolde's *Christus und die Kinder* (1910) [#22] overflows with celebrative laughter, the animated excitement of boisterous encounter, bodies pressing in on one another standing in the busy streets, while the tight-lipped disciples hem and haw in disapproval behind Jesus' back. Christian artists do well to take their tradition of European christian faith seriously, pick up the institutional cross of the church too (see Matthew 16:24–25), and practice the giving in forgiveness rather than fall into the curse of resignation where, as another Anselm Kiefer watercolor, *Jeder Mensch steht unter seiner Himmelskugel* (1970) [#23] shows, when every human being stands resolutely under one's own private dome of heaven, the outside becomes a forsaken uncultivated wasteland.

Hundertwasser grapples with the importance of habitation, cities, and the problem of the earth's becoming a global high-rise. *Blutende Häuser* (1952) [#24] shows how seven skyscrapers in ungainly spatial proximity crowd out any place for trees, any spot for walking—there is no breathing room. Empty black squares for windows reveal this anonymous complex as a rather impersonal location, hard to make into a friendly home. *On the Sunny Side of the Street* (1953) [#25] keeps one in the city; but the yellow rectangle is warm next to the red shadows (on the left side), and all the primary colors swim pleasantly around as if clothes are waving on clotheslines outside. It makes me think of the Swiss square in Geneva I once happened upon (1989) [RA #140] where a group of men were playing chess together in the city with chess pieces half a meter tall. Maybe some of those men lived in a *Rainbowhouse* (1976–77) [#26] where myriad kinds of activities go on and it is messy, lived in, crisscrossed by a rainbow of grace.

Artists need to show city-dwellers, church people, manual workers, bureaucrats commuting—there is not time to illustrate everything—that artists understand *la misère et la gloire* of others' lives, and give the neighbor new eyes to see, new ears to hear, to experience in a restorative, imaginative way that societal life is a marvelous gift needing to be redeemed from despair and loneliness and kept human, to be surrounded by the halo of a rainbow, whether the times be happy or sad. If you as artist can go to a societal institution and cajole them into accepting your artistic enchantment, as Britt Wikström did with a school in Rotterdam, then the children will daily have, instead of a blank wall outside the school entrance, Noah's Ark floating on tiles of blue water [*NA* #18] filled with fantastic animals—anteater, frog, stork, kangaroos, dove, and penguins—as fellow playmates in God's rainbowed world.

Christian artists need, I think, art-informed middle-persons like Knaeps and La Rivière, who are not artists but know art's worth—managers, brokers, agents, mediators!—to link artists to societal institutions, get them commissions. Could not co-operative projects like that take concrete practical shape among christian artists, for the good of the European Community? Christian artists only need to become ("networking") professionals, after an apprenticeship, who serve the neighbor with imag-

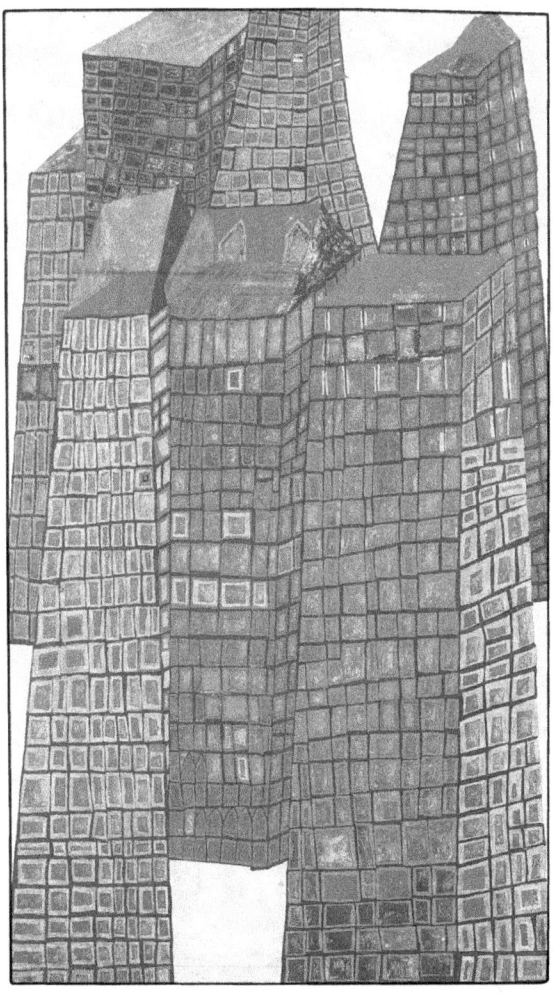

[#24] Hundertwasser, (151), *Bleeding Houses*, 1952

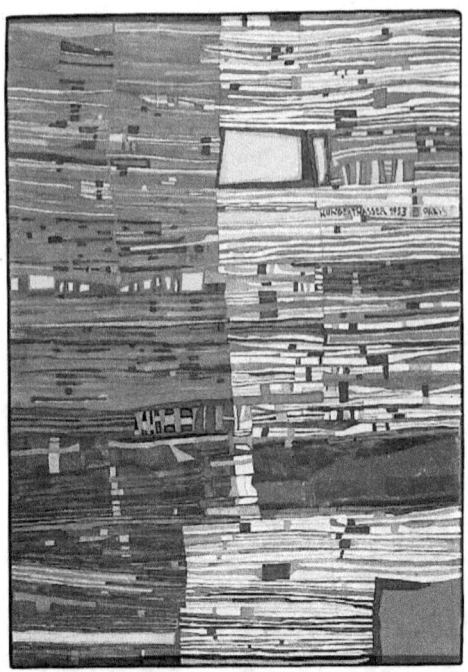

[#25] Hundertwasser, 166, *On the Sunny Side of the Street*, 1953

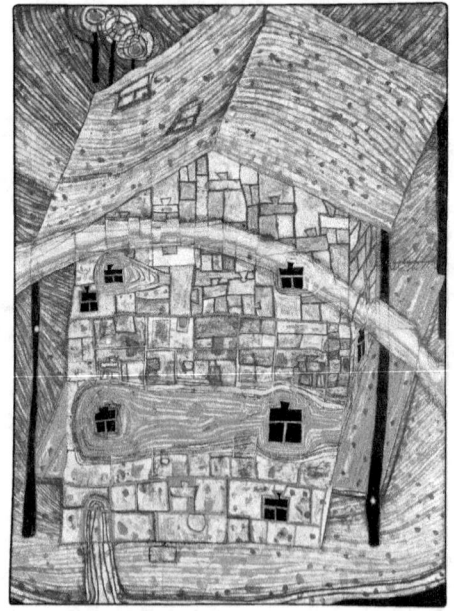

[#26] Hundertwasser, 763, *Rainbowhouse*, 1977

inative gifts, not superstars. One does not have to go for the international Olympic bronze, silver, or gold as christian artist. Just become a precious regional or local reliable ruby.

I end with the encouraging remark that artists may not even be in the European Union kitchen with the too many head chefs of government, corporate finance, and those mysterious advisers who set the menu. But christian artists can be waiters and waitresses who serve up fresh imaginative food from the reformed European tradition that will nourish building up the European Community. An artists' union has no place in trying to muscle in on setting the European Central Banks next interest rate, but a christian artists' union can raise the consciousness of the public to grasp that artistic workers can be worthy of their hire in society (see Luke 10:1–11) if we indeed reenchant the unimaginative neighbor to become alive to the crevices of surprises in God's world. If we artists are found faithfully bringing wholesome, spicy food (see Colossians 3:5–6) to table when the Lord returns, says Scripture, then we waiters and waitresses will be put in charge of all creation's riches (Matthew 24:45–47).

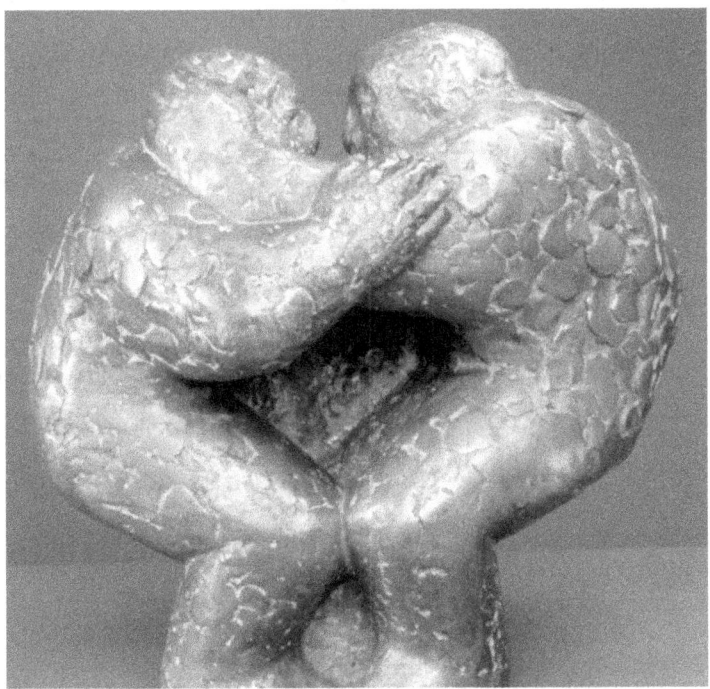

[#27] Britt Wikström, *Jacob and the Angel* (other side)

Meanwhile, christian art is to commemorate with verve human joys and bear with love the neighbors' burdens (Galatians 6:2), as Violet Holmes' piece [*RA* #37] does for any woman who has tried to extricate herself from an abusive relationship: amid a cascading explosion of purple-red troubles around one's head, forced to cry black tears to shut out what doesn't end, the set of her chin says this woman will still come through. God keeps all her tears in a bottle, as Psalm 56:8 says. Or, as Britt Wikström's wrestlers [#27] show grappling with each other toe to toe, knee to knee: if you examine the other side of Jacob and the Angel and the LORD in struggle, you see that they are locked in a supportive dance together. When the Angel touches your thigh, you limp forever afterward but as a blessing.

> I know, my Lord, you keep good track
> of all the pain and trouble,
> collect my tears like broken jewels
> and save them in a bottle.

Bibliographic Sources

Bastide, Roger. *Arte e Sociedade* [1945; 2nd ed., 1971; as *Arte et Société*, 1977] (Paris: L'Harmattan, 1997).

Becker, Howard S. *Art Worlds* (Los Angeles: University of California Press, 1982).

Berman, Morris. *The Reenchantment of the World* [1981] (New York: Bantam, 1989).

Bianchini, Franco and Michael Parkinson, eds. *Cultural Policy and Urban Regeneration: The West European experience* (Manchester University Press, 1993).

Boorsma, Peter B., Annemoon van Hemel, and Niki van der Wielen, eds. *Privatization and Culture: Experiences in the arts, heritage and cultural industries in Europe* (Dordrecht: Kluwer, 1998).

Chaplin, Jonathan. "Subsidiarity as a Public Norm," in *Political Theory and Christian Vision: Essays in memory of Bernard Zylstra*, eds. Jonathan Chaplin and Paul Marshall (Lanham: University Press of America, 1994), 81–100.

DiMaggio, Paul J., ed. *Nonprofit Enterprise in the Arts: Studies in mission and constraint* (New York: Oxford University Press, 1986).

Goudzwaard, Bob. *Globalization and the Kingdom of God* (Washington, DC: Center for Public Justice, 2001).

Goudzwaard, Bob and Julio de Santa Ana, "Globalization and Modernity," in *Globalization: The imperial thrust of modernity*, ed. Ninan Koshy (Vikas Adhyayan Kendra, Mumbai India, 2002), 1–33.

Grasskamp, Walter. *Kunst und Geld, Szenen einer Mischehe* (München: C.H. Beck'sche Verlagsbuchhandlung, 1998).

Haskell, Francis. *Patrons and Painters: A study in the relations between Italian art and society in the Age of the Baroque* (New York: Knopf, 1963).

Hitters, Erik. *Patronen van Patronage, Mecenaat, protectoraat en markt in de*

Kunstwereld (Utrecht: Jan van Arkel, 1996).

Kempers, Bram. *Kunst, Macht en Mecenaat: Het beroep van schilder in sociale verhoudingen 1250–1600* (Amsterdam: De Arbeiderspers, 1987).

Kolb, Bonita M. *Marketing Cultural Organizations: New strategies for attracting audiences to classical music, dance, museums, theatre and the opera* (Dublin: Oak Tree Press, 2000).

North, Michael, ed. *Economic History and the Arts* (Köln: Böhlau Verlag, 1996).

North, Michael and David Ormrod, eds. *Art Markets in Europe 1400–1800* (Aldershot: Ashgate, 1998).

Pears, Ian. *The Discovery of Painting: The growth of interest in the arts in England, 1680–1768* (New Haven: Yale University Press, 1988).

Wielemaker, Christof. "Proceedings of the discussions at the 11th International Christian Artists Seminar held at De Bron, the Netherlands, August 5–11, 1991," in *Art AD 2000. The role of arts in Europe on the way to integration: A debate on social and cultural issues with political implications*, ed. Leen LaRivière (Rotterdam: Commission to the European Communities, 1992).

Zuidervaart, Lambert and Henry Luttikhuizen, eds. *The Arts, Community and Cultural Democracy* (London: Macmillan, and New York: St. Martin's, 2000).

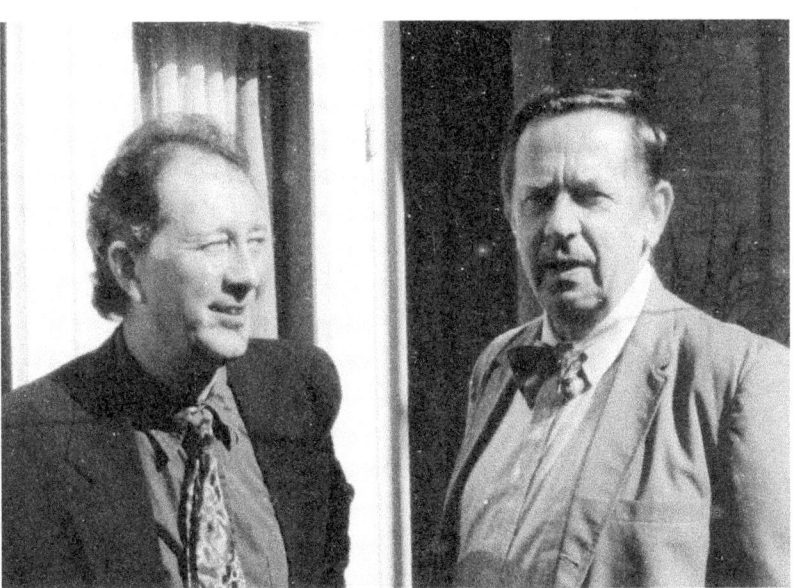

With Graham Birtwistle, Professor of Art History,
Vrije Universiteit, Amsterdam, The Netherlands, 2001

HUMAN MULTICULTURALITY:
INVITATION TO ENRICHED IDENTITIES

Let's start by saying a culture is a particular way a certain societal group orders its interacting patterns of life and death, into which newborns and foreigners can be fitted. A human culture is a formed tissue of doing things in a roughly specific manner one is wont to do that constitutes an ongoing tradition of what is appropriate in society.

For example, an elderly woman hostess I noticed was offended when the Japanese student just ahead of me in the receiving line, upon introduction, asked, "And how old are you?" The gracious Swiss lady was taken aback at such a blunt personal question because she did not realize that the remark was a deferential token of the utmost respect in traditional Japanese culture.

Another example: Princeton professor Kwame Anthony Appiah who is multicultural, Asante Ghanaian-British American, tells of his christian father's being confirmed as hereditary leader of the family clan after his great-uncle's death by throwing a sacrificial lamb into the river and having his offering snatched first and eaten by the crocodiles (*In My Father's House*, 182–183).

In a given culture one assumes as normal, normative, various customary acts, foods, rituals, even a demeanor and spirit, that may strike those outside its cultural boundaries as somewhat unusual.

Defining "multiculturality"
When a microbiologist wants to grow a culture of bacteria or fungi in a laboratory saucer, he or she needs the nutritive substrate of agar as an environment in which the organic culture can flourish. My working idea of a human culture is that **an ethnic culture is a definite physiognomy**

Presented in 2004. First published in *Multiculturality: Blessing or Nightmare.* Report on the 24th International Christian Artists Seminar (Rotterdam: Continental Art Center, n.d. [June 2005]), 4–17. Organized by CNV-Kunstenbond, EZA, and Commission of the European Committee.

of kindred actions that grow in the nutritive bed of language, a living mother tongue. So an ethnic human culture for me is not based in the blood of race, is not exactly identical to nationality, but is best distinguished, I propose, by its matrix of language, including its dialect variations. Germanic culture, Chinese culture, the non-territorial gypsy culture roaming the earth: **every ethnic culture has a kind of kith and kin character whose identifying familiarity breathes the peculiar diversity and humanity nourished by the idiom of a certain language.**

Much more needs to be said, of course. Every ethnic culture is complex, hybridic, with much more serious depth and milling around developing going on in its multi-layered nature than shows itself in a stereotypical Dutch or American tourist on vacation in the Barbados Islands. Ethnicity is not engineered to a formula, and is also not a *bricolage* of tattered bits and pieces of *objets trouvés* tossed together: an ethnic culture does have typical traits, a usual code of conduct, a rather cohering identity distinct from other language-based cultures. **"Multiculturality" simply names and claims the reality of there being various different cultures in the world in which persons are more or less members.** A bare minimum response to that fact, as Jacques Derrida puts it, is that a definite culture needs to be simultaneously aware of itself as an other culture to other cultures (10). And that is where the rub begins.

Just as three people who do not know the strange languages of the other persons have trouble understanding one another—and it does not help discussion much just to shout louder in the language the others cannot grasp!—just so, people who have not met a foreign culture firsthand tend to be puzzled, offended by, or mistake the human meaning in the exotic praxis of eating fried termites or handily marrying off your offspring when they are children. Unfamiliarity and ignorance can breed a hasty judgment of "our way of doing things is better than the others' cultural practices."

When the Hellenistic Stoa (c. 250 BC–180 AD), who always counseled apathy toward matters that might upset your mental equilibrium, broke through the ancient Greek parochial racism that considered any people that did not speak Greek or live within a polis to be "barbarians," the Stoic cosmopolitan approach backed the world-conquering ambitions of Alexander the Great (356–323 BC): world citizens should be open to world cultures, Persian rugs included. But when the French Revolution (1789–99) proclaimed "Give me *liberté, égalité et fraternité*, or it's the guillotine," and promulgated that tricolor culture to the world as the New Day of enlightened humanity, which would end all schismatic "religious" wars, tribal turbulence, and superstitious cultural folderol, the gambit of encouraging an open-minded cosmopolitan appreciation of ethnic cultures was faced with checkmate. Any free human culture, said the Revolutionaries, will be thoroughly **rational**, cleansed of odd impurities.

Fast Forward to our generation: "Globalization," like the monster of Victor Frankenstein (Mary Shelley's novel, 1816), roams the earth seeking whom it may conform to the culture of Technocratic Pragmatism, which will make everybody healthy, wealthy, and internet happy—world without end: Who could be so stupid as to opt out of the "rational" Western Juggernaut culture of "life, liberty, and the pursuit of material happiness"?

Despite the strong homogenizing force of global Technocratic Pragmatism, the reality of multiculturality is still in play. It is unfortunate that in the unwholesome dialectic occasioned by the push to get, if not a Volkswagen in everybody's garage, at least a cell phone in everybody's hand, we have the phenomenon of **MulticulturalISM**: giving multiculturality an exaggerated importance because ethnic culture is an endangered species.

In its standard form proponents of MulticulturalISM promote minority cultures, letting them jockey for power and a (subservient) place in the sun of the dominant reigning culture, a kind of laissez-faire acknowledgement of diverse cultures in society. In its extreme form MulticulturalISM lives with the conundrum of cultural relativism: every culture is as good as any other culture; so hands off our Finnish culture! our African-Zulu culture, our Tibetan culture, lest we perish! MulticulturalISM easily mutates into **ethnocentrism**: our culture is sacrosanct!

Robert Frost's old quizzical, ironic poem is still relevant, gently chiding the ethnocentric position that believes "Good fences make good neighbours" ("Mending Walls," 1914). But since 1989 when the Berlin Wall came down and 2004 when the Israeli Wall started going up, the struggles to protect ethnic multiculturality with multiculturalISM have become more fierce, the air has soured, the stakes are higher, because as William Butler Yeats once wrote ("The Second Coming," 1921):

Things fall apart, the centre cannot hold....
The best lack all conviction while the worst
Are full of passionate intensity.

Many ethnic cultures and languages are threatened with obscurity if not extinction. And a people will fight to keep its culture and language alive in a glassy sea of American-English business transactions and academic conferences. Since 1 May 2004 the European Community faces the problems of multiculturality as never before. How can we foster ethnic cultural diversity *and* champion a European unity? **How primordial and crucial is an ethnic culture to a community of people in our high-rise world society?**

Societal bearings

Critical for grappling with the problems and prospects of multi**culturality** is getting our systematic bearings in society so that we can **distinguish and relate rather than confuse matters of injustice worldwide from difficulties of sharing ethnic cultural life**.

Systemic mistreatment of women in society, neglect and the paternalistic indulgence of us able-bodied people toward the varied handicapped persons in society, the terrible suppression of the weak, misfits, and outcasts of society scream for pro-active correction; but they are not ethnocultural matters, although they are often tangent to multicultural affairs. And if every legitimate partisan interest group, like Greenpeace for the environment and a Humane Society to prevent cruelty to animals, tries to squeeze itself into the ethnocultural discussion, all you will get is a muddle of claims and indiscriminate "culture wars."

Every human creature today is born of parents and is by nature interindividually constituted. Everybody is intrinsically neighborhooded (*Mitsein*), you could say. That is a pre-political, historical given, whether you live in rural Botswana or urban Tokyo. Your own identity, which is your responsibility, is inextricably bound up with your being recognized by other human persons, whether they be tribal fellows, family, friends, strangers, or enemies. And this basic mesh of shared living as society asks us human creatures to recognize others as significant to our communal well-being on earth. **Neighborhoodedness**—irrespective of one's faith orientation—**underlies the fundamental human right to be different than your neighbor with whom you are together. This ontically mutual bond grounds and limits**, I would claim, **the whole variety of social, economic, legal, and ethical entitlements established by the various institutions in society for its members.**

It is important to realize, from my perspective, that in our differentiated society a labor union has a different task than the state, which has a different authority than a school, which has a different competency than a neighborhood, which has a different call upon us than the Church, the Muslim imam, or a Masonic Lodge brotherhood may have. Different ethnic cultures will color these institutions of society differently too; but my point is that Slavic, British, or Mexican cultures have such institutional formations (or comparable arrangements) indigenously in place for the good of everybody. There are these structural societal girders in God's world that receive plural, ethnically carpentered concretion. And it would be helpful to **keep the ethnic cultural coloring and building styles distinct from the fundamental normative task of the kinds of societal institutions** one is examining.

I understand that a good labor union would work co-determinatively with management for fair wages for able labor, a safe workplace, and strive to give the workers respect for the job they do (something much more important if intangible than money in the hand) so that valuable resources be generously delivered for people's needs, and the whole economic transaction remain human. I understand that a good state order has the police power to protect its citizens and aliens within its territory from injustice by law, and actively enables other institutions like schools and families and media to practice their rightful tasks for the commonweal. I understand that a good schooling setup, in an oral or in a literate tradition, will have skilled, reflective elders train the rising generation to think, speak, imagine, and know how to operate wisely and well in daily life, with a rich memory of things past and with hopes to pass on—a wholesome heritage for the generations still coming. I understand that a good neighborhood will have healthful housing that is not overcrowded, where public spaces like the streets and possibly a vacant lot (park) will be people-friendly, and residents feel secure enough in their homes to be welcoming to strangers, offering the rites of hospitality. . . .

I briefly rehearsed this fragment of a societal institutional framework on labor union, state, school, and neighborhood, to say this: whether the Canadian Mounties wear Sikh turbans or French berets and the government be a constitutional monarchy or a council of chiefs with ruling elders, whether the workers and bosses lunch on pizza or bagels, whether the school be classy Upper Canada College in Toronto or a multiclass one-room schoolhouse like I went to as a boy in New York, and whether the neighborhood be in downtown Athens or a country village in Slovakia: **the ethnocultural features attend the institutional activity but they are not the determining factor in whether the labor union, state, school, or neighborhood fulfills its principled calling in society.** The norms for a capable, thrifty, factory business, for a just state, a sound school, a friendly city neighborhood, must not be conflated with ethnocultural manners and norms, because you cannot solve, I believe, problems of corrupt commerce, a tyrannical state, a defective school, or a bad neighborhood by emphasizing, sponsoring, and celebrating multiculturality.

Trouble comes when defective institutions blame ethnocultural accouterments for their respective institutional failings. Trouble also comes when ethnic cultural leaders try to trump or violate bona fide societal institutional norms, especially when the intersection happens in public space and is backed up by claims arising from one's rock-bottom faith and trust in God, the risen Lord Jesus Christ, Allah, the Venerable Ancestors, Reason, or wherever your Buck stops.

Problems around multiculturality

I'll mention just a couple of the most tenacious problems on our hands today where multiculturality seems to occasion or exacerbate or get blamed for strife in society.

(1) To avoid old-style "religious wars" where the rule was that a country followed the faith of its leader into battle, the modern nation-state after the Treaty of Westphalia (1648) in Europe gradually assumed the stance that its democratically elected government governs as a religiously neutral umpire, adjudicating human rights to everyone regardless of their class, race, or creed. Every single citizen has equal rights to be free from unlawful seizure and violation of your personal property. So long as your private decisions like your personal faith and spirituality do not intrude upon public matters, they also are protected.

Problematic about this position is that the professedly secularist state is not "neutral" (void of commitment) but is (liberal) Humanist in perspective, and a person's faith is not truly "private" but shows through in all one's deeds, especially in crises. **In our post-christian era where many other traditional faiths have also been traumatized and uprooted, many people seem to rely on ethnocultural customs for their identity, held with an almost religious tenacity.** But are ethnocultural peculiarities "private" or "public"? When Turkish Muslim migrant workers in Germany need *halal* meat, fine, it can be arranged; but do they have the right to build a mosque and issue their public interval calls to prayer? When Sudanese refugees arrive in Canada and become "landed immigrants," is it right of the Canadian government to forbid (Pharaonic) clitoridectomies of Sudanese girls when that grandmotherly act is as important an ethnocultural rite of purity and passage as circumcision or *bar mitzvah* is for Jewish boys?

It is fascinating to trace how the mass immigration of German, Swedes, Poles, Irish, and others from Europe to the United States of America from 1880–1940 were melted down together by the Americanization program of American public schools teaching English, the pledge of allegiance to the flag, and patriotic songs. Afro-Americans, however, were still in separate schools until desegregation heated up in the 1950s with the Civil Rights movement. Legally forced integration was taking place until Black Muslims challenged the policy in the later 1960s: "We don't want to be integrated = assimilated—Black is beautiful!—we want to be separate and more than equal, to make up for lost time." Thus was born multicultural history in the USA. Everywhere in the North American libraries and media now February is Black History month. Hispanic culture came to be recognized in the 1970s–1980s in America, and now Spanish, spilled over from Mexico, is the second most spoken language in the US, to the resentment of various chagrined citizens there.

So far as I can ascertain, there is a grudging recognition of unassimilated foreign cultural elements in their midst today, but with the expectation that an eventual made-in-USA integration will take place by the time the third inter-married, more affluent generation rolls around. The strong Enlightenment political stance on equal rights for **individuals** (in the USA) seems to obscure a willingness to provide "equal rights" for the ethnocultural claims of **groups**. For example, every individual is free to speak his or her mind—free speech—in court, but is expected to speak not in Spanish but in American-English.

As the European Community faces a similar (but not the same) pressure of ill-fitting residents (like national revolutionaries [Basques in Spain], "fourth world peoples" [the Algerian minority in France] and Roma) and an influx of "strangers," can we maybe learn that **any overt concerted attempt to push for assimilation of strong ethnic cultures that do not want to be just an ingredient in the cultural bouillabaisse will encourage reactive moves by those who are considered "outsiders."** Then the best *modus vivendi* comes to be an unhappy detente.

(2) Particular cultural configurations, as I have defined them—**a tradition of typical kindred actions rooted in a language**—are many and varied (multiculturality), and each ethnoculture can become defensive for fear of being snuffed out. An aboriginal people loses the heart of its oral history if it loses its tongue. Why should Arabs and Malaysians

adopt Western business suits to get loans from the World Bank? After the Soviet Union breakup Uzbek has become the official language of Uzbekistan; although Russian (the voice of the former colonial power) is used for world cultural dissemination, *uzbekchilik* (=uzbekization) is needed to unite the *makhala* (traditional communities) into a cohering peoplehood. While ethnocultural traits do not define our **humanity**, they certainly make evident a telling feature of our colorful human **identity**, which should not get lost.

Problematic, however, is the position, when it is taken, that our specific ethnocultural wonts are absolutely right for us and not subject to change or adulteration. This ethnocentricity wrongly assumes one's particular historically worked-in culture is autonomous and can exist in grand self-sufficient isolation, hostile to others if necessary, but not about to kowtow to any "majority" or bland dominant "globalized" culture that would fundamentally sully or ruin our proud ethnic birthright and heritage.

But wait a minute: **a given ethnoculture is not necessarily normative**; no ethnoculture is pure, monolithic, and without internal dissenters and correctives. And a puristic ethnocentric stance is very disruptive in society if certain of its peculiar practices seem inhumane, hurtful, or criminal, especially if they be driven by a religious faith. Such a fundamentalistic ethnocultural approach needs to be put into question.

Because the Hindu culture for centuries has had a caste of untouchables and in certain states countenanced that widows immolate themselves on the funeral pyre of their deceased husband does not mean it should continue in India in perpetuity. Because *Shari'ah* law revealing Allah's order—which goes to the core of Islam—formulates specific details on clothing, hygiene, cutting off a hand for theft, stoning for adultery, and is now legal (although being disputed) for "domestic and civil matters" in Ontario, Canada, if all parties in dispute wish to apply it, does it matter that a Muslim woman is greatly disadvantaged in such household and divorce contentions (whom *Shari'ah* law declares is worth only half a man for inheritance rights)?[1] And "crimes of passion" and "honor killings," which may still surface in Sicily although not sanctioned by the Church, have a long folk tradition of vigilante justice that bespeaks a hardened heart of ethnocentrism.

As the European Community finds its legal-political feet in weighting power balances among regions, national interests, and a central(?)

---

1 *Qur'an*, 4:11, 13–14.

Brussels administration; and as the European Common Market struggles through economic disparities, agricultural subsidies, and the rising euro among world currencies: honoring the ethnocultural paragraph in the Amsterdam treaty of 1995[2]—which is not a thorn in the flesh but a striking sign of hopeful wisdom!—will be the least of European worries, it seems to me. Those in positions of economic and political power must not fault ethnocultural realities for the European Community's failing to act justly and fairly in legal and commercial-labor areas; instead, **the leadership needs to support the ethnocultural diversities so they can each become exciting voices in the whole societal choir.**

The most formidable ethnocultural problem I think Europe faces is how to imbricate the ethnocultural stipulations of the Islamic faith with its *Qur'an, Sunnah* and *hadith*, where a quite different center than Yeats envisioned ***does*** hold, till death takes its toll. The Islamic code that shapes the Muslim consciousness, if I understand the writings correctly, says that only the Godly state ruled by *Shari'ah* (= the Way) is acceptable, with the austere lifestyle it implies.[3] All the rest, the shoddy Western civilizational glory, power, and dominion, is sham, as Sayyid Qutb proclaims: the Jihad of Islam against apostates and the not yet Muslim world of infidels will someday be won over and a universal Caliphate will rule the earth.

Dare the European Community claim that certain ethnocultures

---

2   Article 151:
1. The Community shall contribute to the flowering of the cultures of the Member States, while respecting their national and regional diversity and at the same time bringing the common cultural heritage to the fore.
2. Action by the Community shall be aimed at encouraging cooperation between Member States and, if necessary, supporting and supplementing their action in the following areas:
—improvement of the knowledge and dissemination of the culture and history of the European peoples;
—conservation and safeguarding of cultural heritage of European significance;
—non-commercial cultural exchange;
—artistic and literary creation, including in the audiovisual sector.

3   "Another objective of *jihad* is to establish the Islamic social order and defend it. It is an order that frees man from the tyranny of other men, in all its forms, by urging the submission of all to the one supreme Master. No individual person or class or group has the right to dictate laws or morals over other people or control their lives through ideology or legislation. The authority of individuals or institutions can only be valid or legitimate if they are representing or implementing God's law, or *shari'ah*, and have had that duty entrusted to them by the community. Individuals have of themselves no authority to introduce ethical or legal concepts, principles or rules as they like, because that is the prerogative of God alone." Sayyid Qutb, *In the Shade of the Qur'an*, 1:329.

in the world have more humanly normative features than others?[4] Can the European Community find a way to admit the secular republic of Muslim Turkey into its councils and encourage Turkey's cultural leaders to extend the policies Mustafa Kemal Ataturk initiated in 1923, who constructed a new official language with a modified Latin alphabet and a vocabulary of vernacular Turkish speech, abolishing the old Arabic alphabet and vocabulary and thereby removing a subtle control of a Muslim *ulema* elite? Edy Korthals Altes in the *Nederlands Dagblad* (21 August 2004) recommends that Turkey be given a place in the European Union in order to become a bridge between an Islamic world and the erstwhile "christian" Western Europe. Would Turkey allow Christians to build churches unhindered in its territory?

Promising steps to take in the European Community

If an assimilating conformity and an intransigent ethnocentrism are both pitfalls to avoid in dealing with multiculturality, and assuming ethnocultural matters not be confused with failings in structural institutional concerns in society like taking steps toward citizenship, obtaining living wages, affordable housing, and peaceable places to worship one's god: what principled steps could one take to enlist ethnocultural diversity into a joyful European unity among humans worldwide?

I will make just a few programmatic suggestions before I close with an utterly brief illustrated comment on the service christian European artists might give to other cultures.

(1) Enlarge your personal identity by becoming multilingual.

Most current Europeans are at least conversationally trilingual. If one, however, can come to groove in the literature of another mother tongue, a native language, then you have learned to love your ethnocultural neighbor, and maybe begun to understand them. Until that time, I dare say, a person operates on hearsay.

Let me extend this thesis to touch on the matter of specialized professions that C.P. Snow treated more than a generation ago: if it is difficult for the artists present to take in lectures on labor and political problems in the world today, remember it may be as difficult for the labor and political leaders present to take seriously your artistic performances, because professionals work in different universes of discourse. It is important for the good of society that professionals in diverse fields give quality time

---

4   See Bhikhu Parekh, chapter 9, "Logic of Intercultural Evaluation," in *Rethinking Multiculturalism: Cultural diversity and political theory* (2000), 264–294.

to find out where the other is coming from and how we together might proceed to serve our neighbors, rather than just "do your own thing."

(2)   Could we **rethink the nature of nationality and its connection to state structural processes?**

Nationality is close to those elusive ethnocultural traits that mark a peoplehood. The Greek language, Dutch, the Polish mother tongue, are a partial clue to the stuffings that infuse a kind of distinctive rallying commonality in those groupings of people we call a "nationality." But a nationality is a diffuse, different kind of community than a state, which sets the laws for socio-economic, civil, and political rights within its jurisdiction, and minds the military enforcement of its legal order. So maybe "the nation-state" is an obsolescent concept flawed by the old Romantic idea of "*das Volk*," which so easily contributes to Nationalisms and their manic racist evils (sometimes faintly recognizable, one might say, when Euro/World Cup matches turn ugly).

Perhaps the time has come to recognize that a multination state makes jurisprudential sense (even though the arrangement is not problem-free). The country of Canada is a multinational state: English-speaking provinces, Quebec, and the First Nations territories, with so far only two official languages. The new South Africa has eleven official (nation) languages. Is a multinational state not precisely what the European Community is inching towards, with twenty-one declared official languages?

Also, while the state structure does well to allocate legal responsibilities on the principle of subsidiarity,[5] forestalling both totalitarian and individualistic exercises of power, a hierarchical reading of that principle is not adequate for relating **ethnocultural decisional authority** to political jural forces, to the business-labor sphere of authority, and to other circles of responsibility, because the subsidiarily structured state is final arbiter in matters of just standards but is not the final arbiter over all the spheres of human life. Neither labor unions nor arts organizations (nor schools) are to be agencies of the state, although the state must do its part (at arm's length) to enable these other communities to fulfill their rightful tasks.

So one must not expect or allow a European Community **political** structure to mess internally with regulating folk festivals of its various **nationalities.** A unified copyright law for artworks, maybe cross-border legal holidays from work, subsidies for bona fide societal artistic projects,

---

5   "Subsidiarity" is the policy and practice in which one does not assign to a higher authority matters that a lesser/subordinate authority can handle. See the papal encyclical *Quadragesimo Anno* (1931), par. 79–80.

yes: setting the annual program of the Concertgebouw Orchestra, or deciding who wins the Eurofest in song, no.

(3)   **Realize that the European Christian culture is a minority contribution in God's world, and translate it joyfully with tears into the lingo of the neighbors.**

The "christian" cachet of European Community culture is a sometime thing as the recent flair up (March 2003) of a long-standing trouble (since 1989) *l'affaire du foulard* in France testifies. Instead of allowing Muslim girls to wear the *hijab* to school classes, the French government declared schools to be a secular arm (*laïcité*) of the state, thereby overreaching its proper state task, in my judgment, to superintend **academic** standards of schooling and obliterating the (christian Dutch) possibility that there could ever justly be taxpayer-supported Muslim schools next to Jewish schools, parochial Catholic as well as Enlightenment Humanist schools.

Also, the European legacy of colonial imperialist exploitation of the continental resources of other peoples will continue to plague our christian genes through the coming generations of our riches and the two-thirds-world's degrading poverty. It is very messy to enact restorative justice for historical cultural wrongs (e.g., Indian land claims in Canada), especially when the claims of the injured would be punitive.

But it is time humbly to accept the fact that European culture may no longer have primacy in the world. That will take time for us to get used to. Yet maybe it will liberate God's faithful people in Europe from the territorial burden of "Christendom"—**conquering** the world—and free the *corpus Christi* to act culturally more like their Lord Jesus Christ: **to be communally at home with the psalmodic mission to giveaway shalom to neighbors so long as the LORD gives you breath.**

Gambian Lamin Sanneh argues persuasively that despite much accompanying evil a century ago, the genial act of (Protestant) Christian missionaries to respect indigenous languages so much they took the time to learn the local vernacular tongues in order to get the Bible translated into them: that anti-colonial! practice gave aboriginal peoples glocal self-respect, the gift of literacy, and gradually the wherewithal to become critical of the Western conquistador mentality hovering nearby. My suggestion is that we Europeans not do hit-and-run evangelism in the world or mass distribute our pop culture cheap as others may do. Instead, **let us painfully by rapt listening learn the neighbors' cultural languages and put up for translation any biblical ethnocultural glory we may**

still be holding in our earthen vessels.

Translating good news artistically

Just as you cannot show hospitality if you do not have some kind of home base, just so, if you have no sure ethnocultural identity you cannot giveaway your treasure in translation to enrich the neighbor. At best you become a muddled pastiche of multiple cultures superficially tasted or a nondescript parasitic nomad. For myself as a biblical Christian I find Sander Griffioen's advice very wise: **hold onto your committed faith position** (with your Latvian- Italian- British-European cultural gifts, I would add) **and hold onto your neighbor to keep up a continuing mutual sharing,**[6] **since translation can bring both languages and both ethnocultural participants a mediated enrichment to their respective humanity.**

To be sure, certain offerings from one's "home" position to a "foreign" neighbor can be embarrassing. For example, if Western missionaries show a Victorian drawing-room, gentleman Jesus to natives of New

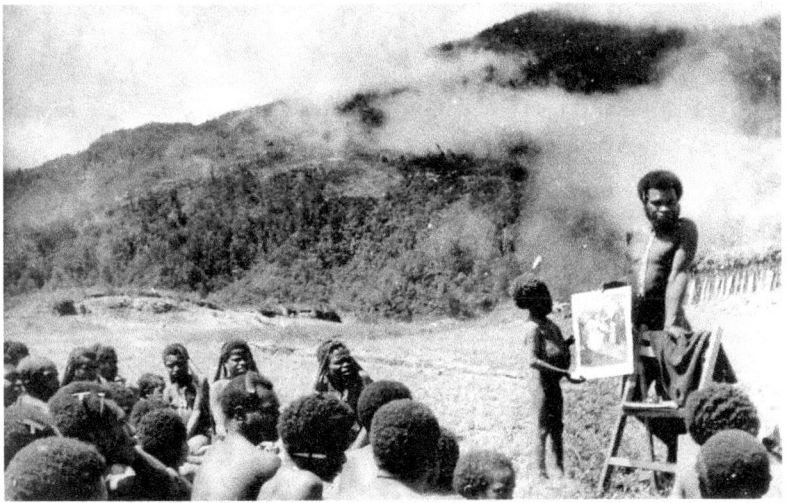

[#28] Papua New Guinea missionaries teaching Jesus to the nations

---

6   Sander Griffioen, *Moed tot cultuur* (Amsterdam: Buijten & Schipperheijn, 2003), 191: "Van de 'verzuiling' valt heel wat goeds te zeggen. De zwakke stee was evenwel de verleiding de levensbeschouwelijke organisaties te zien als 'eigen' organisaties en die vervolgens een quasi-private bestemming te geven. Een publiek ethos beteknt dat men zich geplaatst weet in een ruimte waarin ook anderen zich bevinden, en dan ook de communicatie zoekt. Hier is een dubbele vasthoudendheid geïmpliceerd: zowel vasthouden aan eigen overtuigingen, als ook (en in andere zin) het vasthouden van anderen: het gesprek niet voortijdig afkappen."

Guinea (1960s) [#28], that offering can distort their view of
the Savior of the world. Watanabe Sadao, however, not only
translated Bible stories onto
crumpled *shibu-gami* paper with
a light folksy touch, but with
Kiku (1960) [#29] quietly presents an aged *sensei* figure bent
forward **listening** in an almost
stained glass fashion that bespeaks a medieval troubled solitude, as if Watanabe had become
an ethnocultural "soul" neighbor of Georges Rouault (*Il serait
si doux d'aimer*, 1914–48).

Sometimes the aboriginal
playback of the christian message is accusatory: Piqtoukun's
Priest and Nun (1995) [*RA #26*]
show the priest and nun have no
ears, because they never listened
to us in **our** language, says Inuit

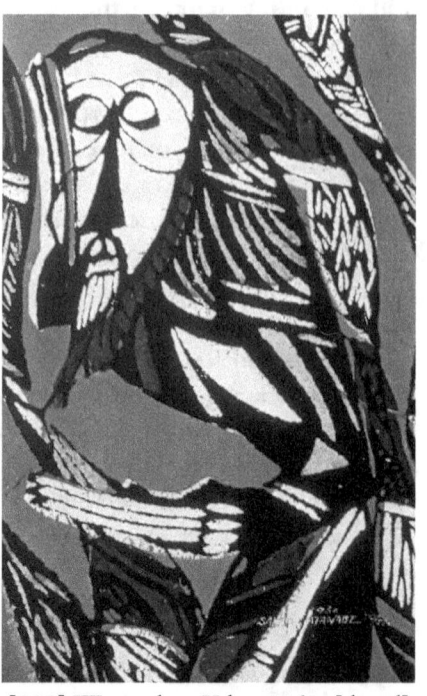

[#29] Watanabe, *Kiku*, 1960, [detail]

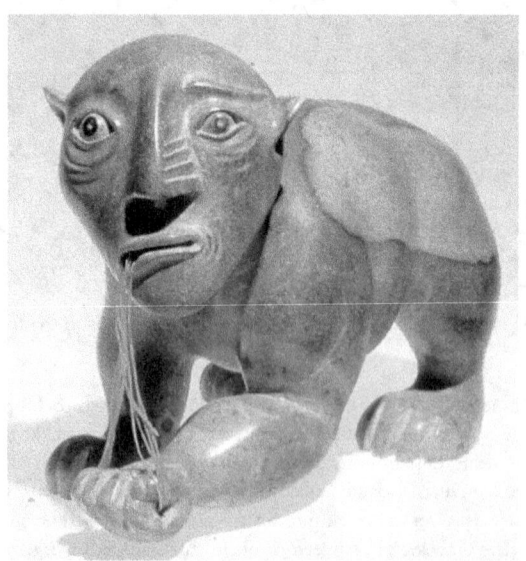

[#30] Piqtoukun, *Drawing Out Evils*, 1995

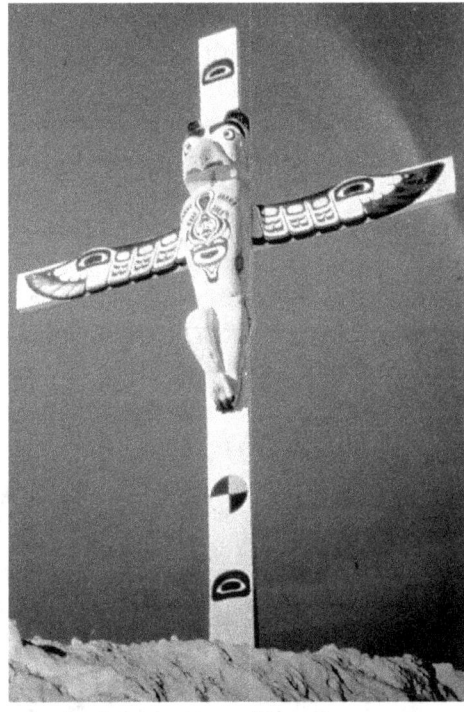

[#31] Stanley Peters, *Totem Cross*, 1975

Piqtoukun; so our Artic culture (*Drawing Out Evils*, 1995) [#30] in-gested poisonous thongs that have stuck in our throats, and we cannot pull them out.

Othertimes the translation of the Newer Testament message to re-mote cultures resonates in a hallelujah: Canadian Tlingit Indian Stanley Peters exults with his *Totem Cross* [#31] the Thunderbird messenger of the great God on a cross above the frozen ice of the Yukon. As Moses raised up a bronze snake in the desert (Numbers 21:4–9), and as the Romans hung Jesus Christ on a cross of wood, so we celebrate the to-tem pole Thunderbird to remember the one who died to save the whole **world**, including animals, tundra, and snow (John 3:16–17).

A gifted woman like Käthe Kollwitz (see *Woman with dead child*, 1903) [*NA* #42] knew how to give **living** artistic water to her neighbors because she learned their vocabulary and grammar of destitution and she (see *Resting in the Peace of His Hands*, c.1935) [*RA* #127] translated the loving mercy of Christ's empathetic arms into etched and sculpted im-ages any poor strangers-to-art in the new Europe or faraway world could read.

There is an unusual series of five photographs by the Czech-American Duane Michals that alludes, with a Buddhist twist, to the story of "The Return of the Prodigal Son" (1982) [##32–36]. I will read it to you as **a metaphorical anagram of how translation in our world of multiculturality tensed by unbalanced power relations can lead to enriched identities**: the naked son, like a mirror image of Massacio's Adam expelled from paradise, enters from the right into a room where the father is leisurely scanning the *New York Times*. The startled older man looks at the youth bowed in shame. The father loosens his shirt to protect the other's nakedness, and thoughtfully removes all his clothes to give them to the younger one. Finally the naked old man gingerly gives

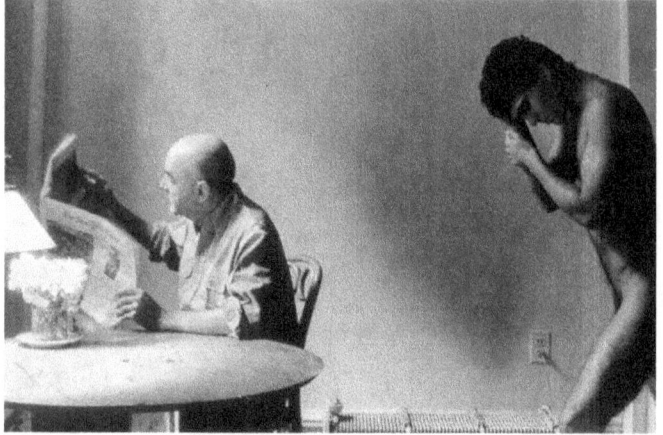

[#32] Duane Michals, *Prodigal*, 1982

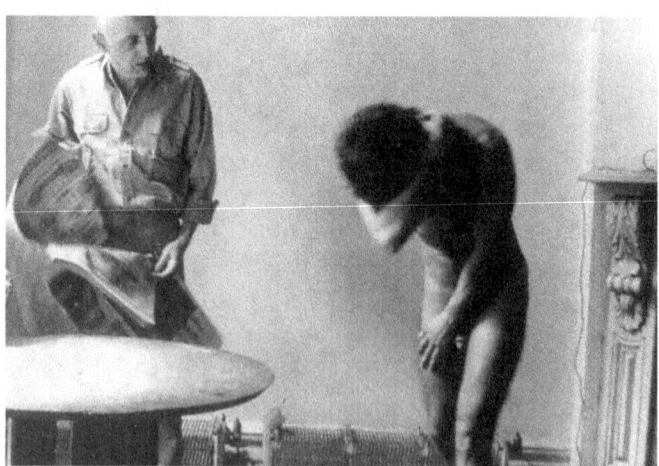

[#33] Duane Michals, *Prodigal*, 1982

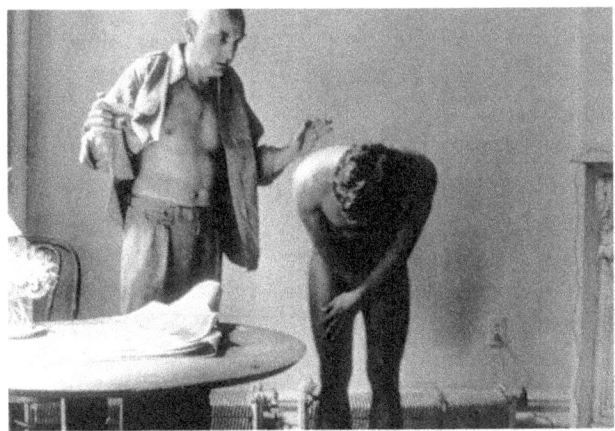

[#34] Duane Michals, *Prodigal*, 1982

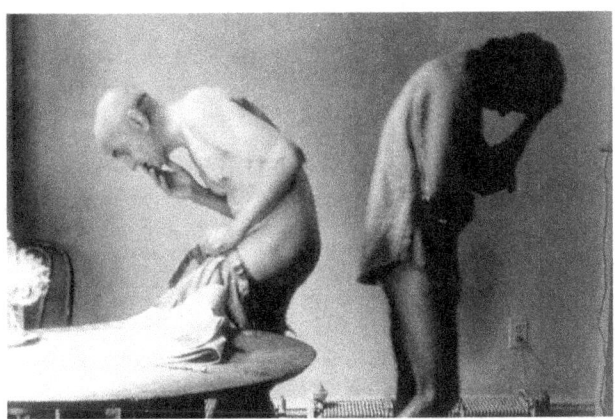

[#35] Duane Michals, *Prodigal*, 1982

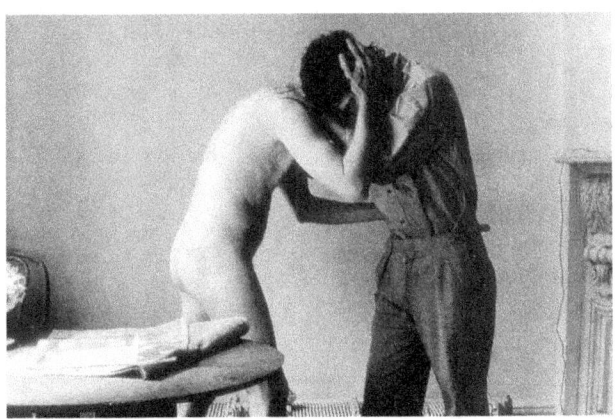

[#36] Duane Michals, *Prodigal*, 1982

the returned son a hug offering reconciliation.

This artwork helps me imagine that we Europeans who have untold stockpiled cultural riches need to be moved to give them away in compassion, translate them, to those around this continent and in the world who appear to us to be naked, and then we shall be surprised to find out that **we spendthrifts are the prodigals**! returning to a humanity for whom God in Jesus Christ went naked. **In translating one's good ethnocultural gifts for the neighbors with a deep respectful awareness and knowledge of their tongues,** *both* **receive clothes to cover our nakedness!**

Since it is Sunday today, when we Christians normally celebrate the resurrection of Jesus Christ and the joy of covering our neighbor with the clothes off our backs (Matthew 5:38–42 and 25:31–46), I'll read in closing Sanneh's translation of what the christian missionaries once brought to the Maasai in East Africa. A portion of their "African (Apostles) Creed" goes like this:

> [God came] in Jesus, "a man with flesh, a Jew by tribe, born poor in a little village, who left his home and was always on safari doing good, curing people by the power of God," until finally he was rejected by his people, tortured and nailed, hands and feet, to a cross, and died. "He lay buried in the grave, but the hyenas did not touch him, and on the third day he rose from the grave. . . . We are waiting for Jesus. He is alive. He lives. This we believe, Amen."[7]

Bibliography

Altes, Edy Korthals. *Heart and Soul for Europe: An essay on spiritual renewal* (Assen: Van Gorcum, 1999).

Al-Qur'an. A Contemporary bilingual translation by Ahmed Ali, rev. ed. (Princeton University Press, 1988).

Anderson, Benedict. *Imagined Communities: Reflections on the origin and spread of nationalism* [1983], rev. ed. (New York: Verso, 1991).

Andringa, Leo and Bob Goudzwaard. "Globalization and Christian Hope: Economy in the service of life," trans. Mark Vander Vennen (Toronto: Public Justice Resource Centre, 2003), 35 pages.

Appiah, Kwame Anthony. *In My Father's House: Africa in the philosophy of culture* (New York: Oxford University Press, 1992).

Benhabib, Seyla. *The Claims of Culture: Equality and diversity in the global era* (Princeton University Press, 2002).

————. "The Liberal Imagination and the Four Dogmas of Multicultural-

---

7 Quoted by Lamin Sanneh in *Whose Religion is Christianity? The Gospel beyond the West* (Grand Rapids: Eerdmans, 2003), 59–60.

ism," *The Yale Journal of Criticism* 12:2 (1999): 401–413.

Bertram, Georg & Karl Ludwig Schmidt, *"ethnos, ethnikos"* in *Theologisches Wörterbuch zum Neuen Testament,* ed. Gerhard Kittel (Stuttgart: Kohlhammer, 1935/1954), 2:362–370.

Botha, Elaine. "The Puzzling Problem of Pluralism," in *Christian Philosophy at the Close of the Twentieth Century: Assessment and perspective,* eds. Sander Griffioen and Bert M. Balk (Kampen: Kok, 1995), 159–173.

Canadian Charter of Rights and Freedoms. Constitution Act, 1982, printed in Roger E. Salhany, *The Origin of Rights* (Toronto: Carswell, 1986), 153–162.

Carens, Joseph H. *Culture, Citizenship and Community: A contextual exploration of justice as evenhandedness* (Oxford University Press, 2000).

Chaplin, Jonathan. *Faith in the State: The peril and promise of Christian politics* (Toronto: Institute for Christian Studies, 1999).

———. "How much Cultural and Religious Pluralism can Liberalism Tolerate?" in *Liberalism, Multiculturalism and Toleration,* ed. John Horton (London: Macmillan, 1994), 32–49.

———. "Subsidiarity as a Political Norm" in *Political Theory and Christian Vision: Essays in memory of Bernard Zylstra,* eds. Jonathan Chaplin and Paul Marshall (Lanham: University Press of America, 1994), 81–100.

Chisholm-Smith, Lisa. *Why Should I Bleed? A conversation with Louise Lander and Lara Owen about the meaning(s) of menstruation* (Toronto: Institute for Christian Studies, M. Phil. F. thesis, 1995).

De Boer, Theo and Sander Griffioen, eds. *Pluralisme: Cultuurfilosofische beschouwingen* (Amsterdam: Boom, 1995).

Derrida, Jacques. *The Other Heading, Reflections on Today's Europe* [1991], trans. Pascale-Anne Brault and Michael B. Naas (Bloomington: Indiana University Press, 1992).

Djumaev, Aleksandr. "Nation-Building, Culture, and Problems of Ethnocultural Identity in Central Asia: The case of Uzbekistan," in Kymlicka and Opalski, 320–344.

Engelstad, Diane and John Bird, eds. *Nation to Nation: Aboriginal sovereignty and the future of Canada* (Concord: Anansi, 1992).

Eriksen, Thomas Hylland. *Ethnicity and Nationalism: Anthropological perspectives* (Boulder: Pluto, 1993).

Glazer, Nathan. *We are all Multiculturalists Now* (Cambridge: Harvard University Press, 1997).

Griffioen, Sander. *Moed tot cultuur: Een actuele filosofie* (Amsterdam: Buijten & Schipperheijn, 2003).

———. "The Relevance of Dooyeweerd's Theory of Social Institutions," in *Christian Philosophy at the Close of the Twentieth Century: Assessment and perspective,* eds. Sander Griffioen and Bert M. Balk (Kampen: Kok, 1995), 139–158.

Habermas, Jürgen. "Warum braucht Europa eine Verfassung? *Die Zeit* nr. 27 (28 June 2001): 7.

Hobsbawm, Eric. "The Nation and Globalization," *Constellations* 5:1 (1998): 1–9.

Kienzler, Klaus. *Der Religiöse Fundamentalismus: Christentum, Judentum, Islam* (München: Beck, 1996).

Kis, Janos. "Nation-Building and Beyond," in Kymlicka and Opalski, 220–242.

Klein, Naomi. "Fences and Windows," spoken on Arts Today, CBC radio, 20 April 2001 (21:00–22:40.)

Koyzis, David T. *Political Visions and Illusions: A survey and Christian critique of contemporary ideologies* (Downers Grove: InterVarsity, 2003).

Kymlicka, Will and Magda Opalski, eds. *Can Liberal Pluralism be Exported? Western political theory and ethnic relations in Eastern Europe* (Oxford University Press, 2001).

Lederach, John Paul. *Building Peace: Sustainable reconciliation in divided societies* (Washington, DC: United States Institute of Peace Press, 1997).

Luzbetak, Louis J. *The Church and Cultures: New perspectives in missiological anthropology* (Maryknoll: Orbis, 1988).

Lewis, Bernard. *The Crisis of Islam: Holy war and unholy terror* (New York: Modern Library, 2003).

Moses, Daniel David and Terry Goldie, eds. *An Anthology of Canadian Native Literature in English* (Toronto: Oxford University Press, 1992).

Narayan, Uma. *Dislocating Cultures: Identities, traditions, and third-world feminism* (London: Routledge, 1997).

National Security Strategy of the United States of America (Washington, DC: September 2002). 31 pages.

Newbigin, Leslie. *The Gospel in a Pluralist Society* (Grand Rapids: Eerdmans, 1989).

Nussbaum, Martha C. *Women and Human Development: The capabilities approach* (Cambridge University Press, 2000).

Opalski, Magda. "Can Will Kymlicka be exported to Russia?" in Kymlicka and Opalski, 298–315.

Othman, Norani. "Grounding Human Rights Arguments in Non-Western Culture: *Shari'ah* and the citizenship rights of women in a modern Islamic state," in *The East Asian Challenge for Human Rights*, eds. Joanne R. Bauer and Daniel A. Bell (Cambridge University Press, 1999), 169–192.

Parekh, Bhikhu. *Rethinking Multiculturalism: Cultural diversity and political theory* (Cambridge: Harvard University Press, 2000).

Qutb, Sayyid. *In the Shade of the Qur'an*, trans. M.A. Salahi and A.A. Shamis, 3 vols. (Leicester: The Islamic Foundation, 1999–2001).

Sanneh, Lamin. *Encountering the West: Christianity and the global cultural process: The African dimension* (London: Marshall Pickering, 1993).

———. *Whose Religion is Christianity? The Gospel beyond the West* (Grand Rapids: Eerdmans, 2003).

Sen, Amartya. "Human rights and Asian values," *The New Republic* 217:2–3 (14–21 July 1997): 33–40.

Snow, C.P. *The Two Cultures* [1959] *and A Second Look* [1963] (Cambridge University Press, 1965).

Taylor, Charles. *Multiculturalism and "The Politics of Recognition"* (Princeton University Press, 1992).

Valadez, Jorge M. *Deliberative Democracy, Political Legitimacy, and Self-Determination in Multicultural Societies* (Boulder: Westview, 2001).

Van Bruinessen, Martin. "Kurds, States and Tribes," in *Tribes and Power: Nationalism and ethnicity in the Middle East*, eds. Faleh Abdul-Jabar and Hosham Dawod (London: Saqui, 2003), 165–183.

Vander Vennen, Mark. "Followers of Jesus, Doers of Justice." Public address 19 April 2004 at Calvin Seminary, Grand Rapids, Michigan (typescript, 20 pages).

Van der Walt, B.J. *Afrocentric or Eurocentric? Our task in a multicultural South Africa* (Potchefstroom: Potchefstroomse Universiteit vir Christelijke Hoër Onderwys, 1997).

Van Nieuwenhuize, C.A.O. *Development Regardless of Culture?*, ed. C.A.O. van Nieuwenhuize (Leiden: Brill, 1984), 1–24.

Wheatcroft, Andrew. *Infidels: The conflict between Christendom and Islam 638–2002* (London: Viking, 2003).

Williams, Melissa S. *Voice, Trust, and Memory: Marginalized groups and the failings of liberal representation* (Princeton University Press, 1998).

Wink, Walter. *Naming the Powers: The language of power in the New Testament* (Philadelphia: Fortress, 1984).

Wink, Walter. *Unmasking the Powers: The invisible forces that determine human existence* (Philadelphia: Fortress, 1981).

Young, Iris Marion. "Ruling Norms and the Politics of Difference: A comment on Seyla Benhabib," *The Yale Journal of Criticism* 12:2 (1999): 415–421.

Special thanks to Jonathan Chaplin, Phyllis Rozendal, Laura Smit, and Peter S. Smith for good bibliographic assistance on books and images.

FROM SYSTEMIC SUPPRESSION OF WOMEN TO ASYMMETRICAL GENDER MUTUALITY: AN HISTORICAL AND SYSTEMATIC INTRODUCTION

It is almost as if near the beginning of history there was a divine curse issued against women—May you be oppressed by men!—since human records from time immemorial seem to detail a vaunting **male perversity to dominate and abuse the female counterpart half of humanity** alive on the earth.

It is also very difficult to deny that only some humans menstruate, can give birth to children, and nurse them with appropriate glands and genitalia, while other humans with a penis lack such amazing bloody, life-giving potential. So there is normally evidence of a **sexual difference between human women and men**, despite the rare occurrence of bisexual hermaphrodites.

And, speaking carefully, today there is worldwide a hullabaloo about gender, since various long-standing distinct cultures now colliding have lived apart with quite fixed ideas, unspoken edicts (*fatwas*) about what in society is **properly a feminine or properly a masculine trait and work task**. Also, articulate lesbian voices call for a multiple gendering process.

I have been asked to introduce and sort out this bouillabaisse of **gender trouble**, and give some historical sense of **why** there is this deep-seated societal depreciation, **disqualification of women and their activity**.

Since I cannot jump out of my historical skin, I speak as an educated Euro-Canadian human of Dutch Huguenot descent who has been husband to a wife for 50 years, with two daughters and one son, two grand-daughters and one grandson. I was the firstborn in a family, with later three brothers and one sister, of a rural New York fishmonger father and legal secretary mother, raised, and became a convicted biblical Christian. So you need to take my remarks with a grain of chocolate.

An unpublished lecture presented at the Christian International Arts conference in Doorn, Netherlands, August 2006.

Since men are indisputably part of the problem in the suppression of women, **we men need to participate by listening to the cries of women and children until we actually hear their aggrieved wisdom so we can suffer through together,** as I understand it, **to what needs doing to foster, also in artistry, a world of promising shalom.**

Naming the evil afflicting us: soft slavery

This beautiful embossed heavy solid bronze artwork [#37] fits around the young African Niger girl's ankle. As she grows up nubile, the bronze anklet is no longer removable and, like a wedding ring, becomes a per-manent shackle hobbling her calloused leg so she cannot easily wander very far from the hearth she tends.

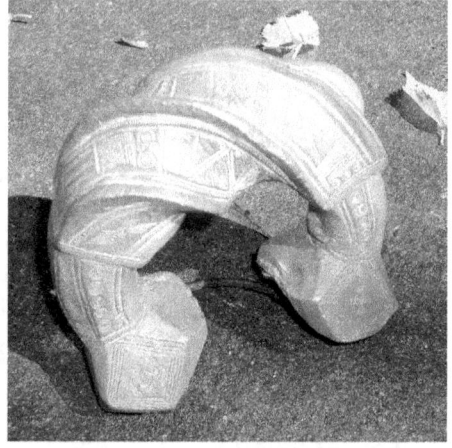

In ancient Confucian Chinese society (following K'ung Fu-tzu, c. 551–491 BC) the benign monarchical fam-ily is central, and women are considered to be weaker, sub-missive creatures who are to be subject first to the father, then to a husband almost as a concubine, and in old age

[#37] Ankle bracelet/fetter, Niger, Africa

governed by her sons. The feet of some infant girls were tightly bound to stunt their growth so that as desired crippled wives they were only good to wait on the Master. (Foot-binding was forbidden in China in 1912.)

Various syncretistic varieties of Hinduism and original Buddhism (following Siddhattha Gautama, c. 560–480 BC) have stigmatized wom-en as reincarnated souls whose earlier life was not ascetic enough to es-cape the cycle of *samsara* (troubles) in our mirage reality (*maya*) and en-ter *nirvana*. A best way to achieve full womanhood might be to enter a nunnery and be occupied in cleansing the temple and cooking vegetarian food for the monks. Lay married women of upper caste and upper class in certain locales of India were traditionally encouraged to prove their *pativrata* (husband-reverence) by immolating themselves on the funeral pyre of the deceased husband. (This ceremonial practice of *sati* was made illegal in India in 1929.)

Ancient Greek myth pitted male gods like Ouranos and thunder-bolt Zeus against female goddesses like fertility Gaia and Olympian

Hera, which gave an undercurrent of hostile struggle to sexual relations for those bred in that mythic culture. Plato (c. 427–347 BC) plumped for a unisex perspective, since "souls"—which define humans—are sexless. It's the incarceration of rational souls in material bodies that causes human troubles. Women have too much body: women are probably sensual reincarnations of immoral men, wrote Plato (*Timaios*, 90e6–91a4). And while philosopher Aristotle (388–322 BC) held out for a more integrated formed-matter creature than Plato, a bespirited body, because he talked enlivening male semen and passive female womb (*De Generatione animalium*, II, 4 738b18–26), biologist Aristotle judged a woman to be, "as it were, an impotent male" (ἄρρεν ἄγονον, Ibid,. I, 20 728a17–20), a disabled male animal (πεπηρωμένον, Ibid., II, 3 737a28). For Aristotle male human animals are superior to female "naturally crippled" (ἀναπηρίαν. . . φυσικήν) human animals (Ibid., II, 1 732a4–10; IV, 6 775a14–16).

Muslim culture built on oral following of the *hadith* (traditions Mohammed observed), which holds modesty be a fundamental female virtue, can lead in different settings to various apparently restrictive customs: simply wearing a *hijab* scarf or veiling *burqa* to signal that womanly beauty is not for public display; keeping a woman in domestic seclusion (*purdah*); or practicing severe infibulation of a girl's genitals (so-called Pharonic circumcision) to insure virginity. The codified *Qur'an* (Medina section) is unambiguous about the authority of men to be in charge of women, because Allah has so ordained it. Take good care of women, says *Qur'an* 4.34; devout women obey God:

> As for those women from whom you have reason to fear rebellion, admonish them; then leave them alone in bed; then beat them. Then, if they pay heed to you, do not seek any pretext to harm them. God is indeed Most High, Great.[1]

Muslim clerics have pronounced Shari'a family law interpreting Qur'anic principles sometimes with severe Wahhabi orthodoxism, other times with a little leeway (*ijtihad*), for example, on the permission granted for polygamy (*Qur'an* 4.3).[2] Muslim leaders like Sufi authority al-Ghazali

---

1 Translation of 4.34 by Adil Salahi and Ashur Shamis in Sayyid Qutb's *In the Shade of the Qur'an* (Leicester: The Islamic Foundation, 2001), 3:135. A quite different "contemporary" translation by Ahmed Ali in the "final definitive" Princeton University Press edition of *Al-Qur'an* in 1994/2001 prints the same text with a starkly revisionist twist as follows: "As for women you feel are averse, talk to them suasively; then leave them alone in bed (without molesting them) and go to bed with them (when they are willing). If they open out to you, do not seek an excuse for blaming them. Surely God is sublime and great."

2 Qutb exposits *Qur'an* 4.3 as a kind of leviratical compassionate way to take care of

(1059–1111 AD) value women and men separately to be "equal but different"; yet such a principled *apartheid* invariably disadvantages women who need to be attached to men in order to survive—a loose woman has no place in Islamic society.

Early Church culture partial to Platonic world-flight tendencies took a different tack: exalting the Virgin Mary churchmen privileged virgins "married to Christ" above ordinary married women. "I praise matrimony," wrote the great rhetorician St. Jerome (c. 347–419?), "But only because it produces virgins."[3] Virginal nuns, it is to be noted, who took refuge in Benedictine monasteries (c. 800 onward), were able to read, learn to write, and make artwork. The mainline medieval Church of Western Christendom, however, imbued with Aristotle's prejudice against women as inferior, derivative, defective men who lack the ability to reason logically and debate discursively, explicitly excluded women from studying at the developing university centers (c. 1200 AD) in Paris, Oxford, Cambridge, and elsewhere. An aristocratic woman like Heloise could arrange for a private tutor like Abelard (from 1108–1118 AD), but women generally were denied education in the faculties of liberal arts, medicine, law, and theology—kept out of the University of Paris until 1868![4]

And this consolidating prejudice, which forbade women to be schooled—women, formed from a **bent** rib of man, being too easily deceived—became an historical factor in hunting down women as prone to witchcraft, being misled by the devil. Three-fourths of the 100,000 or so witches burned at the stake in the countryside that became central Europe (France, Germany, Italy) in the 200 years after the publication of *Malleus maleficarum* (1448) [*The Hammer of Those Who Do Evil*], the "Bible" on witches, were uneducated women tortured, tried, and found guilty by educated male clergy and male university professors trained in "sexless" Aristotelian logic.[5]

---

war widows and unmarried women (*In the Shade of the Qur'an*, 32–38). Ahmed Ali's footnote aligns verse 4.3 with 4.129, and claims the *Qur'an* "virtually restricts the number of wives to one" (73)! After the Caliphate moved to Damascus (661 AD), however, men who could afford it began taking not widows but younger women as additional wives, and polygamy has indeed proliferated where Islam has spread.

3   *Libellus de virginitate servanda* (384 AD), a letter to Eustochium: ". . . laudo nuptias, laudo coniugium, sed quia mihi virgines generant" (20,1), translated by Paul Carroll, "How to Live as a Nun in a Profligate Society" in *Satirical Letters of Jerome* (Chicago: Gateway, 1956), 31–38, especially 37.

4   Prudence Allen, *The Concept of Woman: The Aristotelian revolution, 750 B.C.–A.D. 1250* (Grand Rapids: Eerdmans, 1985), 415.

5   Prudence Allen, *The Concept of Woman: The early humanist reformation, 1250–1500*

Our story of forced womanly submission to a male imposed order, confinement, and deprivation, does not get prettier as we get closer to home in our secularized "enlightened" apostate day.[6]

The French Revolution (1789–1799) of *liberté, égalité et fraternité* did not mention *soeurité*, and the American Declaration of Independence (1776), which emphasized that "all **men** are created equal," hid their bias that women are non-voting home-bodies relegated to motherhood, child care, and not wanted "in the streets," like prostitutes, or mixing it up in public power politics. Further, when industrialization reduced workmen to wage-earners, piecework hirelings in factories, women were hit with a double whammy: your endless, thankless labor of housework and home maintenance—your womanly responsibility—was not considered "productive work" to be paid for; and if you were poor enough as a family so that your unskilled hand labor for bit work outside the house was necessary, as woman you still always had to face the "second-shift" of domestic care after hours, lest family life—your womanly responsibility—suffer a breakdown.

When European colonialization policies exported this family-alienating commercialistic setup to foreign lands, converting rural self-sufficient households with unified work and food community into an urban market cash-economy, because of traditional mores available only to men, the women with their many children had to add to their burden of continuing subsistent farming an increasing **isolation** from the commuting husband in thrall to the dominating cash-nexus society. (Women could join the new order only by selling their bodies for a price.)

Freud's (1856–1939) influential psychoanalytic theories and praxis evince a phallocentric neurosis that denigrates women to be essentially embittered sexual predators—that is their feminine mystique! And as "modern" society becomes increasingly unruly, a godless contest for autonomous survival, women can decorously accept their Freudian sexualization and aspire to be attractive waitresses, secretaries, even minor "bosses," or flaunt their mystique to entertain and frustrate the aggressive, possessive male scrutiny, or unsex themselves and brazen it out as an independent agent in a man's world, no quarter asked or given. But no matter which move a "modern" woman makes, she is caught, it seems to me, in an unsatisfying, cockeyed enslavement fighting or overcompensat-

---

(Grand Rapids: Eerdmans, 2002), 533.

6   Friedrich Schiller's exasperated comment came to mind: "Das Zeitalter ist aufgeklärt. . . . woran liegt es, dass wir noch immer Barbaren sind? (in *Über die Ästhetische Erziehung des Menschen in einer Reihe von Briefen*, 8:3).

ing a resident harassing, male-determining hegemony that is violently disruptive for the lives of men, boys, and girls, as well as of women.

What I hear from the sorry historical notes just told is a tale full of demeaning trouble signifying hurt undergone by generations of women often silenced. Women in all world cultures past and present have suffered what I shall call the stifling cruelty of **soft slavery**. Like Ralph Ellison's *Invisible* [Black] *Man* (1947), **women have been used by men as if women were a male prosthesis and had no independent existence with a subjective will of their own**—slaves.

Sometimes the violence against women as persons (*Gewalt*) is brutal and vivid, like their rape by soldiers of war or in police custody, or as booty: when pirates attacked fleeing Vietnamese boatpeople in the China Sea in the 1960s, the boat offered up its virgin girls to be violated, and then shunned the victims ever after. Often, however, the enslaving abuse of women is not an individually premeditated hard event, but is an on-going generic practice of power (*Macht*) assumed to be normal and "natural": wearing out a woman's belly annually to produce progeny, like a domestic animal, to breed kids to work the fields or beg in the cities—it's "necessary." Or, there is a soft eroticized reduction of women to "models" in the ubiquitous advertising of *Time, Cosmopolitan, Time Out,* or TV media, which is **so flatteringly common that the full human nature of a woman beyond her sexuality is made invisible**.

It is such pervasive systemic cultural exploitation of women (frequently accepted by women themselves as their lot) that men who have power in the societal setup simply by virtue of being male are often **not conscious** of as to its hidden denigrating oppression. The condescension within such witless, male-centered, ruling control, making one's fellow female human being utterly **dependent** on thoughtless male whim, is the violation of women and their worth I understand to be "soft slavery." And that stupid power trip diminishes both man and woman into a dreadfully arrogant monstrous biceptual male human and a desecrated slavish edible female human locked in an everlasting destructive standoff world without end.

Before I try to add my voice to others who would transform the slow ruination of women **and men** by the systemic closeted violence in the world society we inhabit, and try to complicate the life-problematics we share and offer a vision of gender that might offset the gender trouble with gender joy, let me briefly and carefully treat a strain or two in the "feminist" attempt to alter the reigning oppressive "patriarchal" consciousness and debilitating action still extant. As bell hooks puts it:

If we do not change our consciousness, we cannot change our actions or demand change from others.[7]

Different waves of feminist correction

There have always been figures in history who have spoken up for women and men to engage each other in respectful conversation and chaste, caring love relationships. Jesus Christ practiced such correction in the rabbinic society he encountered, which questioned whether Samaritans, let alone Samaritan women! could be considered one's neighbors (John 4:5–30, 8:3–11, 11:1–53, 20:11–18, Luke 10:25–42). The apostle Paul flummoxed his legalistic Jewish antagonists too by teaching in the Newer Testament a reciprocal mingling of women and men in their daily christian life and service in Church activity (Ephesians 5:1–6:29, Romans 16:1–20, 1 Timothy 3:1–15, 5:1–22).

Later on, while African bishop Augustine (354–430 AD) struggled to slough off the Platonizing unisex thought tradition, Augustine affirmed that no sex is superior to the other since "both sexes will remain after the resurrection"; "a woman's sex is not a blemish but her nature."[8] Singular women like Benedictine abbess Hildegard von Bingen (1098–1179), Beguine Mechthild von Magdeburg (1210–1297), and Dame Julian of Norwich (1342–c.1420) showed that disenfranchised women could nevertheless produce oeuvres of finely written reflective texts that unpolemically assumed they as women shared fully a co-humanity with men who practiced philosophy. But it was especially literary artists like Guido ("Donna mi prega") Cavalcanti (1255–1300) and Giovanni (*De claris mulieribus* [*About famous women*]) Boccaccio (1313–1375) who envisioned women not as degendered, unreal Platonic ideals like Dante's Beatrice and Petrarch's Laura, but as wise, virtuous, earthily engaged persons—the *Decamerone* (1348–53) has intelligent **women** telling most of the gutsy, worldliwise stories.

With the European Aufklärung, however, come concerted, argued briefs in public to correct the subordinate status of women.

> We women are the **same** rational human creatures as men; therefore we women deserve **equal** legal-political and socio-economic **rights** as men (to be voting citizens, able to own property, to participate in higher education,

---

7 *Talking Back: thinking feminist, thinking black* (Toronto: Between the Lines, 1988), 25.

8 ". . . utrumque sexum resurrecturum esse; . . . Non est autem vitium sexus femineus, sed natura." *De Civitatis Dei*, XXII,17. Augustine goes on to say in the same section: "So our Lord denied that there would be marriage after the resurrection. He did not say there would be no women" ("Nuptias ergo Dominus futuras esse negavit in resurrectione, non feminas").

not be blacklisted from certain jobs and professions).

This push for equality objecting to male supremacy, from proto-suffragist Mary Wollstonecraft (*Vindication of the Rights of Women*, 1792) to the failed Equal Rights Amendment in the USA (1982), played down sexual-gender differences, and in good Anglo-American Lockean empiricist fashion based its claims for equality on the inviolate autonomous individual every one of us is, male or female. And over the generations, important concessions have been grudgingly granted by a stubborn male establishment as a result of lawsuits and labor union action. But equality based on sameness has the drawback of reducing mutual acceptance to legal equity and of canceling out certain special rights needed, for example, by child-bearing women for family work-leave, or single mothers, and **spurs on women to be like men fighting** for space on the upwardly mobile, bourgeois paleface careerist ladder, everybody cut to the same mold. Even the Victorian Titanic ethic—Women and children first!—is considered a paternalistic cover for the patriarchal assumption that women are the weaker sex; so special preference for women must go.

Such a WASP-ish middleclass "liberal" movement for a sprawling "equality" based on sameness with men partially gave way, let's say, sometime between post-World War II and 1968, to two other waves of women collectively intent upon ending the disadvantaged, devalued condition of women worldwide: (1) those who celebrate womanhood on the basis of recognizing their **sexual difference** from men instead of sameness—I'll call it the "Womanist" wave (to adopt Alice Walker's good term); and (2) what has been called "radical feminism," a medley of attempts to overturn abusive male dominance in society on the basis of upholding an **anti-male or** a "neutral," **neutered sexuality**.

(1) When "fourth world" (=a relatively powerless minority within the "first world," e.g., Afro-American women) and "two-thirds world" women (the global multi-ethnic majority who are not the white Western affluent minority) found their voice, new "feminist" notes were heard, because marriage and motherhood were humanizing protective experiences rather than a curse for black women after the abolition of racist slavery in America; and Asian Indian and South Pacific women forced into unwanted, pre-arranged marriages, who were denied basic education, or women wearied by an incessant Latino machismo, or women blanketed and isolated by a repressive man-made religious ideology in the Near East, did not want a "liberation" to act the same as males! or like leisure-class females to hold highfalutin seminars on "women's-lib" or parade bare-breasted through Toronto streets. Their non-Western repres-

sion was of a deeply different kind and needed different remedies.

I understand the Womanist wave of feminist correction to be say-ing: we cannot escape living in **intimate** co-existence with the oppressor. So **we need control of our own womanly sexuality, its identity and glory**. Sisterhood is a fortifying, unifying bonding around the world, **but we must find a** *modus vivendi* **relationally** *with* **men**, men amenable to relinquishing absolute power; since both of us, male and female (in the presence of extreme poverty or AIDS, for example) necessarily depend on each other for survival in our multi-faceted society and workplace.

The Womanist wave of reform breathes a more communitarian and kinship spirit than the individualistic Enlightenment fixation plumping for the "same equality." An aboriginal matrilineal, not to say, "matriar-chal" order backgrounds the Womanist dedication to develop somehow a sexual companionship in our multi-faceted society and workplace.

(2) A common theme among the quite diverse exponents of "radical feminism" is the corrective challenge to reject maleness as the norm and, as it were, to remove the secrecy, even privacy, around the matter of sex-uality—"let it all hang out," because clandestine "sex" fosters evil against women. And it is true, if a girl or a woman has been sexually molested, wantonly or ritually abused by trustable men, I can understand they may want to castrate any man they meet on the street, practically criminalize malehood (Mary Daly), and go so far as to construe heterosexuality as a compulsory affront to women (Adrienne Rich), a conspiracy for male pleasure that legalizes rape in the "institution" of marriage.

Thoughtful lesbians, struggling for a strong womanly consciousness not formed in the shadow of male hegemony, unwilling to play the role of "victim," resort to a philosophically nominalist, performative concep-tion of sexuality (Judith Butler): the human "body" is an unsexed site (Simone de Beauvoir) for "consciousness" to construct its LGB (lesbian, gay, bisexual) "nature"; so there are more than two strictly defined sexu-alities that a person can choose to appropriate even though at birth the medical authorities declare, "It's a girl!" or "It's a boy!" Rather than be apologetic female wimps bemoaning their plight in "a man's world," vari-ous practitioners of "Queer theory," as it is called, boldly proclaim, "We are not ugly ducklings in a paddling of ducks swimming around: we are swans!"

There are a few thoughts I should like to distill from these waves of femi-nist correction, because it will take on-going wise, mediating discussion and years of restorative action to alter the soft slavery women endure throughout the world. We need to have not only rape phone lines and shelters for battered women in Western cities, but condom help for rural African women against HIV-infection from philandering husbands, and give internet notice to the Malaysian "Sisters in Islam" (begun 1988) who are battling intolerant *ulama* by showing that the *Qur'an* (Meccan section) can be interpreted to allow for an updated just dignity for women.

The Americo-Eurocentric fight against discrimination for equality based on sameness is not adequate to combat worldwide oppression, I think, because "equal rights" will remain a tug of war geared to the "other's" superiority and "my" assimilation. Also, the current promotion of heterophobia, like homophobia, is disastrous for building sound sexual relationships in society, because to live out of fear (or hatred) is not humanly healthy, and replaces genuine reform with **conceptual violence** and scapegoating.

I find the Womanist resolve to accept female and male sexual difference as a given reality to be reckoned with the most promising perspective. Rather than argue and contend for one's "pound of flesh" within an "equality calculus," **we need to work toward differential equity of opportunity, gift-recognition, and just deserts within a horizon of sexual and gender mutuality, aware of the multiple factors contributing to the inequities oppressing women** and other unfortunate "outcasts" of society, like the poor. Humans are not defined by one's genitals. And the soft slavery of women is not caused solely by male sexual cruelty. So we need a larger cosmic picture in which to frame the abuse of women, and to zero in on a way to convert antagonistic gender trouble into mutual gender joy.

More needs to be said about the problems of socio-economic equity in an increasingly multi-ethnic, plural-faith conglomeration that is drastically affecting the family, school, nationhood, church-synagogue-mosque heritage of our erstwhile Christian Humanist Europe, I would like to follow up the introductory historical setting I have given with a couple of systematic points on our actual societal setup worldwide, before I slip in a perhaps controversial note on "gender."

Our complicated societal setup liable to manic disorder
We would do well to stop talking about "Others," and reactivate the biblical insight that each of us lives among neighbors, no matter how different they may be. Further, this primal inter-individual mesh of being neighborhooded as humans, at its peril, overlooks or denies **the dated/located reality of a circle of institutional grips on our lives in so-**

ciety, each of which is meant to facilitate and protect (pace Foucault) **our well-being together.** The transportation network of dusty roads or underground trains, the hospital or field health clinic, the extended or nuclear family, a university, an art museum, restorative sanatorium, the tribal council, constitutional monarchy or one-party government, a prayer center for exercising the faith of your choice, a village or metropolis, the newspaper or internet media: a variety of precincts with limited authority and circumscribed purpose are in force, at different stages of development or disrepair, so to speak, to minister to our commonweal.

Also present in any historical societal make-up, including our societies today, often unaccounted for—you may not believe this—are strange compelling forces, it seems, that drive communities of people manic. Racist Nationalism, Imperialistic Democratism, Functionalistic Pragmatism, Militaristic Nihilism, Rationalistic Agnosticism, Idealistic Consumerism, Sexist Hedonism: underneath any powerful ISM, which often competes against or joins other ISMs to drive the hearts and lives of people, lies the uncanny surd you are not supposed to talk about in polite, contemporary society—sin. I don't mean peccadilloes or immoral deeds. Sin, as I understand it, is a powerful corrosive Evil (σάρξ) that can infect humans like a virus, swell to fill them up like a cancer, and blot out sanity with Fundamentalist fervor, so that I eat while you next to me starve, I murder you while you sit relaxing in God's sunshine, we destroy . . . ourselves and loved ones by becoming zombies in destructive missions while being dead to the living God and dead to the world of **neighbors.**

The simple point of this set of remarks is this: when cultural institutional leaders in various fields come under the sway of one or another invisible, cancerous sinful "Principalities" (ἀρχαὶ, ἐξουσία, δυνάμεις, see Ephesians 6:12), humans who follow the élan of such zealous leaders like a herd of swine over the ISMatic cliff, throw society out of whack and wreak wasteful havoc in God's world. And the possibilities are legion!

For example, when thousands of Frankish youth of the medieval Church, stirred with zeal to free "Holy Land" real estate in 1212, trusting that their naive innocence (being 12 years old) would work miracles so they could succeed where previous crusades of knights had failed, the complex endeavor of "the Children's Crusade," which embarrassed Pope Innocent III, was touched, it seems to me, by mania. When the current political leaders of the USA, believing a *volonté générale* will always freely elect Jeffersonian democratic governance, and presuming it should use its enormous global clout of trade embargoes and monetary sanctions to cow countries around the world to embrace this ideology, the complicated geo-political fallout of miseries strikes me as fraught with a blind-sided mania. When Muslim and when Zionist Fundamentalists turn education into hateful indoctrination, hospitals into rocket launching pads, and neighborhoods into walled-off dead-ends, **believing** that forgetting a history of still resident injustice, taking retaliatory vengeance, and pursuing total separation is the only way to forge "a just peace" between enemies, must one not recognize that some kind of mania is distorting their daily lives, stymieing commerce, media, family life, blocking out shalom/shalam?

Apropos our topical focus on the centuries of soft slavery endured by women: different mania warping different institutions in the societal complex have twisted the lives of women (and men) into multi-sorts of contortions—there is no one simple cause or solution. A constant, grinding, continuous poverty—not knowing whether you have a next meal coming to hungry you—is debilitating not because you are female but because the rich do not share their goods. You are an "untouchable" Dalit in the Hindu caste system or an illegal Mexican immigrant in Texas and you cannot flourish culturally, not because you are female rather than male, but because Brahmin **women** shun you and white supremacist **women** will hire you only as working poor maids. That is, class, ethnicity, race, education, divorcement, orphanhood, monolinguality, foreign mores, even rigorous personal morals can and do enter into the oppression of women. So, **much more than male/female relations in society need to be straightened out before the injustice done to women can be remedied**.

And it may be worth mentioning *en passant* that women themselves, like men, need to be wary lest they fall prey to a ruling passion or *idée fixe* loose in the world breathing disorder, such as the principality of Consumerism: Pleasure-for-me is #1. Then women could daydream to be starlets in Bollywood (a secularized replay of age-old fertility cult routines), maybe yearn to wear steel stiletto high heels (unaware that you are voluntarily adopting the ancient yoke of back-wrenching, foot-binding deformation); or, more conservative, you may decide to watch Harlequin romance type sit-com shows on TV (where virginal romantic tension, domestic security, and sexual excitement all together let you drift off subconsciously into Never-neverland, escaping the oppressive circumstance you actually inhabit). Those who serve short-term hedonistic Consumerism, however, women or men, become themselves consumed; your subjectivity is objectified into a prop put up for sale—humanity snakily checkmated.

A phenomenological approach to human gender

Is there some way to relate gender to female/male sexual difference without freezing "feminine" and "masculine" into stereotypes at loggerheads, and also to provide merciful place for human neighbors who are predisposed to a mixed gender identity, perhaps because of an indistinct or conflicted sexuality?

For fun let me make a start by trying to describe phenomenologically how to understand our intricately interwoven humanity, sexuality, and gendered corporeal nature that would position us women and men to develop in sharing an asymmetrical gender mutuality in our consciousness and praxis.

Diagram #1: A clay jar model of human creaturely consciousness.

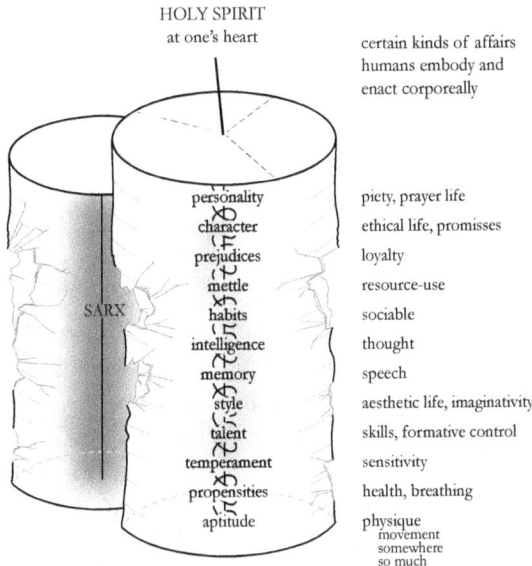

HOLY SPIRIT
at one's heart

certain kinds of affairs
humans embody and
enact corporeally

SARX

personality — piety, prayer life
character — ethical life, promises
prejudices — loyalty
mettle — resource-use
habits — sociable
intelligence — thought
memory — speech
style — aesthetic life, imaginativity
talent — skills, formative control
temperament — sensitivity
propensities — health, breathing
aptitude — physique
movement
somewhere
so much

Humans, unlike animals, plants, and mountains, let's say, are flesh-and-bloody based, life-breathing mortal creatures whose subjective corporeality consists of varied irreducible ways of acting. Neighborhooded humans are so big, somewhere, able to move, who have a measure of strength, are vital, feel, can normally control various things, imagine, speak, think, be sociable, employ resources, act (un)justly, be (un)friendly, and are able to pray. Peculiar about us human creatures is that all the ways we are here and can be functioning are centered by our willingness to dedicate our many splendored kinds of activities to Something—Humanity, Allah, Pleasure, the God revealed in Jesus Christ, Nihil, or Whatever. . . . As Bob Dylan sang, **"Ya gotta serve Somebody"! That is what makes you peculiarly human—the willingness to lay down your life for someone or some "cause." That is also why we humans are susceptible to mania and cruelty.**

As for sexuality: as Camille Paglia says, "If you menstruate, you are a woman. Else not." Michael Foucault (1926–1984), who spawned much current imperious denial of constant sexualities, may be correct in thinking ". . . it is sex itself which hides the most secret parts of the individual"; but Foucault is mistaken, in my judgment, to believe "our sex harbors what is most true in ourselves."[9] **Sexuality is fundamentally vital to a person's existence, but is not central or definitive.**

As a man I can only imagine how the fact that a woman usually bleeds monthly for a long period of her life, and could give birth to a new creature—could also be assaulted at that precarious depth level of one's existence—covertly affects her everyday bearing, almost the way tidal waters on earth are affected by the monthly phases of the moon, because such a regular reminder of female sexuality is not buried in my male unconscious. Motherhood does not define womanhood any more than to remain celibate makes a man less a male. And while a strict binary conception of sexuality often misses noting the important gradations in a person's underfunded or overtaxed, possibly even disturbed or damaged libidinal propensities, and while the performative slipknot approach to sex as "fictive" (Judith Butler, Monique Wittig) rules out any aberrant, pathological sexuality,[10] Paglia's blunt, knowing statement sets real boundaries and holds true on sexuality, as I see it.

Gender is different from but indirectly prompted by matters sexual. Although men are more than testosterone sources of sperms, and women are more than a residence of ovaries, everybody human has the parentage of a male sperm and a female ovum. Our being generated, however, by

---

9 Michael Foucault introduction to *Herculine Barbin: Being the recently discovered memoirs of a nineteenth-century French hermaphrodite* (1868), translated by Richard McDougall (New York: Pantheon, 1980), x–xi.

10 A recent seminar I attended at York University in Toronto (March 2006), entitled *Transgressions: A scholarly and creative conference on subversive practices across the fields of art and visual culture*, was led by many presenters whose spirit of zetetic agnosticism and soft-nihilism assumed that sexuality like gender was completely unfixed, practically a matter of anyone's choice, a virtual "put-on." So one wondered how any condition or act could be "transgressive."

One session on "apotemnophilia"—a person's abiding desire to amputate a limb of one's body to become sexually attractive—proposed that such a state of somebody's consciousness and action might be a quest for defining one's bodily identity, but was not necessarily pathological.

the conjunction of an ejaculated fathering sperm and mothered (until recently) in an egg-friendly womb, and then **being born from a woman's body** as a girl-daughter or as a boy-son, provides me with the link between sexuality and gender.

Without trying to exposit Nancy Chodorow and Carol Gilligan's untangling Freud and Lacan's labyrinth of prejudices toward daughter-mother/father and son-father/mother relationships, let me posit this for your consideration: **the dated/located character of being parented**, of being actually cut from a mother's umbilical cord and growing up from baby to child to youth to adult—father (and siblings) assisting, conflicting, or being absent in the process—**affects your sexual engenderment most significantly**. Daughters are potential mothers (even if never activated), but sons are not. Since mothering is originally constituted by **birthing and betrothed nurturing** (carrying the fetus so many months), it seems sensible to me to expect such **an ethical-organic** contribution to my existence to be the gender spin-off for what will be a particularly feminine predisposition: **feminine gender tends to evince (mothering) life-giving care.** Since fathering is characterized by a **begetting potency and being justly responsible** as a partner, that peculiar male feature leading to my being here prompts me to expect that such a **physical-duty-administering** character might be what serves as a masculine gendered bent: **masculine gender tends to rest on (fathering) responsible potency.** So "gender" is not one, but varies structurally per sexuality.

Such feminine and masculine gendered proclivities, sourced in one's having been mothered and fathered as a girl-daughter and as a boy-son, take on certain modified cachets depending on what the historical, complex societal circumstances specifically be for parenting at the time and place of your parented birth and development (for example, Confucian China, Victorian England, '60s California). Anybody's gender, somewhat like race, is also richly colored by all the other facets of one's creaturehood, as well as by your personal inborn talents and deficiencies. But feminine gender and masculine gender are of a relatively stable nature, each of which is distinct from the other, it seems to me, because each person has been both begotten (from ruling potency) and birthed (out of life-giving care) **as a girl or as a boy. Feminine gender and masculined gender each have a sexually based, parentally induced Gestalt relative to its historical occurrence.**[11]

---

11 Unlike Judith Butler who thinks "drag" performance subverts both gender norms and gender definiteness, I see it as confirming the fact that gender is **not** fictive, if it can be so parodied. Also, even though trans-sexual surgery may dispute a given person's

It makes sense to say today that anybody, female or male, including single unmarried adults, can "father" a project or "mother" an enterprise; and that "fathering" and "mothering" have different nuances corresponding to "masculine" and "feminine," without setting off a gender war. Also, because men can be faithful enlivening persons, and because women have the creatural wherewithal to manifest ruling power, it is no disgrace but entirely normal, like cross-dressing (robes, kilts, pant-suits), for men upon occasion to exhibit feminine traits and for women at times to show masculine lineaments.

Further, gender is integral to friendships. Friendships are relationships of trust between people who feel at ease with each other (an emotionally funded ethically qualified bond), kindred spirits, where each friend normally shares one's gifts to fill the other's lacunae, enriching both. If my phenomenological proposal for grasping gendering Gestalt has merit, we would expect girl-to-girl friendships to highlight not prowess but supportive, intimate inter-individual attachment, and boy-to-boy friendships will enjoy not so much vital closeness as energetic uniting escapades of cooperative camaraderie. One must be careful not to romanticize and stereotype gender differences as the mass media often do, taking young aggressive males and very attractive young females as the gender norms. Then people tend to stigmatize some girls and boys with disqualifying terms like "tomboys" and "sissies." Before puberty one's gender formation is in the process of becoming firmed up by following the role models of parents, teachers (including "pop stars"), or one's older peers. Once erotic desire fully awakens in a male or female youth, friendships naturally become more complicated.

It is my hunch that the experience of pain and pleasure **and friendship** is markedly different for an adult woman and an adult man, if a mature corresponding gender framework is in play. A woman often endures pain without male kick-back remonstrance. A man often enjoys pleasure more as an eventful occurrence than as an exuberant female state of contentment. In a cross-sexual friendship the feminine expectation is lively exercise of shared mutual interests furthering wholeness, and the masculine expectation tends to want to ground the exciting common activities with physical contact. So male/female friendships are rare that do not lead to pledged marriage founded in physically cementing intercourse, or at least to partnered cohabitation while foregoing the stressful joy of

---

sexual identification, such a deep-going body modification (overrating the nature of human sexuality as primordial?), it seems to me, is desperately reaching for a male or a female sexual identity as if such indeed be extant.

bearing children. A mature woman to woman friendship that reaches the erotic seriousness of a lesbian partnership is different in make-up from a homophilic partnership of two adult men friends, even if both gender roles are at work in either given partnership, because the female-feminine sexual underlay in a lesbian bond is a residential mothering, while the male-masculine sexual underlay in male bonding has an existential fathering "distantial" commitment to the union. Persons in any lasting female or male homophilic human relationship experience joys and troubles—communion, conflict, celebration, jealousy, hurts—comparable to any long-term heterosexual human relationship.

The upshot of this brief excursion into friendship of different sorts and human gendering aims to complicate the frequent over-simplification made of gendered sexuality, and commends the mutual sharing intrinsic to any sound friendship for the way to begin overcoming the terrible oppression of women by men, at least in this sexual-gendering aspect of our corporeal human consciousness so prone to trample on or rub out differences.

To de-sex women and men and intentionally confine us to a neutered no-man/no-woman's-land in order to base equality on sameness strikes me as settling for a drab, bitterly conflicted human existence. And to champion homophilic relations at the expense of heterosexual realities in the name of a misconceived autonomous freedom for a person only dislocates the sexual-gender differences and breeds new outcasts for a hostility that will simply continue the historic wrangling and turmoil at a homo/heterosexual level.

The asymmetrical mutual giving of one's distinct gendered endowment to the sexual neighbor is a step out of the barren loveless stalemate we have on our hands, and provides the wisp of a promise toward womanly and manly shalom in God's world.

Normative gender-friendly artistic steps showing loving mutuality

Let me illustrate for you just a few gender-friendly artworks that are brimming with loving sexual-differential consciousness that understands and contributes to restoring justice for women as strong sexual creatures meet for humbled men. It was Jesus Christ who told especially his male disciples **not** to practice the curse of Genesis 3:16, **not** to "lord-it-over" the neighbor as the pagans do, but to minister to your fellow human, to wash each other's feet (see Luke 22:24–27, John 13:1–17).

Henry Moore (1898–1986) as a child rubbed the arthritic back of his mother, trying to ease the corded muscular pain with rubbing alcohol. The wall of the maternal back must have seemed huge to the little helping boy. Ever after Moore's big sculptured women in Brown Horton stone evoke earthy female strength, their thigh-belly-breasts sexuality is unabashed, but **not** eroticized. Moore knows women are vulnerable, with holes in their ponderous reclining bodies, but like this UNESCO artwork [#38] of Travertine marble, a periscope of a neck emphasizes she is femininely on the lookout for the safety of children in the world, inviting girls and boys to run to her as a compassionate mountain of security. Moore's family pieces also always assume that parenting is meant to be a shared task of the man as well as of the woman.

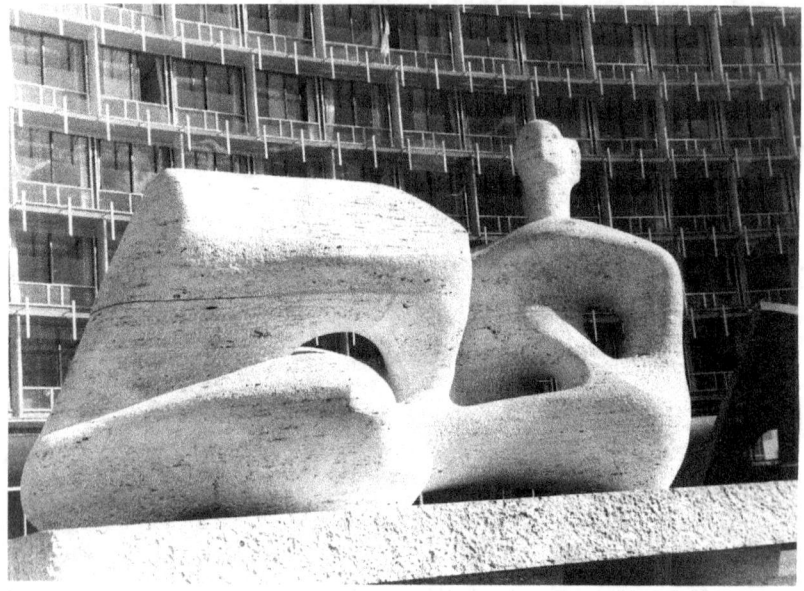

[#38] Henry Moore, *Reclining Figure*,
outside UNESCO Building in Paris, 1957-58

One could reach back to the steady admiration of artist Johannes Vermeer (1632–1675) for the composed women of his day, who were ennobled in pouring milk [#39] with care in the kitchen to serve with fresh bread, who knew that needlework could be an exquisite **profession**. Women dominate Vermeer's painterly oeuvre, usually singled out to highlight their casual dignity, as cultured and desirable near the harpsichord, but at home in their bodies, standing, restrained, a commanding presence, yes, often pregnantly homely, reading a letter from the man out adventuring the map of the world, but still—despite the mores of the day—with a sure will as well as a room of her own. Feminists should not

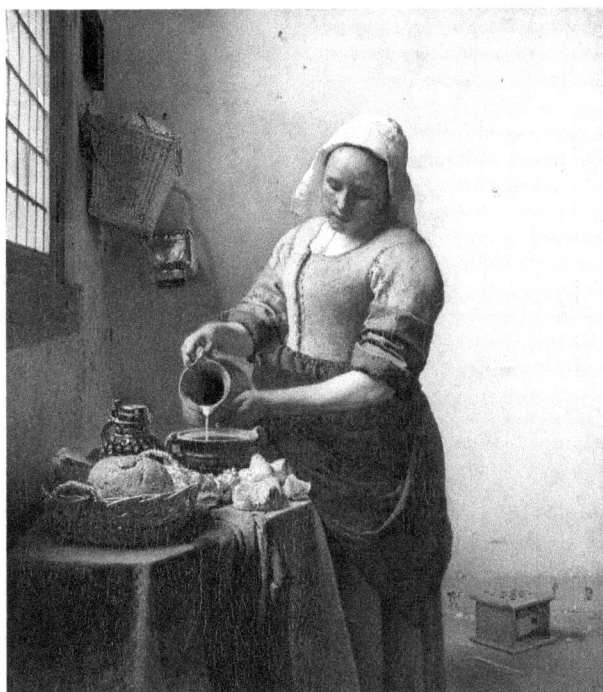

[#39] Johannes Vermeer, *Melkmeisje*, 1658-61

miss that Vermeer's recognition of a woman's sexual appeal and feminine reserve is **not** domesticated, but is perceived as chaste, noble, vitally attractive. Vermeer also hints that the studied compassion a woman is peculiarly capable of, in quietly weighing serious matters, may, we hope, be the way God will judge our lives in the final Day of reckoning.

Käthe Kollwitz's (1867–1945) womanly horror of war is existentially born out of the death of her German son who once was a sleeping child, but was recruited as a youth with drums and parades to volunteer to go kill for one's country. War has always been itself terror (despite disposable Genevan Conventions), depicts the womanly artist Kollwitz, with not only women as tortured casualties discarded like garbage, but also men and children, who at best become prisoners of war, also mentally, ever after. Would that the male-masculine consciousness of power-handy political leaders—"liberal" democratic leaders too, whose institutions now treat women and men indiscriminately as non-sexed, numbered draftable "identities"—could hear the artistic cries and whispers of a woman's deep yearning to protect the young like a human bomb shelter with her inadequate body [#40], and then weep uncontrollably for those killed, in a clumsy lump of sodden flesh manly trying to revive her dead child again within her body. We need masculine woman voices like that of artist Kollwitz to be heard so that our masters of war, male or female, become more feminine in their fateful decisions.

Let me close with a few cheerful hints of mutual gender sharing of female and male sexuality boding shalom. Swedish Bror Hjorth's (1894–1968) couple [#41] has a peaceful erotic joy exploring each other with

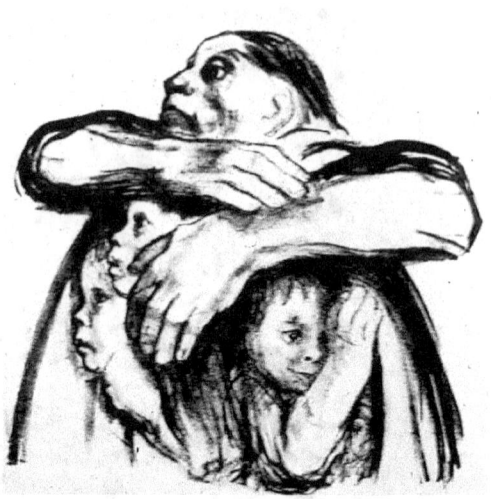

[#40] Käthe Kollwitz, *Mother Protecting Her Children*, 1942

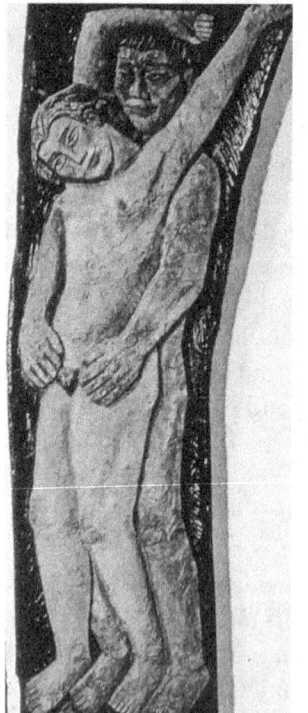

[#41] Bror Hjorth, *Love Scene 1*, 1937

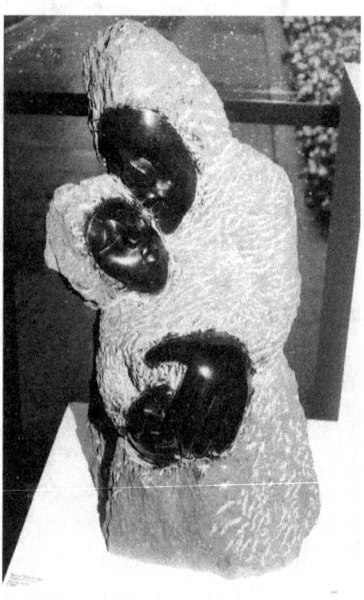

[#42] Marion Nyanhongo, *Comfort of Love*, 2005

all the ungainly naiveté that keeps erotic union **normal, ordinary**, the corporeally wonderful discovery and surprise that happens when a body meets a body comin' through the rye leading to betrothed attachment, not dependency, but a willingness to complement one another as woman and man.

A community of Zimbabwean women sculptors know how to carve stone into a happy melee of women carousing with laughter together in a bundle of jubilant womanly friendship. These women [#42] are poor enough to stare like a Paul Klee angel as they face their difficulties, to offer a pensive tilt of the head; but their unsophisticated, non-Western gaiety—nary a troubled **question** about "gender"—carries an infectious loving care for the neighbor we Europeans would do well to learn, male or female.

And Britt Wikström's (born 1948) moving bronze *Caritas* [#43] shows us two men, the one tending the other with a solicitous feminine touch, gently clothing him so as not to aggravate any hidden wounds, while the other man allows the helping hands, quietly wondering at such tenderness. This is human homophilic sexual intimacy of amazing purity. Wikström's human pair together present us with the gender mutuality—**the loving care with due respect**—we as a society need man to man, woman to woman, woman and man toward each other, not only in hospitals, but in the home, school, at work, ruling one another, hospitable toward strangers! and even, God willing? toward enemies who also, believe it or not (see Matthew 5:43–48) are neighbors.

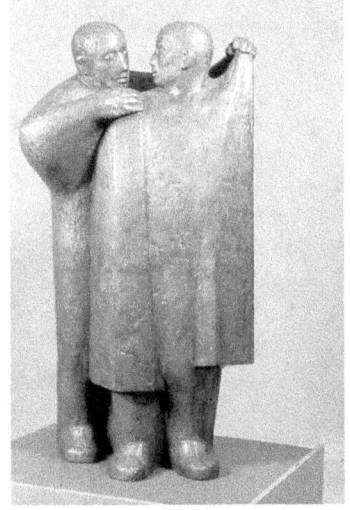

[#43] Britt Wikström, *Caritas*, 2006

Bibliography

* Allen, Prudence. *The Concept of Woman: The Aristotelian revolution, 750 B.C.–A.D. 1250*, vol. 1 (Grand Rapids: Eerdmans, 1985).
* ———. *The Concept of Woman: The early humanist reformation, 1250–1500*, vol. 2 (Grand Rapids: Eerdmans, 1985).
* Asad, Talal. *Formations of the Secular: Christianity, Islam, Modernity* (Stanford University Press, 2003).
Aspetsberger, Friedbert and Konstanze Fliedl, eds. *Geschlechter: Essay zur*

Gegenwartsliteratur (München: Studien Verlag, 2001).

Barbin, Herculine. *Herculine Barbin: Being the recently discovered memoirs of a nineteenth-century French hermaphrodite* [1868], trans. Richard McDougall, introduction Michael Foucault; and Oscar Panizza, "A Scandal at the Convent" [1893], trans. Sophie Wilkins (New York: Pantheon, 1980).

Behi, Jelila. *Sans Contrainte: L'Islam au Féminin. Essai* (Tunis: Nirvana, 2003).

Bell, Diane and Renate Klein, eds. *Radically Speaking: Feminism reclaimed* (London: Zed Books, 1996).

Benjamin, Jessica. *The Bonds of Love: Psychoanalysis, feminism, and the problem of domination* (New York: Pantheon, 1988).

Butler, Judith. *Gender Trouble: Feminism and the subversion of identity* (1990) (London: Routledge, 1999).

Chakrabarty, Dipesh. *Provincializing Europe: Postcolonial thought and historical difference* (Princeton University Press, 2000).

Chodorow, Nancy. *The Reproduction of Mothering: Psychoanalysis and the sociology of gender* (Los Angeles: University of California Press, 1978).

Cixous, Hélène. *Neuter*, trans. Lorene M. Birden (Lewisburg: Bucknell University Press, 2004).

Conley, Verena Andermatt. *Hélène Cixous* (University of Toronto Press, 1992).

Courtine-Denamy, Sylvie. *Three Women in Dark Times: Edith Stein, Hannah Arendt, Simone Weil, or Amor fati, amor mundi* [1997], trans. G.M. Goshgrian (Ithaca: Cornell University Press, 2000).

Diop, Cheikh Anta. *The Cultural Unity of Black Africa: The domains of patriarchy and of matriarchy in classical antiquity* [1959] (London: Karnak House, 1989).

Freud, Sigmund. "Femininity" [1924–1931], in *Works, Standard edition*, trans. James Strachey with Anna Freud, Alix Strachey and Alan Tyson (1964). 22:112–135.

Friedan, Betty. *The Fountain of Age* (New York: Simon & Schuster, 1993).

* Gilligan, Carol. *In a Different Voice: Psychological theory and women's development* (Cambridge: Harvard University Press, 1982).

Göttner-Abendroth, Heide and Kurt Derungs, eds. *Matriarchate als herrschaftsfreie Gesellschaften* (Bern: Edition Amalia, 1997).

Goodwin, Jan. *Price of Honor: Muslim women lift the veil of silence on the Islamic world* (Toronto: Little, Brown and Company, 1994).

Gormick, Vivian and Barbara K. Moran, eds. *Women in Sexist Society: Studies in power and powerlessness* (London: Basic Books, 1971).

Hartsock, Nancy C.M. *Money, Sex and Power: Towards a feminist historical materialism* (New York: Longman, 1983).

Hess, Thomas B. and Elizabeth C. Baker, eds. *Art and Sexual Politics: Women's liberation, women artists and art history* (New York: Macmillan, 1971).

* hooks, bell. *Talking Back: thinking feminist, thinking black* (Toronto: Between the Lines, 1988).

Hubrath, Margarete, ed. *Geschlechter-Räume: Konstruktionen von 'gender' in*

Geschichte, Literatur und Alltag (Köln: Böhlau Verlag, 2001).

Illich, Ivan. *Gender* (New York: Pantheon Books, 1982).

Irigaray, Luce. *Speculum of the Other Woman* (1974), trans. Gillian C. Gill (Ithaca: Cornell University Press, 1985).

Kassam, Zayn. "Politicizing Gender and Religion: Love for women, love for Islam," in *Love, Sex and Gender in the World Religions*, eds. Joseph Runzo and Nancy M. Martin (Oxford: One World, 2000), 223–237.

La Cocque, André. *The Feminine Unconventional: Four subversive figures in Israel's tradition* (Minneapolis: Fortress Press, 1990).

Leghorn, Lisa and Katherine Parker. *Woman's Worth: Sexual economics and the world of women* (London: Routledge & Kegan Paul, 1981).

Lewis, Stephen. *Race Against Time* (Toronto: House of Anansi, 2005).

Lloyd, Genevieve. *The Man of Reason: "Male" and "Female" in Western philosophy* (1984), 2nd ed. (London: Routledge, 1993).

Minh-ha, Trinh T. "Difference: 'A Special Third World Woman Issue,'" *Feminist Review* 25 (Spring 1987): 5–22.

Moglen, Hélène. *Trauma of Gender: Feminist theory of the English novel* (Berkeley: University of California Press, 2001).

Moraga, Cherrie L. and Gloria E. Anzaldúa. *This Bridge Called My Back: Writings by radical women of color*, 3rd ed. (Berkeley: Third Woman Press, 2002).

My Hanh, Isabelle. *Kinder, Küche, Karma: Die Frau im Buddhismus und Konfuzianismus, Zwischen Matriarchat und patriarchal Ideologie* (Bern: Edition Amalia, 1995).

Nelson, James B. *The Intimate Connection: Male sexuality, masculine spirituality* (Philadelphia: Westminster Press, 1988).

Nouraie-Simone, Fereshteh, ed. *On Shifting Ground: Muslim women in the global era* (New York: The Feminist Press at the City University of New York, 2005).

Nubile, Clara. *The Danger of Gender: Caste, class and gender in contemporary Indian women's writing* (New Delhi: Sarup, 2003).

Offen, Karen. "Defining Feminism: A comparative historical approach," *Signs* 14:1 (1988): 119–157.

Paglia, Camille. *Sex, Art, and American Culture: Essays* (New York: Vintage, 1992).

Plath, Sylvia, "Daddy," in Camille Paglia, *Break, Blow, Burn* (New York: Pantheon Books, 2005). With Paglia commentary, 164–176.

Prost, Antoine. "Public and Private Spheres in France," in *History of Private Life: Riddles of identity in modern times* [1987], trans. Arthur Goldhammer (Cambridge: Belknap Press of Harvard University Press, 1991), 5:1–143.

Rich, Adrienne. "Compulsory Heterosexuality and Lesbian Existence," *Signs: Journal of Women in Culture and Society* 5:4 (1980): 631–660.

Rosaldo, M.Z. "The Use and Abuse of Anthropology: Reflections on feminism and cross-cultural understanding," *Signs* 5:3 (1980): 389–417.

Rubin, Lillian B. *Intimate Strangers: Men and Women together* (New York: Harper

& Row, 1983).

Salin, Sara, ed. *The Judith Butler Reader* (Oxford: Blackwell, 2004).

Scott, Joan W. "Deconstructing Equality-versus-Difference: Or, the uses of poststructuralist theory for feminism," *Feminist Studies* 14:1 (1988): 32–50.

Scott, Joan W. "Gender: A useful category of historical analysis," *American Historical Review* 95:5 (1986): 1053–1075.

Snitow, Ann, Christine Stansell, and Sharon Thompson, eds. *Powers of Desire: The politics of sexuality* (New York: Monthly Review Press, 1983).

Spivak, Gayatri Chakravorty. *In Other Worlds: Essays in cultural politics* (London: Routledge, 1988).

Stewart-Van Leeuwen, Mary, ed. *After Eden: Facing the challenge of gender reconciliation* (Grand Rapids: Eerdmans, 1993).

* Stewart-Van Leeuwen, Mary. *Gender & Grace: Love, Work, & Parenting in a Changing World* (Downers Grove: InterVarsity, 1990).

Vander Walt, B.J. "A Liberating Message for Women in Africa," in *When African and Western Cultures Meet: From confrontation to appreciation* (Potchefstroom: Institute for Contemporary Christianity in Africa, 2006), 228–280.

Walker, Alice. *In Search of our Mothers' Gardens: Womanist prose* (San Diego: Harcourt Brace Jovanovich, 1983).

Weedon, Chris. *Feminism, theory and the politics of difference* (Oxford: Blackwell Publishers, 1999).

* Wilton, Tamsin. *Sexual (Dis)Orientation: Gender, sex, desire and self-fashioning* (London: Palgrave Macmillan, 2004).

* Sources of particular note

Note: My daughters and daughter-in-law have educated me in many ways over the years to be critical of chauvinist assumptions common to my training and generation. For this study I am grateful to my wife Inès Cécile Naudin ten Cate for support, surprising observations, and newspaper clippings. I am especially grateful to my friend Phyllis Rozendal for the best books to read, and for conversation informed by her teaching "Women's Studies" in past years at York University. I thank Institute colleagues Jim Olthuis and Nik Ansell too for giving me initial readings on the topic. The text here printed makes clear I have only begun to understand the wonderful, precarious gift of being gendered.

CULTURAL DIALOGUE AS HUMAN RESOURCE FOR THE INTEGRATION OF EUROPE—AND WHAT ABOUT THE DEVELOPMENT OF CITIES?

Every word of this theme is loaded and needs to be unpacked, so we don't just ramble on about cabbages and kings in Alice's "Wonderland."

Cultural dialogue

Two monologues do not constitute a dialogue. At the very least for a dialogue you need a common topic, a roughly acceptable framework for discourse, and language that is mutually understandable by the two parties talking to one another. Even then, if you are in dialogue with a bully, the weaker person is humanly mistreated in the discussion. For me Plato's so-called "dialogues" are imperial setups for Socrates to confirm his heterodox position, since his conversational partners are reduced to only saying "yes" or "no." The fact that the Irish recently said "No" to the proposed Lisbon treaty (2007), which aimed to give legal subject status to the European Union, maybe because many believed the Lisbon treaty would commit them to a militarist stance . . . does a **legal** veto mean an end to **cultural** dialogue?

What is this human resource called "cultural dialogue"? If you hold an international dance festival and the Russian male troupe performs a vigorous black booted cossack dance, and then Spanish women dancers present colorful, stylized, sensuous flamenco pieces, and everybody in the audience applauds both sets, is that "cultural dialogue"? Is the soccer European Cup an exercise every four years in "cultural dialogue"? Or is the fabulous on-site blend of Eastern and Western guitar musical rhythms, sounds, and melodies achieved by Jason Carter a model for "cultural dialogue"?

This unpublished lecture was presented at the artists and labor conference sponsored by CNV-Kunstenbond/Europäisches Zentrum für Arbeitnehmerfragen in Doorn, Netherlands, August 2008.

The 1990s dispute of the Council of the European Community with the USA reading of the 1947 international GATT accord on regulating the distribution of cinematic productions, and the European intent in 1986 to restrict "*Télévision sans frontières*" so that 50 percent of TV time in Europe be European productions,[1] highlights a fundamental difference on what is "cultural." For the Americans "culture" is high art, philosophy, and refined literature, but if the artwork is popular audiovisual entertainment, it is considered by them commercial merchandise, subject only to the rule of market price and demand. For the European negotiators in this dialogical dispute, films and CDs are not just copyrighted items "for sale" but embody a specific cultural vision of human life and its meaning and, as François Mitterrand said in his 1993 Gdansk University speech,[2] any people that is not free to choose which images inundate its public environs becomes an enslaved society.

For me "cultural dialogue" is serious stuff, because "culture"—whether it be Glenn Gould piano playing Bach or a staged Noh theatre, comic strips, or the ubiquitous digital internet media enveloping us—**"culture" is never innocent**, but embodies a fundamental world-and-life-vision, breathes a captivating spirit, and coaxes a Way-of-life out of its practitioners and recipients that blesses or/**and!** curses what is human about us.

If "cultural **dialogue**" is indeed a human resource—dialogue does not abide one side's monopolizing the exchange—is cultural dialogue possible between a strict young Shi'ite Muslim *Gastarbeiter* in Germany willing to be a martyr, and an apostate well-educated, free-wheeling *bon vivant* Frenchman in Paris? Or, are certain matters and peculiar kinds of people to be excluded from "dialogue"?

Since the Berlin Wall came down in 1989, is there still impetus to forge a cohering identity via dialogue among the nations of Europe with whatever our cultural praxis be, so that we not move again here as have Zionist Jews there to build an Israeli Wall cutting through Palestinian farmlands to make it more difficult to shoot missiles at one another?

---

1   Canada achieved this protection in 1988. The regulation was strengthened in 1999 to 75 percent.

2   Mitterrand presented these remarks upon receiving an honorary doctorate, 21 September 1993. ". . . c'est . . . l'identité de nos nations, le droit pour chaque peuple à sa propre culture, la liberté de créer et de choisir nos images. Et il ajoute qu'une société que abandonne à d'autres ses moyens de représentations 'est une société asservie,'" as reported in *L'Express*, 14 October 1993 (31), quoted in Caroline Brossat, 384 n697.

Europe

The draft treaty (2003) to establish a Constitution for Europe, which the French and Dutch citizens rejected (2005), holds a significant clause for our topic that follows up article 128 of the Maastricht Treaty (1992) and article 151 of the Treaty of Amsterdam (1997):

> The **Union** shall respect its **rich cultural and linguistic diversity**, and shall ensure that **Europe's cultural heritage** is safeguarded and enhanced. (Article 3, par.4) [my emphasis][3]

That a (political) Union can house "cultural diversity" is not so strange, since **diversity is not possible without unity**. A structural problem, however, that has bedeviled a generation of European Union dialogue is how do an **economic** union and a legally constituted (super) **state** relate to "culture," understood to include artistic performance, scientific research, youth education, practice of sport, information technology, and communication media.[4] And how is **cultural diversity** to respond to a unified European Comm**unity**?

Canada has two official languages, and soon Inuktitut may be official in the provincial courtrooms for Nunavut. South Africa post-Mandela and the Truth and Reconciliation Commission (1995–1998) has eleven official languages.[5] Will there eventually be highly paid work for a raft of versatile translators in twelve to twenty languages in Brussels? And can you imagine that "Wilhelmus" (1569–72), "God Save the Queen" (1745), and "Deutschland über alles" (1841) could be melted down into a single European anthem to sing for athletes on the Olympic winners' podium?[6]

---

3 The 2007 Treaty of Lisbon (rejected by the Irish referendum in 2008), regarding the **functioning** of the European Union, seems to pull back a little: "Action by the Union shall be aimed at encouraging cooperation between Member States and, **if necessary** [my emphasis], supporting and supplementing their action in the following areas: improvement of the knowledge and dissemination of the culture and history of the European peoples; conservation and safeguarding of cultural heritage of European significance; non-commercial cultural exchanges; artistic and literary creation, including in the audiovisual sector" (article 167, par.2).

4 The Cultural Commission of the Assembly of the Council of Europe was expanded like topsy to include all these affairs: culture (1956–61), and scientific (1961–69), and education (1969–).

5 Afrikaans, English, IsiNdebele, IsiKhosa, IsiZulu, Sepedi, Sesotho, Setswana, Siswati, Tshivenda, Xitsonga.

6 It should be noted that although I have heard this **first** stanza of the *Deutschlandlied* chanted at large sportive events in Europe when the national German team has won a match, only the **third** stanza of Fallersleben's poem sung to Haydn's melody serves as the official German national anthem: "Einigkeit und Recht und Freiheit für das

Yet first, before I try to allay such cynical fears—my title intimates that "cultural dialogue" can be conducive to the (unspecified) integration of "Europe"—we still need to ask, "What is Europe?" Is there, could there be, should there be "a European culture" (singular)? Or is it proper to be satisfied with European cultures (plural), especially now that the original six member countries of the European Union[7] have become twenty-seven member states?[8]

Maybe you know the ancient Greco-Roman Hellenistic myth[9] about the lovely royal damsel named Europa with whom the philandering, unfaithful father god Zeus became infatuated, metamorphosed himself in a noble, deceptively gentle bull, seduced her into sitting upon his back so he could fly off away with her to Crete, and as stud enjoy having her bear noble demi-deity sons.

Neapolitan Luca Giordano's (1632–1705) expertly saccharine oil painting entitled "Rape of Europa" [#44] uses the myth to pander to his Humanist viewers the erotic availability of female flesh with revealing flapping clothing, garlanded pútti and a bevy of attentive, aroused nubile young women, as she waves goodbye to her fatherland. Giordano's seicento Mannerist unraveling of the prodigious Italian Renaissance glory is so patently unreal, a world where rape is not a dirty four-letter word and shameless misogynist crime again womanly humanity: this art is not "Europe's cultural heritage" the proposed European Union constitution pledges to "safeguard" and "enhance," is it?

The Dutch Jewish pacifist artist I came to know, Flip van der Burgt (1927–77), retells the myth more truly [#45]: a naked Europe is abducted from her homeland that has been ravished by war and is over-filled with crosses of the dead. The heedless Guernica bull-of-a-god has left devastation behind, as if it did not care.

Myths oversimplify and do not tell the truth. It is the spotted good-**and-bad history** of a person, of a people located somewhere on earth

---

deutsche Vaterland, danach lasst uns alle streben, brüderlich mit Herz und Hand...." To sing the first stanza today, "Deutschland, Deutschland über alles, über alles in der Welt" makes most Germans uncomfortable, since this first stanza was the only stanza allowed to be sung as national anthem during Hitler's Dritte Reich.

7   France, Germany, Italy, Belgium, Luxembourg, Netherlands.

8   Present member states of the European Union as of 2007: Austria, Belgium, Bulgaria, Czech Republic, Cyprus, Denmark, Estonia, Finland, France, Germany, Greece, Hungary, Ireland, Italy, Latvia, Lithuania, Luxembourg, Malta, Netherlands, Poland, Portugal, Romania, Slovakia, Slovenia, Spain, Sweden, United Kingdom.

9   Narrated by Moschus of Syracuse (c. 150 BC).

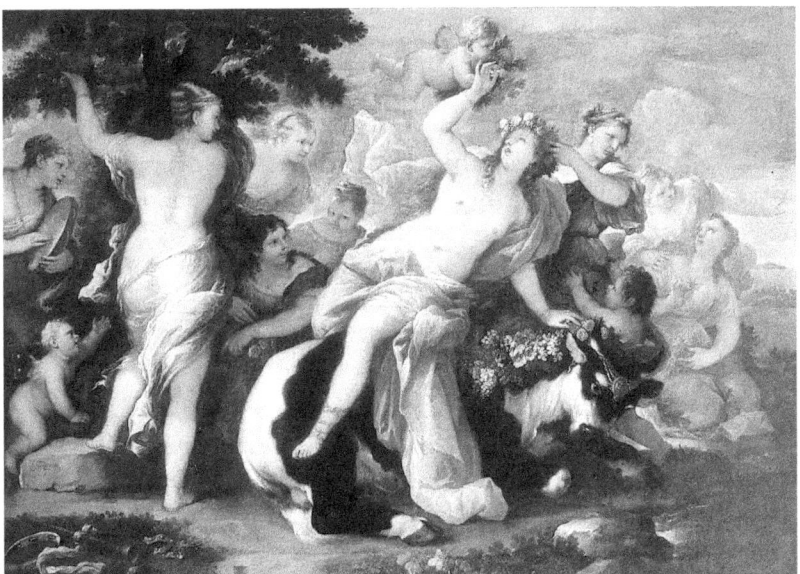

[#44] Luca Giordano, *Rape of Europa*

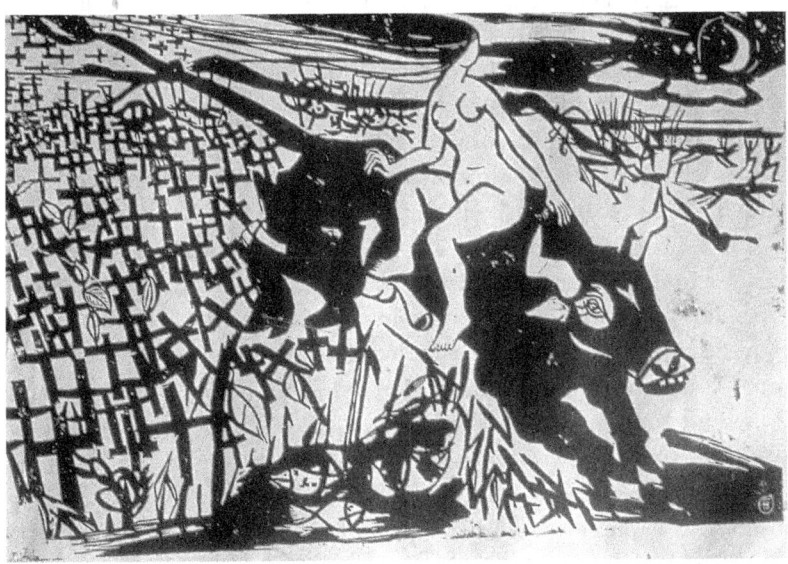

[#45] Flip van der Burgt, *Europa*

and dated that must be recognized as formative in the make-up of your on-going identity. And "Europe" does have, I believe (and I count myself as a European, despite my New York birth and Canadian citizenship), a rich historical cultural heritage—both the Acropolis and Auschwitz—that distinguishes its character today from African, Asian, and American rich cultural inheritances and complex identities.

Let me foolhardily attempt to sketch briefly, without chauvinism, the ethos of Europe today—the European community bounded by the Mediterranean, Atlantic Ocean, Artic, and Black Sea—before I mention two major challenges besetting **and encouraging** "the integration of Europe" and explore the structural problem I mentioned—how state and human culture interrelate. And after that I'll dare give a few closing ideas on how and why we christian artistic laborers might proceed with "cultural dialogue," especially in cities.

The complex cultural heritage of Europe, and update
"Europe" is not a beautiful woman on the back of a lusty god, but is the centuries-old mix of peoples on the land mass stretching during the Roman Empire from Egypt over the Alps to the British Isles, and during Charlemagne's reign from Spain north to the German tribes as far as the Baltic Sea. The ancient Greek Athenian and Spartan civilization of privileged intellectuals, skilled craft people, and slaves permeated the rich and poor feudal societies that followed, although the Stoic idea of universal humanity and the Roman Republic conception of individual property and legal contracts melded with the Judeo-Christian ethic of personal responsibility, fidelity, and a communitarian injunction to neighborly compassion.

Christians, with Muslim scholars, preserved the pagan Greek cultural inheritance in a synthesis that sifted out to favor a Humanist multilingual rationality. And the Church, which dominated this European area for centuries (especially after the 1054 AD schism with the Eastern Orthodox Church) as an imperial papal Christendom with Crusades and Inquisition, serving itself as background occasion for barbaric "religious wars"—remember Jeanne d'Arc (1412–1431)—suffered the corrective Protestant Reformation and finally met its match in Napoleon who revoked the Concordat with the Vatican in 1801 AD.

Killing wars between our nation states aforming is part of European history—no "melting pot" ideology in force here. The *cujus regio, eius religio* compromise (the religious faith of the ruler holds for that country's territorial subjects) was a brake against rampant anti-clericalism, while it slowly fostered separation of earthly state powers from "heavenly" church authority. With the advent of the French Revolution (1789–1791) and its *Déclaration des droits de l'homme et du citoyen* came a push for postchristian adoration of REASON as god to guarantee societal *liberté, égalité et fraternité*. But wars continued as nations large and small plied their mercantilist trade initiatives abroad, often sanctified by an Idealistic colonialist missionary overlay to bring our "civilization" to benighted foreign cultures. A harsh polluting industrialization and impoverishing factory humiliation of human workers at home followed apace, before trench warfare (1914–1918) and the cruel Nazi blight with *sho'ah* (1939–1945) deeply stigmatized the European *mentalité.*

Curiously, in the past sixty years Europe seems to many to have undergone a sea change. The old Christian Humanist temper recognizing freedom of conscience fueled by the Enlightenment spirit of *sapere aude* (dare to know) has been softened by post-war prosperity for many more people, so that a more leisurely cultivated, hedonistic—**my** pleasure—society is counted as a public good and human **right**! Especially since 1989 good folk from the Eastern reaches of the continent and even south of the Mediterranean Sea have been flocking to "Europe," some for its cultural heritage of rule under law for social justice, but most often, I think, for the unspoken promise of a better if not a decent standard of living with food and drink, work, health, and habitation; and many arrive not knowing the ins and outs of the enabling differentiated institutional societal infrastructure hammered out over centuries of struggled diligence. Persons born in Western Europe itself after 1960 may also have a weak awareness of the multilingual, historically conscious, reflective Humanism that has formerly constituted the European cultural heritage. And **what people know and remember, and do not know or remember, affects their identity**.

Challenges for an on-going European identity
The way French culture set the standard for the European landscape in the 1700s AD, culture made-in-USA has tended, after so-called World War II, to blanket countries of the world **and Europe** with its particular technical mass production line of goods and efficient services, from McDonalds to the Bill Gates internet. "Europe" has become practically indistinguishable from "the West," and "the West" is ostensibly defined by "American."

Time was when classical philologist Erasmus who would debate Luther on "free will" and write a light, erudite ironic book, *Stultitiae Laus* (c. 1509, *Praise of Folly*), was quintessentially European next to an important American figure like diplomat Benjamin Franklin who signed the United States Constitution and penned *Poor Richard's Almanack* (1733–57) with its maxims on "how to get ahead in the world." Montesquieu's *L'Esprit des*

Lois (1748) is Europeanly different from brilliant American slave-owner President Thomas Jefferson and his Neoclassically designed Monticello. Kant's *Kritik der Urteilskraft* (1790) and Heidegger's *Der Ursprung des Kunstwerkes* (1935–36) are quite unlike racy John Dewey's *Art as Experience* (1934).

I am not saying one is better than the other, but the two—European and American—have been importantly different and bring valuably different wisdoms to the dialogical table of world affairs. I am suggesting it is worthwhile not to erase the difference, but to speak in an idiom and voice with European resonance that will not be confused with hip American lingo. Otherwise a species of cultural identity will go extinct.

(1) I do think that a major threat to "the integration of Europe" and its identity, much worse than internal fragmenting national rivalries and the fear of small European countries to be marginalized by larger countries like Germany and France's throwing their political weight around, is the insidious external, practically intangible but all-powerful GlobalISTIC drive to serve Mammon. Americans may still presently seem to hold the reins to the Beast, but it would not surprise me if it soon becomes a Chinese dragon. This supranational financial corporate hydra of IMF, World Bank, WTO, GATT, Disney, Microsoft, and etcetera Megacorporation hosts, which uncannily is both privatized and anonymous,[10] operates by the same principle of competitive Survival of the Fittest, which does not brook dialogue but peremptorily compels standardized, monopolized following of economic orders. The GlobalISTIC version of multiculturality is that all ethnicities and cultures fit our single Commercialized Consumerist credit plan of obtaining new (disposable) products; join our worldwide enterprise and you will find happiness.

In my judgment, if the European Union abandons working out its reflective patrimony and clutch of diverse mother tongues for this pragmatic, monotonic, coercive scheme for quick, satisfying success, the European Union will have sold its rich Christian Humanist birthright for a thin, heartless mess of sagging dollar potage. Again, I am not demonizing America, because the fascinating monolithic GlobalIST dynamic that divides and conquers anything small and beautiful in its way has been turning my birth country into a rapacious militarist Monster.[11] A Midas idol

---

10 Ignacio Ramonet, " L'idéal démocratique dévoyé," préface in Joest Smiers, *État des Lieux de la Création en Europe,* pp. 12–13.

11 Cf. "The National Security Strategy of the United States of America," article 5 (June 2002).

is so deceptive: who can be against GNP Growth! and material Progress!? except those who are dead on their leaky boat attempt to reach the streets paved with "freedom" and gold.

(2) A second major challenge facing our tenuous process of firming up European identity is the influx during your lifetime of millions of Muslim families settling down as immigrants, refugees, and illegals in member nations of the **European** Union. This great number of Muslims are here to stay, and many are now well into a second generation. Just as a Dutch emigrant living in rural Neerlandia, northern Alberta, Canada, often acts more Dutch than a Dutch person living in cosmopolitan Rotterdam, the Netherlands, so Muslims moving into strange lands where Muslim customs of dress, gender roles, ritual slaughtering of animals for *halal* meat, the regimen of praying five times a day, Ramadan fasting and the like cannot be taken for granted: you tend as a family and Muslim friends, especially if you are not so educated, to cling to those patterns of life you know, for stability. A people's faith and one's language—both of which are portable—provide ghetto security in unsettling circumstances. And there comes the rub. Muslims have not been accustomed to live as a silent minority in a country, and Europeans are not accustomed to being, as it were, colonized on our own territory! by demands for a quite foreign way-of-life. And mutual ignorance soon compounds misunderstandings into full-fledged fears and antagonism.

The fact that Muslims are enormously ethnically diverse—from Morocco, Iran, Indonesia, Turkey, Algeria—and that Sunni, Shi'ite, and Sufi Muslims compare to something like a nominal Roman Catholic, premillennial Baptist, and Russian Orthodox mystic, telltale how unjust it is, as most of us and the media usually do, to refer to "Muslims" en bloc, a stereotype. And why quote *Qur'an* 2:256—"There is to be no compulsion in the matter of faith" (or, for that matter, Jesus' word from Matthew 5:44: "But I say, 'Love your enemies'")—to settle an argument? since how many Muslims, or Christians, **practice** what their sacred book commands (and both Qur'an and *hadith* as well as the Bible are currently subject to multiple interpretations). That is a problem within most non-Muslim countries: there is no representative Muslim voice. And many imams lead prayers in the mosques far from Mecca and Cairo's Al-Azhar University and, like many priests in the medieval period far from Rome who could not read and study the holy scriptures in the original language(s), so often fill their duties by rote, following old *fiqh* traditions and picked-up local popular prejudices.

Deep down, however, in the many Muslim positions is the root conviction that faith permeates culture; faith is a public affair and is not to be shunted off to an individual's private, purely personal life. So it is a question whether even the third generation of displaced, active Muslim believers will be "assimilated" into secularized European society—possibly as a "Euro-Islam" middleclass variant?—as many Jews have done over the centuries: you mind the religious holidays, eat strictly kosher at your *seder*, but do not particularly let your faith be noticeable in your daily, ordinary, or professional life. This is why many devout Muslim thinkers do not trust Christians to follow through on their basic christian faith convictions in public, because so many Christians have meekly privatized their faith. Genuine biblical followers of Jesus would dispute, would they not? rather than join the race for heedless Growth and Moneyed Progress! Are biblical Christians afraid they might be called nasty "Fundamentalists" by the laid back majority of current-day Europeans who are generically "nice" people but piously profess not to believe in much of anything?

However, the presence of Muslims all around us Europeans has revealed in *l'affaire des foulards* in France (from 1994 on) the petty, parochial lengths to which a post-christian **Secularist** "Fundamentalism" will go: girls may not wear a head-scarf (*hijab*) or crucifix jewelry to school! Such a political move seems to me to prohibit "cultural dialogue" and plans to reduce any future "integration of Europe" to a barren, lowest common denominator, uniform inhumane conformity.

Underlying structural problem:
the interrelation of faith, culture, and the (nation) state

A core problem, as I understand it, is the real complicated matter of how can a political legal state foster cultural activity (particularly literacy, advanced schooling, and imaginative artistry) for the commonweal of its folk without dictating "culture" that becomes by nature a kind of national propaganda, and therefore denature itself.

The 1957 Treaty of Rome organized the European **Economic** Community—a common **market**, so to speak—manifest today in the euro currency, introduced in 1999/2002. The 1992 Treaty of Maastricht formed a European **Union** that by adopting the principle of subsidiarity insures that culture would not be treated just commercially (for example, national treasures **cannot** be put on the international market) but remains firmly in the province of the nation states. The various governmental Ministers of the nation states in the European Union have consistently spoken up for inter-governmental "cultural co-operation," but for decades the same European Ministers have left cultural projects and events proposed by the consultative European Parliament's Cultural Commission underfunded. Such underfunding is understandable since the Ministers who hold the cultural purse strings have the Foreign Affairs portfolios in their nation states and are focused on **European political unification**; so they naturally give cultural artistic activities less priority (also since culture is reserved for internal **national diversity**). **The regrettable result is that "cultural dialogue," though touted as an essential domain in our European life together, is treated more like an unwelcome stepchild.** And the test of whether the "cultural dialogue" deserves moneyed support tends to become whether the **cultural** activity makes **political-economic** sense.[12]

So the conundrum is how to get national cultural diversity thriving in dialogue that promotes European unity without becoming political propaganda for democracy or simply commercially viable, homogenized popular entertainment able to pay for itself.[13] Another unsettling fact is that newer member states of the European Union, which after 1945 were forced into the Soviet orbit, where the Stalinist-like state controlled cultural production absolutely, may come to discover that their new-found "freedom" in the European Union means they operate under the tyranny of Capitalistic power: if your "culture" does not sell, it becomes backwater insignificant activity.

As leaders of the European Union decide whether to forego a supernational federal state and develop a confederated political union of sover-

---

12 The "Culture 2000 Programme" states explicitly that "the concept of culture also covers popular culture, mass-produced culture and everyday culture," and "Culture 2000 emphasises the role of culture as an economic factor and as a factor in social integration and citizenship." See http://europa.eu/legislation_summaries/culture/l29006_en.htm.

13 "Le chemin vers une union européenne comprend le politique, l'économique et le culturel. Le but de l'action de l'Assemblée est la création de l'unité européenne à laquelle contribue le domaine culturel.

"La position dominante au sein de la commission des Questions culturelles et scientifiques est alors l'affirmation du devoir de l'Assemblée d'aller vers une unification complète de l'Europe. La culture peut être un moyen de parvenir à l'unité en aidant à la création d'une conscience populaire en sa faveur. L'Assemblée doit être prête à utiliser tous les moyens de l'éducation et de la propagande pour y arriver . . . puisque ce sont essentiellement les nationalismes culturels qui sont à l'origine de l'opposition à l'union de l'Europe. D'un autre côté, l'unité européenne est la condition de la survie de la culture européenne." Caroline Brossat, *La Culture Européenne: Définitions et Enjeux*, 274.

eign states with a common ethos of undefined "humanity," or settle for a multi-national conglomeration of nations (like the "United Nations Organization") forming a commercial cartel, with a kind of European multi-personality, it will need to be decided what are the nonnegotiables for peoples to belong to a European Union. Must the government of Turkey allow free building of churches, or not?

Since I presently believe a politically confederated European Union might best serve the people of this continent at this time in world history, I should like to sketch a vision of process that could guide us who are "cultural" workers. I take my cue from Denis de Rougemont who wrote:

> Those who wish to participate in the European culture ought to integrate themselves into the community that has transmitted this culture and that has given the conditions of its reality, nature, and a certain meaning.[14]

But in the very next breath I add Paul Ricoeur's caveat: merely to conserve past virtues in antiquarian, taxidermist fashion is false leadership; **proper dynamic reflective and cultural activity is to be busy positing enduring norms anew for lives today.**[15]

Glocal cultural dialogue
to build mutual understanding for a European ethos

There are three steps to what I will call a **glocal** approach, a global-local, bifocal committed world-and-life-vision that is "globally" aware (worldwide historically) and prompts action first-of-all "locally," with your own particular gifts in whatever place you call home.[16] This is a Way, I believe, to foster cultural dialogue that can build consensual experience from the

---

14 "Celui qui veut participer à la culture européenne doit s'intégrer à une communauté, qui a transmis cette culture et qui lui donne ses conditions de réalité, de création, de signification," Denis de Rougemont, quoted from *Fédéralisme culturel* (Neuchâtel: Ed. de la Baconnière, 1970, 191) in Pamela Sticht, *Culture européenne ou Europe des cultures?*, p.63.

15 "Cette mémoire volontaire diffère d'un inconscient collectif qui garderait simplement l'empreinte du passé et un prolongerait le retentissement par simple inertie affective. . . . Ainsi, une civilisation ne conserve des valeurs anciennes que par une mémoire qui est l'envers d'une création de valeurs nouvelles. . . . La conservation historique de valeurs définitivement acquises est un faux problème. . . . Telle est la 'fidélité créatrice', pour reprendre Gabriel Marcel, qui ne conserve que ce qu'elle crée." Paul Ricoeur, "Le chrétien et la civilisation occidentale," 97–98.

16 See my "Glocal culture" in *That the World May Believe: Essays on mission and unity in honour of George Vandervelde*, eds. Michael W. Goheen and Margaret O'Gara (Lanham: University Press of America, 2006), 45–66; "Cities as a Place for Public Artwork: A glocal approach," CD #15 (Hamilton: Work Research Foundation, 2007). {See *RA*: 233–261}.

bottom up, so to speak, rather than try to impose a common European style artificially from the bureaucratic elite top down, and end up with something like a literacy in Hollywoodese or Esperanto.

I must be overly brief, and may be provocative.

(1) Prospective and by-birth Europeans need to be invited/seduced to **take fresh root in the biblically christian source of the rich cultural heritage of Europe**. Humanistic warmed-over Rationalism and **lackadaisical** indifference do not have what it takes to withstand the ruthless, aggressive influence of Global TV advertising culture or to answer the fair moral questions of strict Shi'ite believers on our doorstep. Trust in a military-industrial "rationality" bodes the prospect of our becoming "Americanized," and our leaving most Muslims to carve out a parallel, separate existence. Everybody vaguely knows there is christian DNA in our cultural heritage, but the "christian" has become more like dried-up glue in the backing of books—it is cracked and weak. The only way for a people, the European peoples, to pull together in our post-christian climate, I believe, is to have the common gut of a living, spirited *Heimat* following the wisdom of Jesus Christ.

By a Bible-breathing, Christ-following *Heimat*, home base, I do not mean a despotic "Fatherland" of orthodox prohibitions, or an idyllic "homeland" ghetto of sanctimonious bourgeois churchgoers who really crucify their Christ-made-of-Bibles [#46] and project the Savior of humankind like a driftwood relic in a rosy red tinted room for contemplative prayer-room observation [#47]. No, I mean that a person comes to feel at home with the pulse of the gritty Older Testament psalms you know by heart, and are gripped by the Christ's compassion for the unfortunates as Käthe Kollwitz's art shows with a mother keening for her dead child [see *NA* #42]. Africans, Asians, Americans, or drifting nomads without a fertile cultural identity can take up the

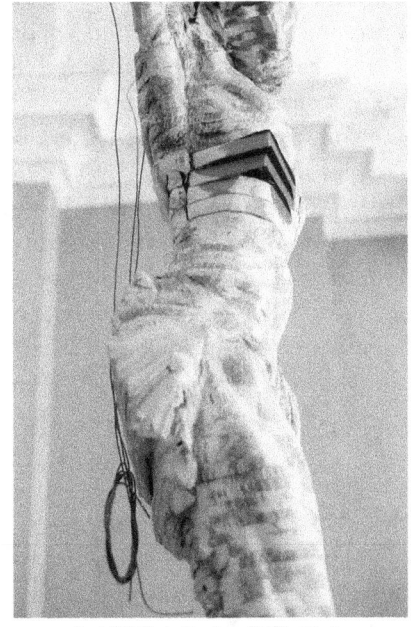

[#46] Wim Botha, *Bible Christ*

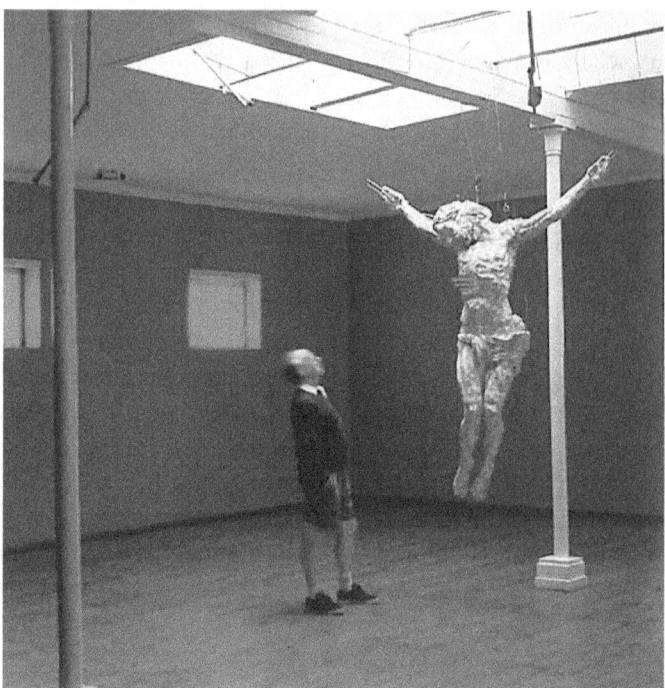

[#47] Wim Botha, *Bible Christ, with voyeur*

christian strand of Europe's cultural heritage by living into a communion breathing the *Book of Hours* [#48] devotion at work serenity, the brusque forthrightness of Luther, the droll humor of Cervantes, the worldly wisdom of Shakespeare, the intricate wiry musical lines of Heinrich Schütz, the pointed barbs of Pascal, the sober wood sculpture of Ernst Barlach, the tense cinematic loveliness of Bergman [#49]. All these cultural workers I just mentioned did **not think the Bible was a dead letter book, but let its live-wire testimony to the gentle lordship of Jesus Christ obliquely spire their artwork.**

Anybody present is invited to join such a "cultural dialogical" communion, be transplanted here, take root—we're talking long-term educated maturing, not a quick fix—and become rooted truly European in a vital way.

(2) The second glocal step, once a person or a community has decided to own its *Sitz im Leben* is European in this biblically convicted dimension, is to **give priority to *Ortskultur* and to honor the rich ethnic and institutional openings nearby in one's neighborhood.** Instead of training to be an Olympic superstar who sets the pace of the artistic universe, a

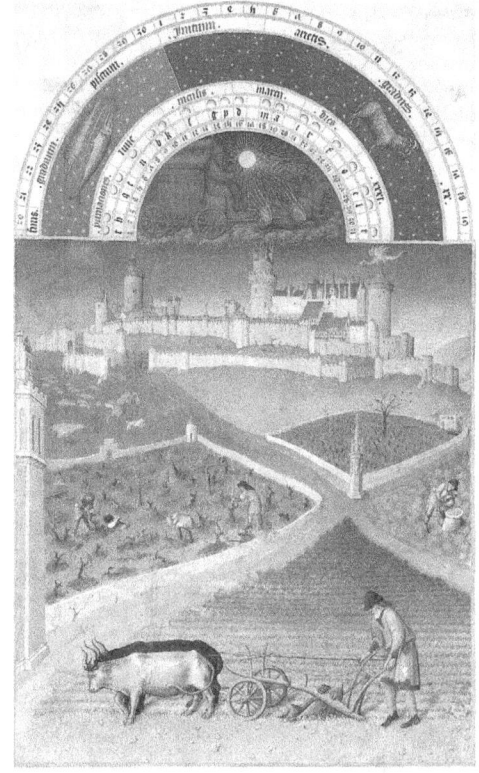

[#48] *Book of Hours,* 1412-1416

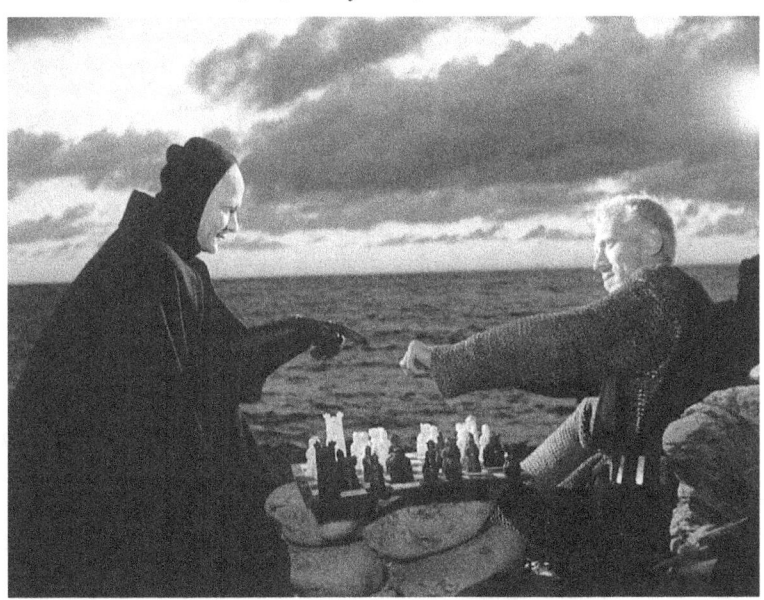

[#49] Bergman, from *The Seventh Seal,* 1957

faithful European cultural worker will begin by **exercising one's imaginative contribution proximately**. When artists focus work on the local territory they know, the mix of neighbors whose needs, interests, and stage of imaginative development can be met, you don't have to sport a multicultural ideology: the very variegated nature of public society and quirky expectations of your fellow citizens encourage a colorful diversity that is still integrated with people's lives.

Britt Wikström's artwork for the lost corridor space [#50] between the original Belgium hospital and its constructed addition through which doctors, nurses, and patients need to walk, lightens their troubles with

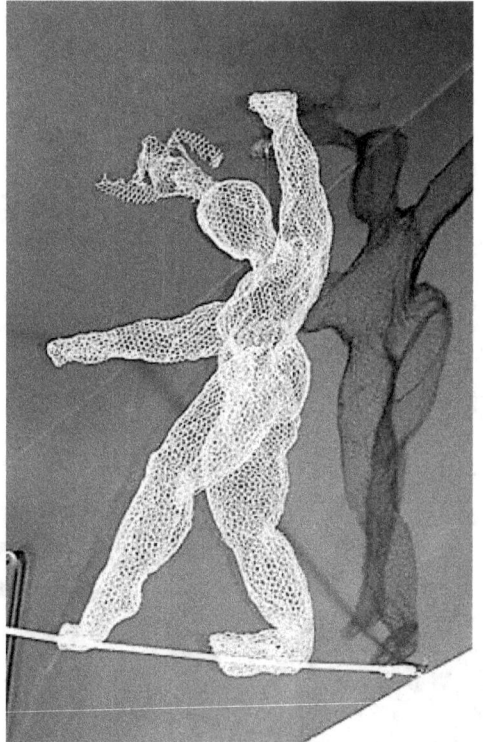

[#50] Britt Wikström, *Circus of Dreams*

playful wire mesh animals and a medley of agile circus figures [#51], daredevil tightrope walkers, trapeze artists, lovely floating figures, and jesters to make you laugh. An art piece of suspended rocks [#52] in the Thessaloniki airport waiting room is a dangerous wonder to behold. How in the world was it installed!? A symmetrical thundercloud like an accident waiting to happen. And Hundertwasser's paintings carry on cultural

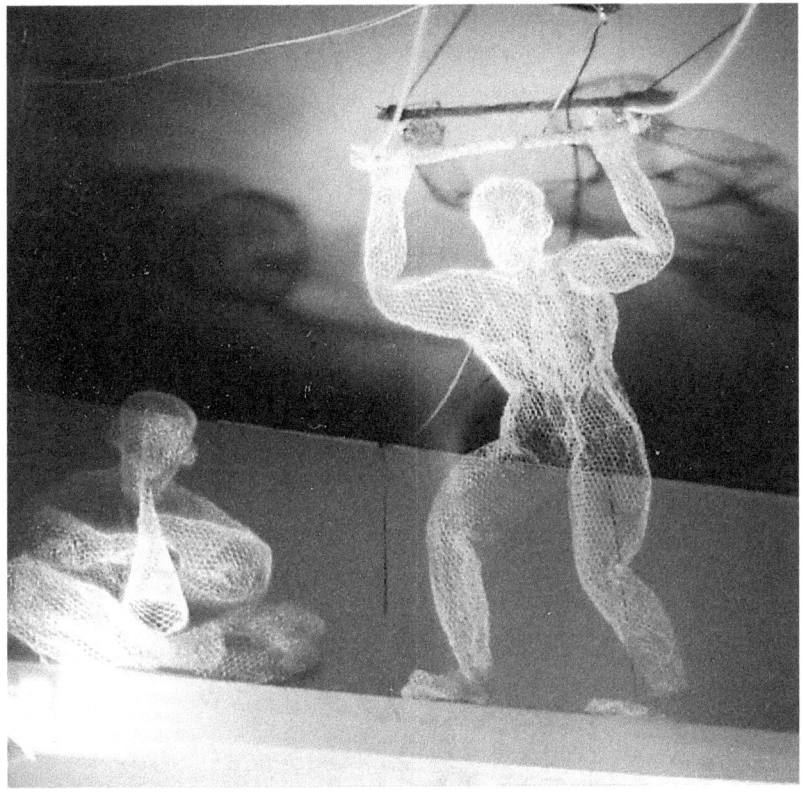

[#51] Britt Wikström, *Circus of Dreams*

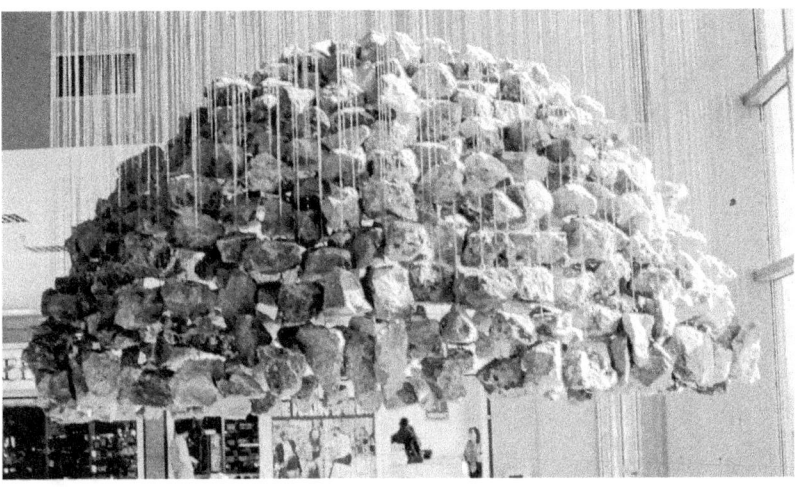

[#52] Costas Varotsos, *Globe*, 1995, Thessaloniki airport

dialogue in a specific European vernacular idiom too: *Good Morning City–Bleeding Town* [#53] characterizes urban Vienna as a sprightly mash of high density living in homely worn buildings, probably wishing them to be as idiosyncratic as his courtyard of homes in Plochingen [#54]. Hundertwasser's take on Malta is entitled *Grass for Those Who Cry* (1974), carrying through his "greening" message—"Singing Bird on a Tree in the City" (1951) [#55]—and motif of human tears worth their weight in gold (*Die Gelbe Trane*, 1959). Wikström and Hundertwasser exemplify for me local placement of art woven into the European web of cultural dialogue that has neighborhooded vitality that, as differentiated artwork, builds community because it smiles and cries and surprises in people-friendly, trustworthy fashion. Its purview is global, but its delivery is local. The artistry is not tribal, not esoteric, not geared for mass reproduction sale, but has, to my eye, a glocal **European** cachet consonant with the spirit of service.

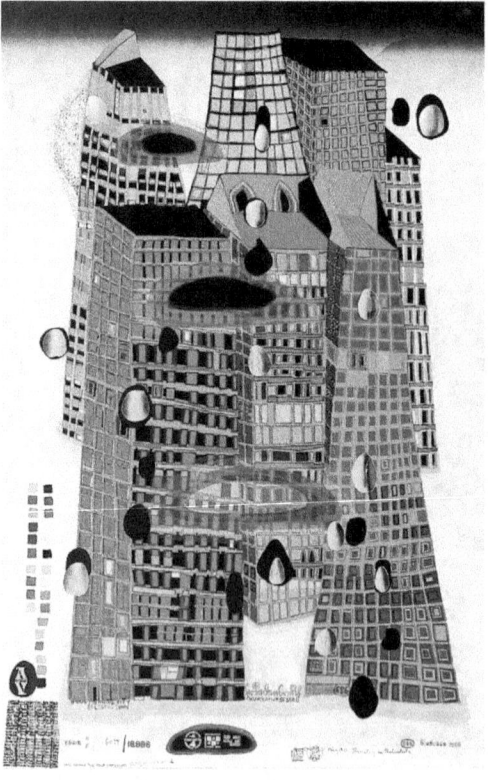

[#53] Hundertwasser, 686, *Good Morning City–Bleeding Town*, 1970/71

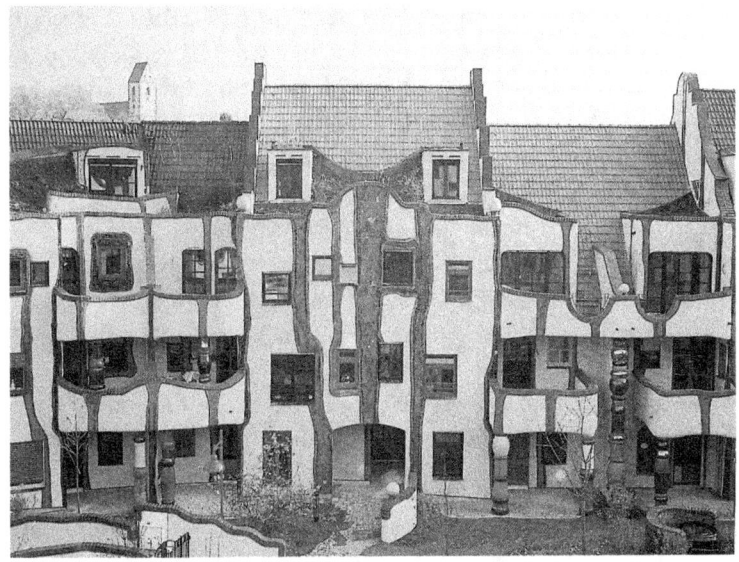

[#54] Hundertwasser, apartment complex, 1993-95, Plochingen, Germany

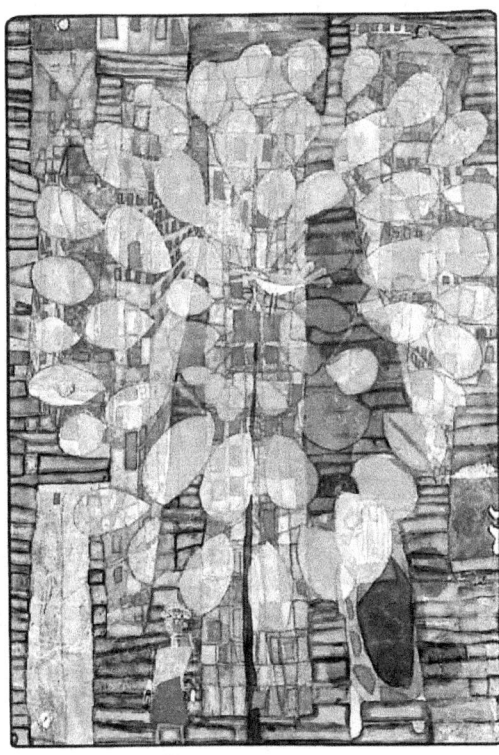

[#55] Hundertwasser, (124), *Singing Bird on a Tree in the City*, 1951

A good way to accentuate **European unified cultural diversity**, I think, would be to make cities one's defining workplace. Developing the culture of cities does not stir up the pride of nationalities, and allows for cross-national sharing of artists. The London Philharmonic Orchestra is not conducted and composed solely of Brits, and it is a Russian-French artist Zadkine who made the moving tribute to bombing the heart out of the Dutch city of Rotterdam [*NA* #30]. "Nations" hype states to be more than legal governing institutions, and patriotism is not evil; but nationalISMs can take on ugly ethno-racist overtones that block close cultural co-operation, not to mention European "integration." But cities are not nation-states. Cities are social institutions limited to municipal rule and have especially local public, civic enrichment in focus along with its global-oriented libraries and musea. Cities as glocal cultural centers can build grass-roots cohesion. For a city to be "cultural capital" of Europe for a year can be a good event if it is used not just to attract stop-and-shop, hit-and-run tourists for a year, but to develop the peculiar cultural, aesthetic life and urban living of quite different quarters of the city, as Rotterdam did in 2001.[17]

A good city museum can expand one's cultural dialogical horizons too, like exposing Europe-bound citizens to the sandstone calligraphy with plant decoration of Outb Minar (c. 1192 AD), or view an ancient Qur'an manuscript [#56] (Cairo, 1376 AD), to ready one to appreciate an Arabic letter-word [#57] for "Nihil" looking like a snake in a cage (*Heech*

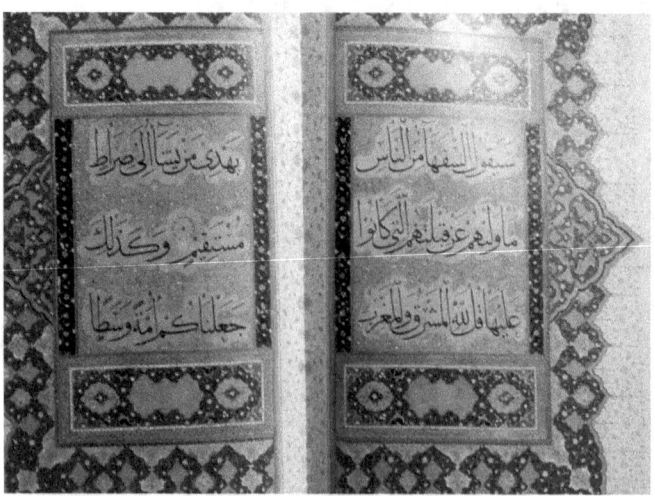

[#56] Qur'an manuscript

17 See Jan Buursink, "The Cultural Strategy of Rotterdam," at http://cybergeo.revues. org/1203

in a Cage, 2005), commemorating in 2005 the death of hundreds of Shia in the desert 680 AD. . . .

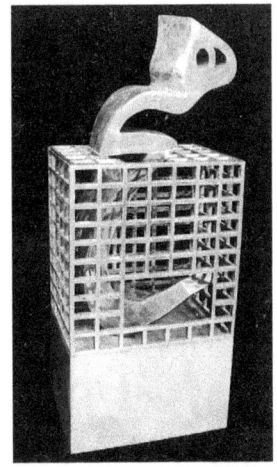

(3) A third step in a glocal cultural dialogical approach to ferment **cultural** "integration" (unifying diversity)—not lockstep "assimilation" (becoming like the dominant whole)— in Europe, once one is prepared to build and walk across ethnical neighborhood bridges in a spirit true to the biblically christian, non-imperialist commitment I mentioned earlier, is this: **passionately giveaway your artistic offerings that do justice and bespeak peace to *la gloire et la misère* of your neighbors and strangers in God's world.**

[#57] Parviz Tanavoli, *Heech in a Cage*, 2005

In our technocratically hardened society, to speak up for artistic hospitality may seem old-fashioned. But Martin Buber was right, I think, when he said that cultural dialogue is only possible when it assumes self-critique. To many of us a woman in a *burqa* seems to be confined, kept almost hidden like someone disfigured, out of sight. Before we start to talk, however, can we "Westerners" understand that our fashionable exposure of women on the street in mini-top and jeans, inviting the sexualized stare, may show women not confined, but seem somehow over-exposed, maybe shameless to others? Rather than two monologues, maybe a tentative dialogical outcome could be an Egyptian Coptic figure or well clad young woman who has the resourceful mien, modest dress, and normal eyes of the woman in Proverbs 31?

More than hospitable listening to prepare cultural dialogue, however, producing art that does justice to current realities and even offers notes of hope for peace to the disillusioned and outcasts while confronting the comfortable, and so be art that enters vigorously into honest dialogue and would move toward tête-à-tête communal bonding: such artistry will take the ultimate act of loving one's enemies. I do not understand that impossible injunction of Jesus to be a plea for "liberal tolerance." Britt Wikström's *Cathedral of Suffering* [*RA* #6, 31] with mother, child, and father being brutally crucified, with the empty pole inviting us spectators as we walk away, cries out for justice!—indeed God should follow up Mugabe's boast and "take him away"! and the hardened Israeli zealots who are misappropriating countless Palestinian Naboth vineyards with a wall (see 1 Kings 21) need to be prayed for . . . as enemies! in my judgment.

To pray **for** enemies artistically is no small task. Gert Swart has done so, in my judgment, with his Isandlwana monument (1999) [#58] to commemorate the Zulu warriors who died defending their territory safely against British troops in 1879. Rather than vaunt their spear-wielding

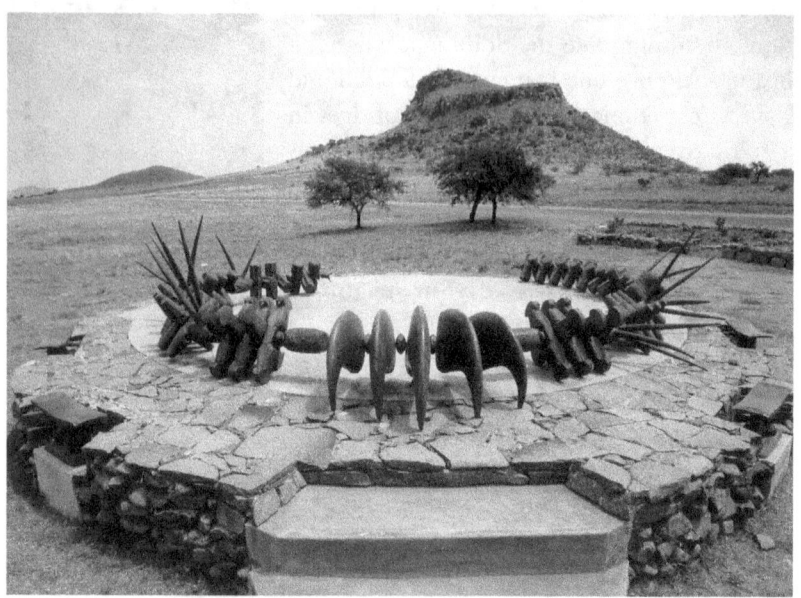

[#58] Gert Swart, *Isandlwana Memorial to the Zulu Fallen*, 1999

heroics, Swart has cast in bronze a large facsimile necklace (*isuqu*) of lion claws and thorns the most brave Zulu fighters were allowed to make for themselves and wear, adding four headrests to symbolize the four Zulu battalions who were swept away to their dreamland. This quiet artistic prayer follows up the agonized *Cathedral of Suffering*'s appeal for God to wake up perpetrators of hatred, cruelty, and war to its devastating futility! so they may turn to doing merciful justice,[18] since the Almighty God of enduring judging mercy **is** indeed present on earth, believe it or not. To forge cultural unity even across faith divides does not mean you have to abandon your convictions: **you just present your artistic gut sacrifi-**

---

18 By importuning his followers to love and pray for one's enemies (Matthew 5:43–48) Christ is asking believers to mature enough so they can plead with God to shame through our efforts those who are evilly harassing others to be so moved that the persecutors turn instead to pursue just-doing (see Luke 9:49–50). It is not biblical wisdom to ask militant "Fundamentalists" of any stripe to change their faith, but rather demand they **practice justice!**

cially. One vulnerably gives away intense artistic wisdom without strings attached, even if a good response is apparently lacking.

Patchwork quilt of Europe
and redemptive saltlick of cultural dialogue
Cultural dialogue breathing a hurt peace-making christian spirit reaching out to neighbors cannot guarantee a cessation of hateful antagonisms. But tough-love **cultural** dialogue can nourish a communal **civic** will, and civility can open up avenues to explore a possible **political** concert of interests. Europe does not need to dismantle nation-states, as I see it, but does need to develop a vision committed to fostering different folk cultures becoming a patchwork quilt that hangs together called "Europe," peaceably respecting minorities and legislating public justice for all peoples, but shunning! the GlobalIST omnivorous commercial Growth cancer.[19] **We need to testify that we Europeans are rediscovering and forming anew the cultural unity of Europe.**[20]

An Anselm Kiefer artwork [#23], *Jeder Mensch steht unter seiner Himmelskugel* (1970), accuses persons of wanting to stand isolated under one's own heavenly dome and let the earth go to hell. Kiefer asks in *Nero Malt* (1974) [#2] what kind of art are you painting, showing, singing, making, and enjoying while foreign cities are burning on the distant TV horizon?

The CNV/EZA/European Commission-sponsored Christian Artists Europe Seminar gatherings in Doorn over the years give a modest answer to Kiefer, following the biblical wisdom, as I understand it, to be a glocal saltlick on the earth (Matthew 5:13–16). Whether it be Nina Astrom singing to women in Russian prisons, Jason Carter doing workshops in

---

19 In his 1970 speech ("La Cité européenne") accepting the Robert Shumann prize, Denis de Rougemont makes most of these points, although he misnames this approach, as I understand it, as his *solution fédéraliste* (developed in an earlier 1969 Paris speech ["Pour une définition nouvelle du fédéralisme"] following Heraclitus and the Chalcedon formulation for the Trinity and the divine-human nature of Jesus Christ [!]). "Il faut admettre la pluralité des allégeances, civiques, politiques, culturelles, idéologiques et religieuses, contra la prétention de l'Etat-Nation à leur monopole absolu. Il faut distributeur les pouvoirs étatiques aux différents niveaux de décision—le communal, le régional, le fédéral—indiqués par la nature des tâches, leur dimensions et celles de la communauté la plus apte à les administrer" (*L'Un et le divers*, 57).

20 Milan Kundera lamented in 1984 that nobody noticed the forced disappearance of "central Europe" after 1945 because "Europe no longer perceives its unity as a cultural unity." Kundera adds the judgment that without **cultural** unity, political machinations to engineer unification will be "artificial" ("The Tragedy of Central Europe," 36.)

Afghanistan, Jukka Leppilampi's throat poetry in Finland, or Jean-Pierre Rudolph with Esther Hege making music in villages of Southern France, and Carlos Martînez fascinating children with mime in Spain and Germany, or British Peter Smith's standing before open doors and cobbling together for exposition in Holland the seasoned ceramics of Romanian Mártha Jakobovits and the graphics of newcomers from some other na-

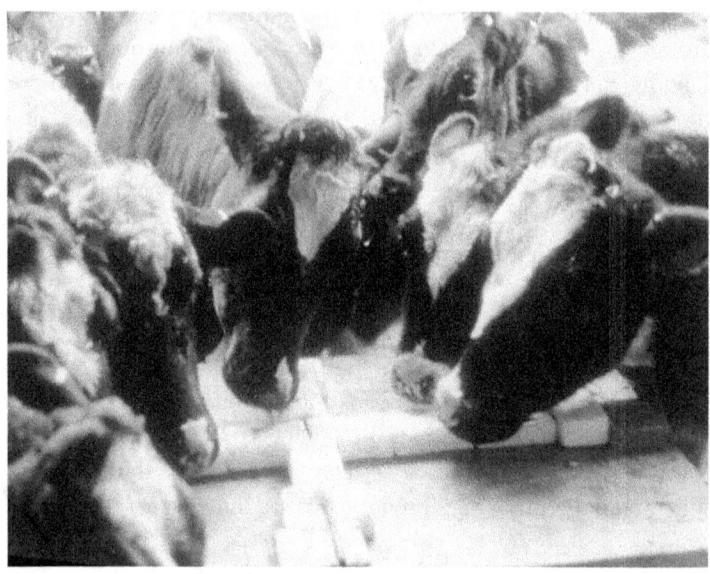

[#59] Ted Prescott, *Salt Lick Cross*, 1991

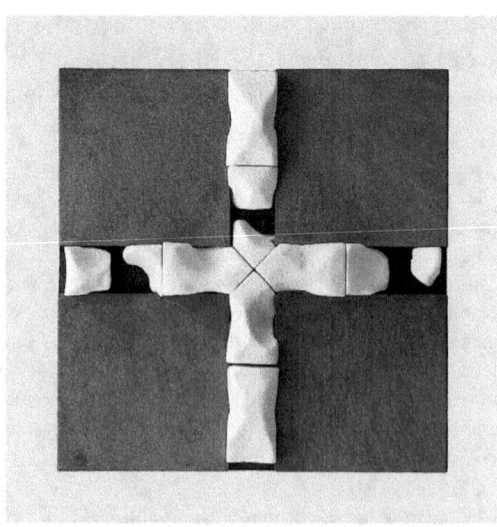

[#60] Ted Prescott, *Greek Salt Lick*, 2011

tion: Christian Artists Seminar—lectures, concerts, artwork, studio workshops, and conversation—constitute a multi-national but common European saltlick cross [#59-60], if you will. A community of Christians not out to convert people—that's the work of the Holy Spirit anyway— but **to give an artistic account of the certain hope within us** (1 Peter 3:8–17) to anybody on the lookout. Like Britt's tombstone [#15] with a bird bath: even in death remember our fellow creatures the birds, while Noah's dove with olive leaf chiseled permanently into the granite shows there is life for the faithful even after the cursed flood of death.

When you have a communal saltlick of sinful artistic saints glocally mindful of neighbors—not a sweet pudding of prima donnas congratulating one another—you will be surprised at its redemptive attraction for all kinds of comers. We workers in **cultural dialogue** are not responsible for enacting a **political patchwork quilt of Europe**. However, we are called by God not to hand out sweets, but to have our artistry and reflection for our neighbors, strangers, and even for the cows God loves (see Jonah 4:11), always be winsome, tasty, gracious salt (Colossians 4:5–6).

Selected bibliography

Beneke, Jürgen. "Foreign Language Teaching and Cross-cultural-communication: A case for a multilingual and multicultural European identity," in *The Role of Intercultural Mediators in Europe* (Stuttgart: Robert Bosch Stiftung, 1987), 39–51.

Brossat, Caroline. *La Culture Européenne: Définitions et Enjeux* (Bruxelles: Bruylant, 1999).

Buijs, Govert J. "The Promises of Civil Society," *Contact*: Newsletter of the International Association for the Promotion of Christian Higher Education, 17:3 (June 2006), insert of 10 pages.

Búrca, Gráinne de. "The European Constitution Project after the Referenda," *Constellations* 13:2 (2006): 205–217.

Couloubaritis, Lambros and Marc de Leeuw, Emile Noël, and Claude Sterckx. *The Origins of European Identity* (Brussels: European Interuniversity Press, 1993).

Gablenz, Otto von. "History and its Role in Promoting Intercultural Awareness," in *The Role of Intercultural Mediators in Europe*, 33–38.

Goheen, Michael W. and Craig G. Bartholomew. *Living at the Crossroads: An introduction to Christian worldview* (Grand Rapids: Baker, 2008).

László, Ervin and Iván Vitányl, eds. *European Culture and World Development* (Frankfurt: Pergamon, 1985).

Goudzwaard, Bob and Mark Vander Vennen, David van Heemst. *Hope in Troubled Times: A new vision for confronting global crises* (Grand Rapids: Baker, 2007).

Graf, Peter, ed. *Religionen in Migration. Grenzüberschreitung als Aufforderung zum Dialog* (Göttingen: V & R, 2006).

Karic, Enes. "Is 'Euro-Islam' a myth, challenge or a real opportunity for Muslims and Europe?" *Journal of Muslim Minority Affairs* 22:2 (2002): 435–442.

Kundera, Milan. "The Tragedy of Central Europe," trans. Edmund White, *New York Review of Books* 31:7 (26 April 1984): 33–38.

Langsted, John, ed. *Studies in Modern Cultural Policy* (Aarhus: Aarhus University Press, 1990).

Lavrijsen, Ria, ed. *Intercultural Arts Education and Municipal Arts Policy* (Amsterdam: Royal Tropical Institute, 1997).

Lipp, Wolfgang. *Heimat–Nation–Europa: Wohin trägt uns der Stier? Standort in Bewegung* (Würzburg: Ergon Verlag, 1999).

Meyer, Steven E. "Israel and Palestine: Why is this issue so difficult?" in *Capital Commentary* 14 March 2008 (Washington, DC: Center for Public Justice).

Newbigin, Lesslie and Lamin Sanneh, Jeremy Taylor. *Faith and Power: Christianity and Islam in 'secular' Britain* (London: SPCK, 1998).

Peckham, Robert Shannan, ed. *Rethinking Heritage: Cultures and politics in Europe* (London: Tauris, 2003).

Potz, Richard and Wolfgang Wieshaida, eds. *Islam and the European Union* (Leuven/Paris: Peeters, 2004).

Ricoeur, Paul, "Le Chrétien et la Civilisation Occidentale" [1946] in *Le Christianisme, quel impact aujourd'hui?* Ed. Alain Houziaux (Paris: Les Éditions de l'Atelier, 2004), 91–117.

Rougemont, Denis de. "The Era of Federations: From cultural unity to political unity," in *The Idea of Europe*, trans. Norbert Guterman (Cleveland: Meridian Books, 1968), 363–434.

Rougemont, Denis de. *L'Un et le divers ou la Cité européenne, Deux discours* (Neuchâtel: Baconnière, 1970).

Rowe, William V. "Difficult Liberty: The basis of community in Emmanuel Levinas," in *From Ghetto to Emancipation: Historical and contemporary reconsiderations of the Jewish community*, eds. David N. Myers and William V. Rowe (Scranton University Press, 1997), 63–74.

Sardar, Ziauddin. "The Ethical Connection: Christian-Muslim relations in the postmodern age" (1991), in *Islam, Postmodernism and Other Futures: A Ziauddin Sardar reader*, eds. Sohail Inayatullah and Gail Boxwell (London: Pluto Press, 2003), 157–188.

Skillen, James W. "Pluralism as a Matter of Principle," in *The Many and the One: Religious and secular perspectives on ethical pluralism in the modern world*, eds. Richard Madsen and Tracy B. Strong (Princeton University Press, 2003), 257–268.

Smiers, Joost. *État des Lieux de la Création en Europe : Le tissu culturel déchiré* (Paris: L'Harmattan, 1998).

Steinhäuser-Carvill, Barbara. "Die Christenheit oder Europa—Eine Predigt," *Seminar* 12:2 (May 1976): 73–88.

Sticht, Pamela. *Culture européenne ou Europe des cultures? Les enjeux actuels de la politique culturelle en Europe* (Paris: L'Harmattan, 2000).

Voll, John O. "Fundamentalism in the Sunni Arab World: Egypt and the Sudan," in *Fundamentalisms Observed*, eds. Martin E. Marty and R. Scott Appleby (University of Chicago Press, 1994), 345–402.

Wiesand, Andreas Johannes. *Kunst Ohne Grenzen: Kulturelle Identität und Freizügigkeit in Europa. Eine Einführung in Gegenwart, Probleme und Entwicklungschancen Europäische Kulturpolitik* (Köln: DuMont, 1987).

"For a Europe founded on its culture," Appeal by the cultural world, July 2004. http://www.europeanwriters.eu/images/files/1792004211744.pdf. Accessed 18 October 2011.

Draft "Treaty establishing a constitution for Europe," June 2003. http://european-convention.eu.int/docs/Treaty/cv00850.en03.pdf. Accessed 18 October 2011

"The National Security Strategy of the United States of America," The White House, September 2002. http://georgewbush-whitehouse.archives.gov/nsc/nss/2002/index.html. Accessed 18 October 2011.

PUTTING HUMPTY-DUMPTY
BACK TOGETHER AGAIN:
THE PROBLEM OF ARTISTS EARNING
A LIVELIHOOD IN SOCIETY

It's not bad to have Martin Luther King dream for racial and ethnic non-discrimination and peace on earth—when you have tasks fitted to your talents that put bread and wine on the table, and you can sit safely, as the Bible puts it, under your own fig or olive tree after a hard day's night of work, to hold conversation with family and friends. But the Irish poet William Butler Yeats diagnosed Europe's trouble back in 1921 when he wrote:

> Things fall apart; the centre cannot hold;
> Mere anarchy is loosed upon the world,
> The blood-dimmed tide is loosed, and everywhere
> The ceremony of innocence is drowned;
> The best lack all conviction, while the worst
> Are full of passionate intensity. (from "The Second Coming")

In our globalized world of corporate blood and oil spills [#61], hard-nosed Fundamentalistic Darwinian Pragmatism, and millions of the damned wretched poor of the earth, where do we artists come in, if at all? Do you realize what the thirty years of Christian Artists International, Leen La Rivière's leadership in the Christelijke Nederlands Vakverbond, and the

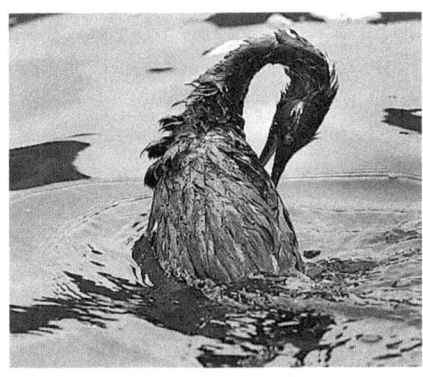

[#61] Pelican in oil, 2010

Europäisches Zentrum für Arbeitnehmerfragen have contributed and

---

Spoken at the Christian Artists International conference in the Netherlands in August 2010.

are contributing in a modest way to "a center that holds" promise for a generation of Christians serious about artistry?

You as a person are more than an artist, I dare say, but who/what are you **as artist** in society, in God's world? Do we need what you have to offer **as artist**?

Are you an individual who constructs your own private imaginative bubble of existence, outside of which is a wasteland of desolate furrows? Anselm Kiefer's watercolor is entitled "*Jeder Mensch steht unter seiner Himmelskugel*" (1970), which is translated in English as "every human being stands under his or her own dome of a heaven" [#23]. Do you pursue your painterly artwork, compose your songs, and make your band music like old Emperor Nero fiddling while Rome, Nagasaki, New York City, Lagos, or Kandahar burns with hatred in the far distance?

I want to rehearse for you briefly the struggle artists have undergone in Europe in the past so that we recognize that our problem of making a living as artists is not new, but has a history that might be instructive as a reality check for us to envision which way we possibly are to walk together.

A History of artisans ("cultural workers") and artists in European society

Ancient open air Greek temples [#62], built as a sacred place to propitiate gods of Aphrodite Culture and Mars War, used slave labor—much as Egyptian pharaohs who were considered deities had used forced labor—to construct monstrous pyramid tombs for their afterlife. Olympian medalists early on were revered practically as demigod heroes with ἀγάλματα (an idol-offering),[1] but the fellows who chiseled the marble were not counted for much: **manual labor is not noble**, believed those who ran the Athenian polis and handed out laurel wreaths to champion athletes and dramatists.

A Churched society with guilds

After the great Roman Empire went the way of all flesh, the Church, which was new on the face of the earth, rehabilitated hand work in a backhanded way by employing carpenters, stone masons [#63], and bronze casters to build and to decorate places where people assembled

---

1 See Dirk van den Berg, '*N Kritiese Besinning op die Moontlijke Invloed van die Vorm-Materie Grondmotief op die Griekse Beeldhoukuns* (Bloemfontein: MA thesis at Potchefstroomse Universiteit, 1972), 169–170, 181.

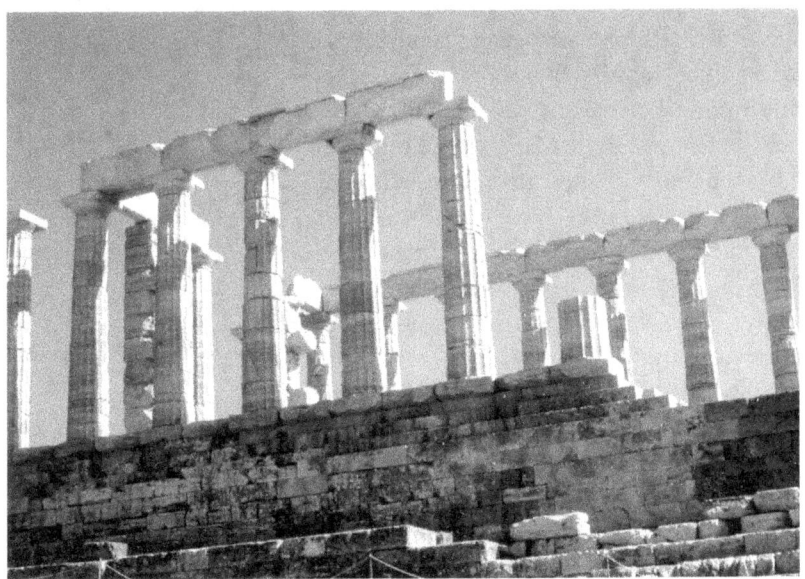

[#62] Temple of Poseidon ruins, Cape Sounion, Greece (1990)

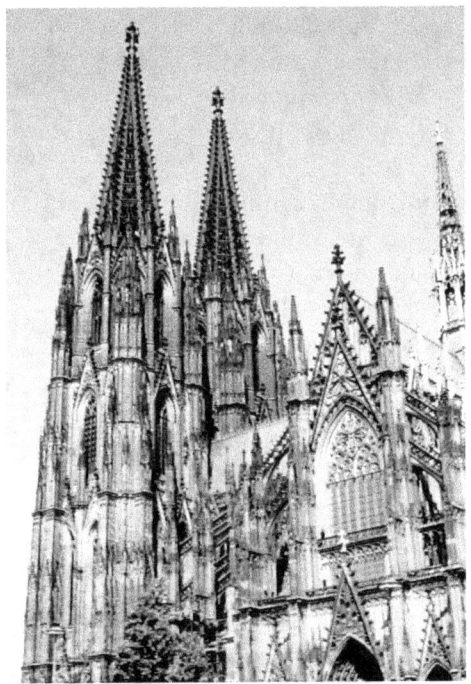

[#63] Köln Cathedral (1954)

for worship. Handicraft was valued for visu-
ally teaching those who could not read the
basic truths of the Bible as interpreted by
the ruling theologians, which came to give
the pregnant Virgin Mary [#64] a glow of
lovely, homely holiness that almost assumed
a co-mediatrix [#65] role with Christ in salvation from the world. Wood-cutters, glass-
blowers, and other skilled craftspeople were
absorbed in the cohering medieval mentality that not only the heavenly Beauty of the
rose window awaited believers, but devils
were real and needed to be scared off by rain-
water gutters [#66] of gargoyles from where
the saints were gathered—**you as artisan
were employed**! Frescoes taught catechism
and emulation of miracle-producing saints,
but carvings also on occasion showed a non-
sanctimonious whimsy [#67] like this wonderful tribute to black African Bishop
Augustine whose honest, agonized
confession was, *Da mihi castitatem
et continentiam, sed nolo modo*[2] (Give
me chastity and continence, O Lord,
but not yet!). Because sin was considered, however skewed, an awful reality in those days, and mortality was
an existential presence—people on
either side of you will die this year
of the bubonic "Black Death" plague
(1348–1350)—there were lay con-
fraternities, quasi-religious guilds, of
trained singing boys and girls [#68],
men and women you could hire, if
you had the money, to sing a mass
at your funeral to save you so many
years in purgatory.

But it would be more or less correct to say, **there were no artists rec-**

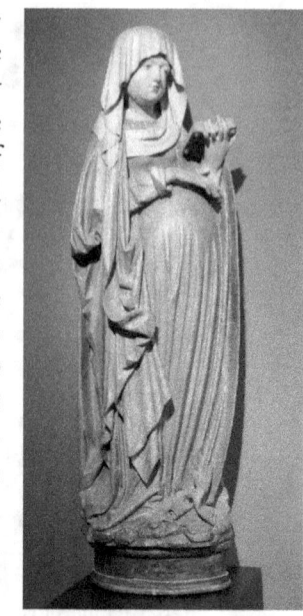

[#64] Swabian Master carver,
Maria expecting, 1500s

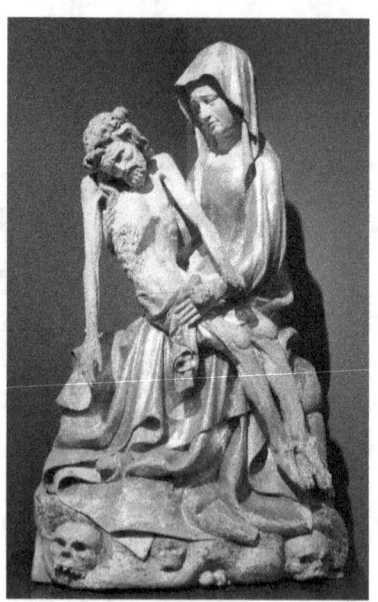

[#65] Middle Rhineland carver,
*Vesperbild, Mary mourning over
the dead Christ*, 1390

---

2 *Confessiones*, VII,17.

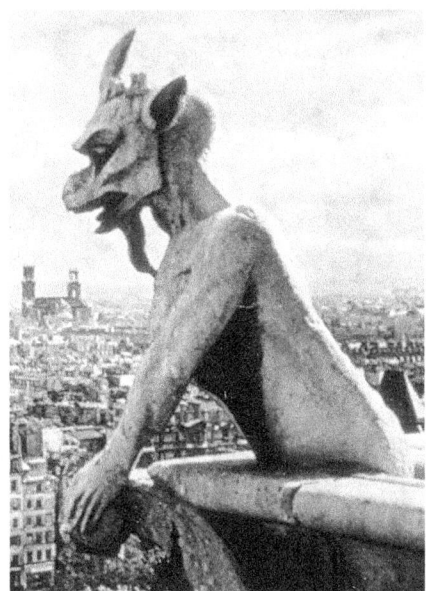

[#66] Gargoyle high up on Notre Dame Cathedral, Paris

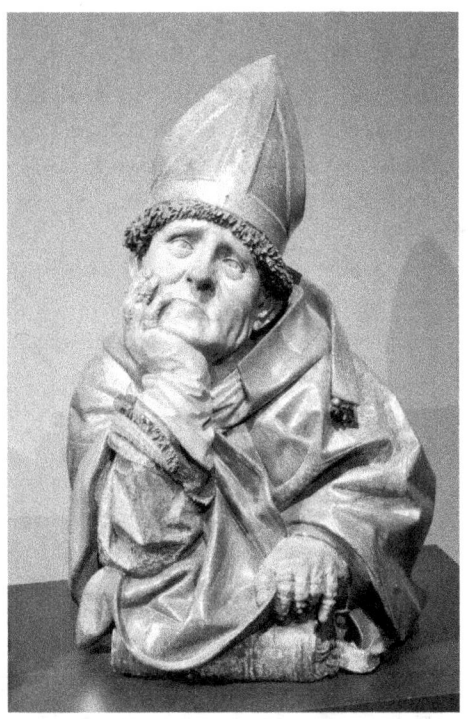

[#67] Middle Rhineland Master carver, *Holy Augustine ?*, 1489-96

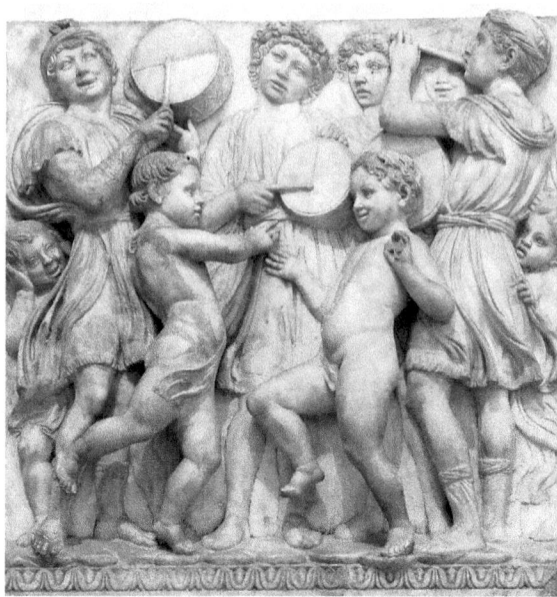

[#68] Lucca della Robbia, detail of *Cantoria* [1431-1438]

ognized as such in Europe until about 1560 AD.

There were certainly these medieval guilds in the Italian cities who had developed a rigorous system of craftsmen and women that regulated the hands-on practice of apprentices (for three to six years) in one's barber/painting/saddle-making/pharmacist workshop—you were all in the same guild—and then supervised the journeymen's use of materials, mixing pigments or drugs, scissors, brushes, tanning leather, to a standard guild quality (another nine months), until finally the novice, now seasoned, knew the trade firsthand and could apply to the *corporazione* directors, upon payment of a fee for himself to become a Master of a guild craft workshop. Guilds were civic organizations of artisans that strove to regulate working conditions, to control especially import, and to export sales of goods and services in a specific field, a community that cared for its members' livelihood (and funerals) more by cost-sharing than price-fixing. **Guilds were composed of very skilled Master manual handworkers with oral traditions.** To be a practitioner of a "profession"—clergy, lawyer, medical doctor, notary public—you had to have a university education (begun c. 1100s AD) and be literate.

Rich princely nobility sparking an Art academy in society
The rich, powerful Medici dynasty of highly cultured bankers centered in Florence, for example, Lorenzo il Magnifico (1449–1492) valued the ex-

traordinary Leonardo da Vinci (1452–1519) and adopted young Michelangelo (1475–1564) as protégé to be personal Medici consorts, as it were, with their studies [#69], paintings, and sculptures [see *RA* #106–108], and catapulted them out of any guild restrictions, fees, and elementary teaching duties. "You paint with brains, not with the hand," wrote Leonardo. Painting is not a manual skill, said Michelangelo, but a "spiritual expression like poetry"[3] (of which he wrote many, many sonnets). And it was Giorgio Vasari (1511–1574) who set up in 1562 in Florence what was called *l'Accademia del' Disegno* (The Academy of Design) for such superior liberal arts-knowing draughtsmen and sculptors and painters, like the earlier Botticelli and his *Il Primavera* (c. 1477–78) [*RA* #105], replete with classical-mythical allusions to Plato, Plotinus, Mercury, Poliziano, and Dante; be-

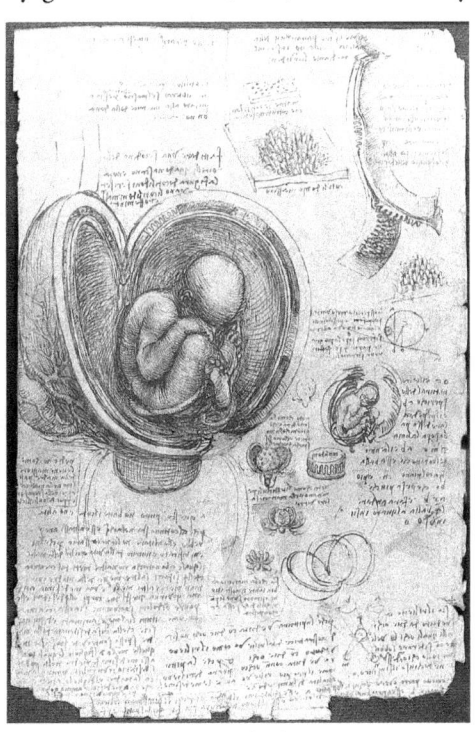

[#69] Leonardo da Vinci,
Studies of Embroyos, 1510-1513

ing so far above the manual guild labor of copying prescribed motifs on leather horse saddles, it is ridiculous to make a comparison—so thought the distinguished superstars invited to be members of the Medici (Rockefeller) appointed Academy. Medici bankers became Renaissance popes too—Pope Leo X (1513–1517) and Pope Clement VII (1523–1534), who spent extravagantly on artworks.

So began the institutionalization of the fateful separation of persons called Academy "artists," whose overwhelmingly impressive works were beholden [#70] to learned, literate Humanist and papal princes. Don't think [#71] is a naked woman being scrutinized by a pianist; this is Art!—about the goddess Venus inspiring Music-making! After **1562 in**

---

3   "Si dipinge col cervello e non colla mano," quoted in Nikolaus Pevsner, *Academies of Art Past and Present*, 33.

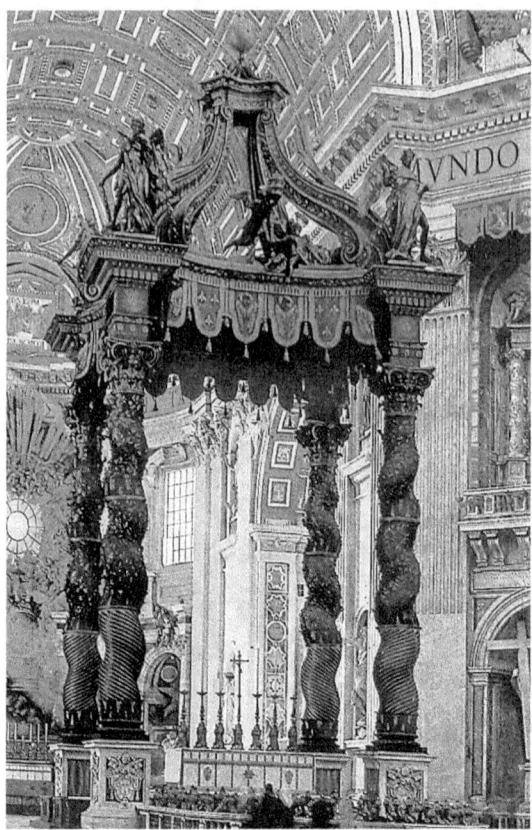

[#70] Bernini, Baldachino over the main altar,
St. Peter's Cathedral

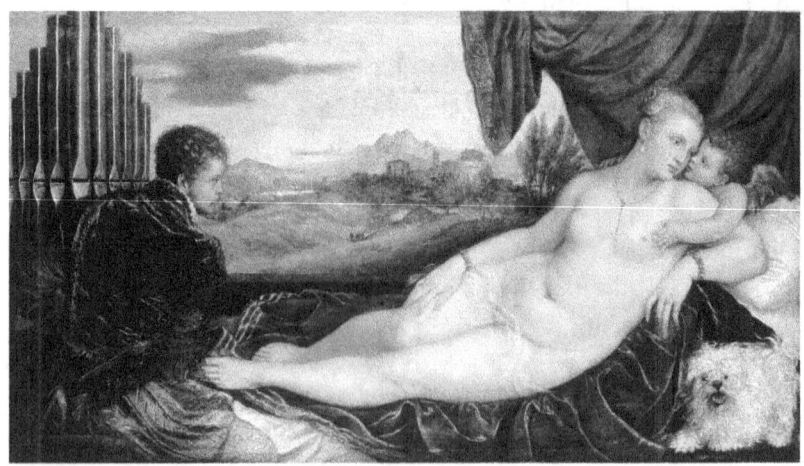

[#71] Titian, *Venus with the Organ Player*, c. 1550

Italian cities "Artists" were no longer considered "artisans," craft persons whose handiwork in the guilds fit a decorative purpose in products serving daily life needs. It is so that in 1579 in the Netherlands, painters, sculptors, engravers, embroiderers, and tapestry makers, formed **a special visual art *guild*** cluster differentiated from the workshop of tradesmen and merchant cartels, to help market "genre" painterly artworks for middle-class families; this action in Reformation-affected North Holland precluded a divide between aristocratically pampered artists and those making-a-living-from-your-labor-with-your-hands craft artisans. Even the second "Academy" started by the Mannerist Zuccari brothers in Rome in 1593, solemnly extoled the virtues of piety and chastity in Art, became a much more mundane "academy" (similar to a guild) trying to teach beginners with life-drawing classes.

The authoritarian royal state defining art-making

However, what became the paragon model for art academies in Italy, imperial Spain, Germany's dukedoms, England, and Eastern Europe was *l'Académie Royale de peinture et de sculpture* in France (1648/1655/1663) under the absolutist rule of Louis XIV, run by Jean-Baptiste Colbert (1619–1683) and Charles LeBrun (1619–1690). **If you wanted to be a bona fide *artist*, you had to join the Royal Academy** by submitting a painting judged good enough to be accepted by the resident academicians (which they then added to the king's collection in the Louvre); and then you were bound to follow the lectures in geometry, anatomy, perspective, and history with life-drawing, compete for the prizes, and sell your artworks at the annual exhibitions. Everything was controlled: a style of impeccably researched, classical grandeur [#72], or of the highly literate, like that of Poussin in painting [#73], and with the sumptuous spread-out elegance of Versailles [#74] that spells royal leisure, promenades, luxury, and feasting—that's the kind of art you are to make for *la gloire de la France!* (Building Versailles gave work to 36,000 artists, artisans, and landscape laborers [Roeck, 1999, 27].)

There is too much to say: the French Art Academy held a monopoly on life-drawing, so you could be fined for doing illegal life-drawing in your private studio with a few friends; if your acceptance piece was a *nature morte* painting, [#75] like that of Chardin, (judged to be the least worthy thematic category) that's what you painted for the rest of your academic artistic life; because Antoine Watteau's (1684–1721) submission piece was so good [#76] but did not fit any of the Academy's categories, they quietly made a new category—*fêtes galantes*—tweaking their

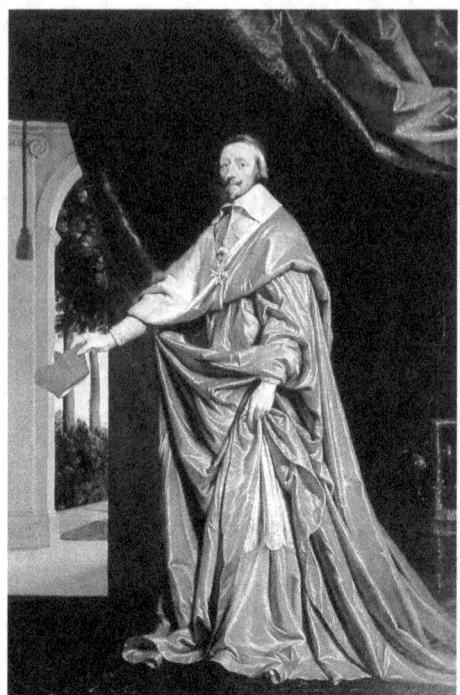

[#72] Philippe de Champagne, *Richelieu*, c. 1640

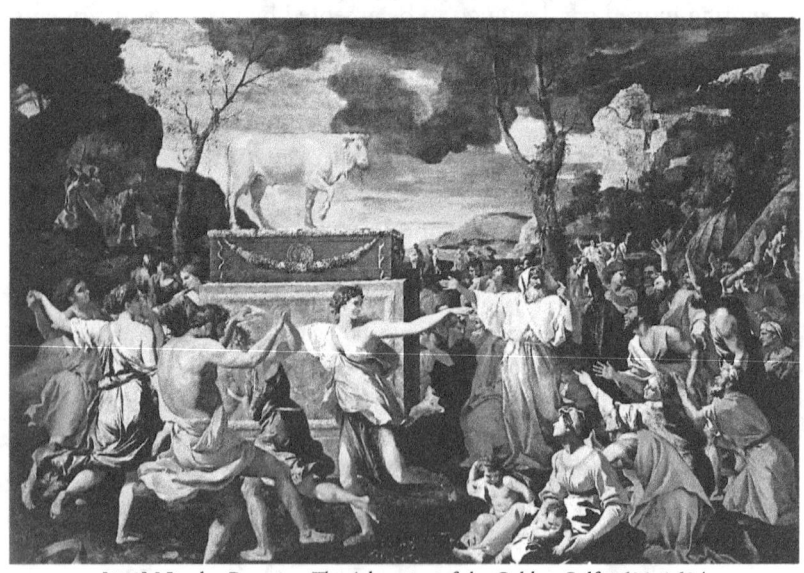

[#73] Nicolas Poussin, *The Adoration of the Golden Calf*, 1633-1634

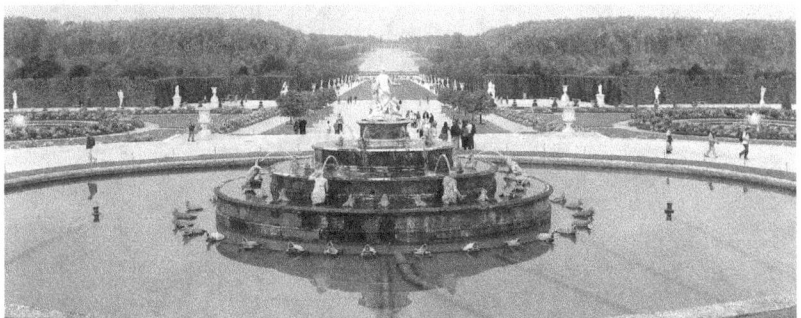

[#74] Gardens of Versailles, conceived by André Le Nôtre, 1661-1668

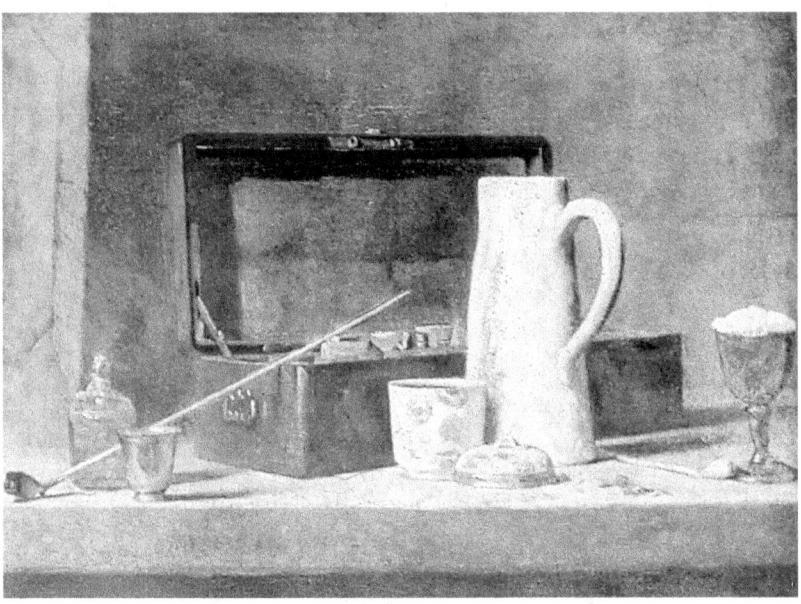

[#75] Chardin, *Pipe and Jug*, 1737

regimen of impressive grandeur to a lighter rococo sensibility. And there were always mavericks: William Hogarth (1697–1764) could not bring himself to paint in the flattering grandiloquent style of British Royal Academy president Sir Joshua Reynolds (1723–1792) [#77] or of the successful high society portraitist Thomas Gainsborough (1727–1788). So Hogarth started his own private St. Martin's Lane Academy (1734) and puckishly threw in the family cat on the back of the chair to the right [#78] when he got a commission from the nouveau riche in England to do a family portrait (*The Graham Children*).

And it is historically noteworthy that in the Dutch Republic of the 1600s, where the Calvinistic faith tradition had no use for large altar-

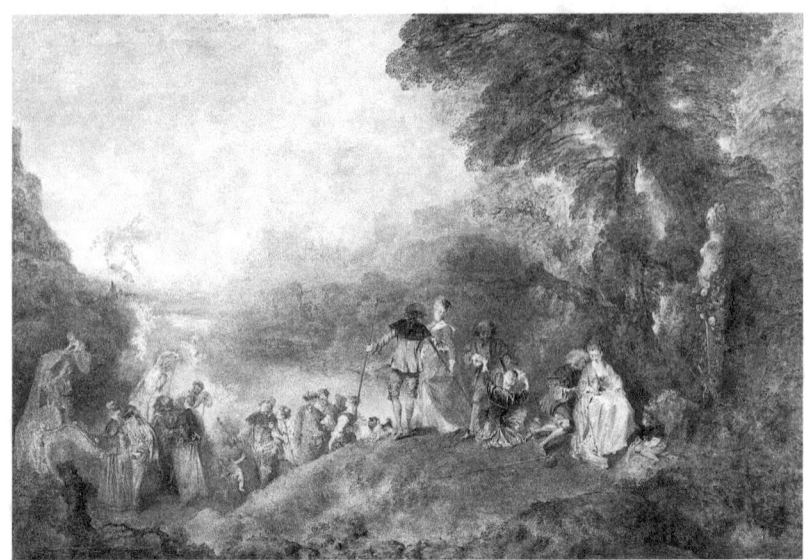

[#76] Antoine Watteau, *Pélerinage à l'île de Cythère*, 1717

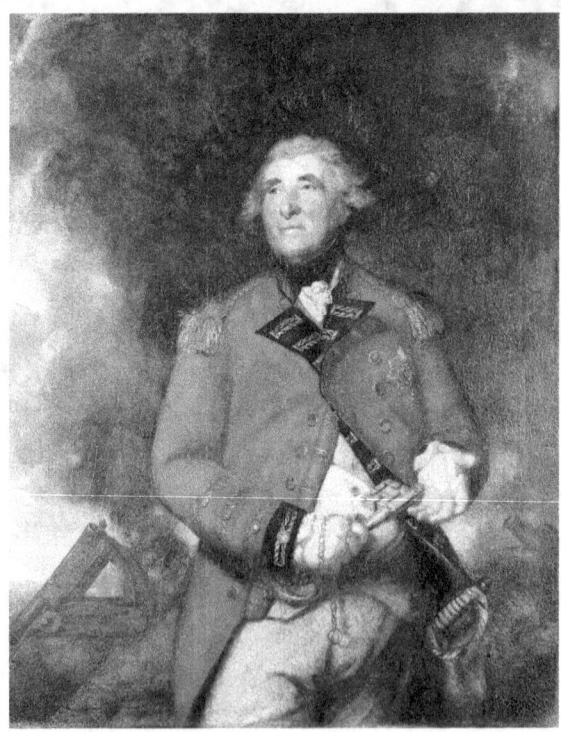

[#77] Joshua Reynolds, *General Eliott,*
Baron Heathfield of Gibraltar, 1787

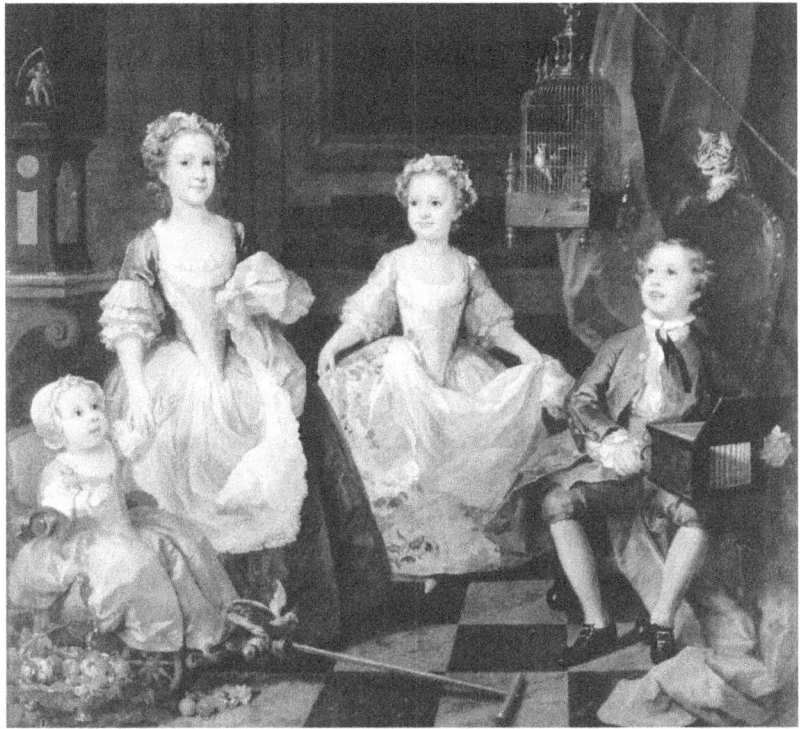

[#78] William Hogarth, *The Graham Children*, 1737

pieces, and where there was no ostentatious court to fund a national Art Academy, the guilds under municipal supervision were thriving. For example, forty-nine painters in The Hague applied in 1655 to form their own *confrérie* distinct from the wood-cutters and embroiderers, leading to *de Haagse school* of painterly art. Without a royal "Art Academy" small paintings of subtle excellence were being marketed by art dealers to people's homes; a few important commissions by small cities [*NA* #56] and even guilds were resulting in striking artworks. Less successful Dutch painters took a second job: Jan Steen (1626–1679) was an inn-keeper; Jan van Goyen (1596–1656) was a merchant in tulips; Hobbema (1638–1709) worked in the wine excise business. . . .

But the point for our purposes is that most of Europe, following the centralized French Royal Art Academy system, geared to trumpet national prestige, combined with a mercantilist bent that translated conspicuous consumptive artistic *dessin*[4] into, say, huge Gobelin tapestries,

---

4 The Renaissance conception of *disegno* (drawing with planned intention) has been reduced by the "Enlightenment" to *dessin* (pure draughtsmanship); the way the multicomplex medieval cathedral becomes reduced to the stark girders of the Eiffel tower.

which you really need in your castle to keep out the draft and dampness: **artists were swallowed up and defined as a privileged aristocratic class of special persons trained to parrot the *refined* taste—*fine* art—of their wealthy, political, not-stupid royal overlords, far from the madding crowd of lowly people working with their hands to make the world go round.**

Academic art to teach morality and the revolt of avant garde geniuses
Yet as it happens, not every artist is a Michelangelo, a Rembrandt, or a Mozart. What do you do with all the mediocre artists being churned out by the art academies around Europe in the 1800s?

Well, you keep producing them in the Idealist mold of *l'École des beaux-arts*. The more self-assured artists survived in the French Revolution [#79], next they deified Emperor Napoleon [*RA* #54] when he became boss. Lesser artists of the Establishment tried to have a part, for example, in the Crystal Palace 1851 Great Exhibition and to begin to consider bending their exalted art activity of design down into ornamental or decorative [#80] purposes. As the practicalist Aufklärung of *sapere aude* (dare to know) mutated into the Neo-Classical cadre of Kant, Winckelmann, and Anton Raphael Mengs, **Friedrich Schiller's basic conservative conviction that art can make us moral beings and**

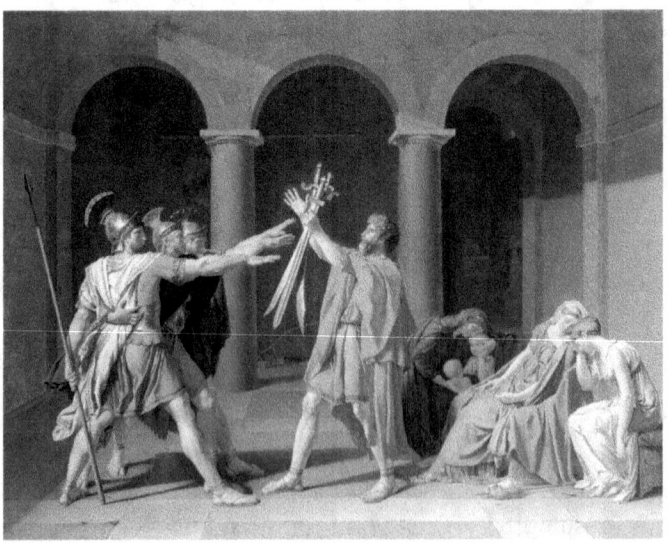

[#79] Jacques-Louis David, *Oath of the Horatii*, 1786

A similar desiccation occurred to Thomas Aquinas' *ratio* in Descartes' *cogito*.

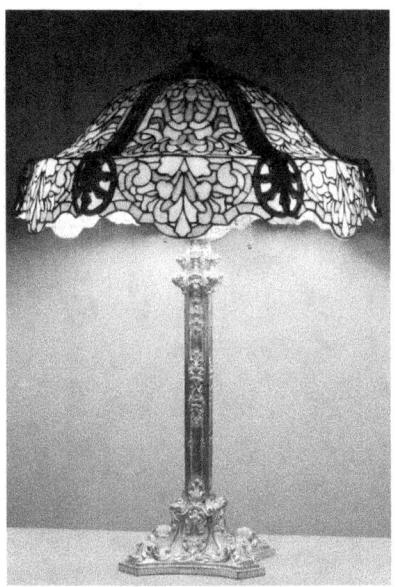

[#80] Lampshade made of Tiffany glass, 1890–1900

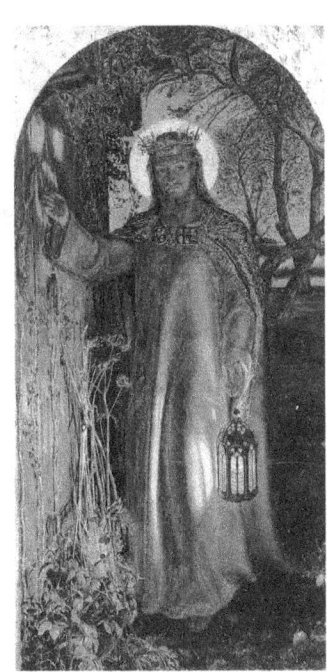

[#81] William Hunt, *The Light of the World*, 1851

pacify our sensualist and rationalist extremist tendencies,[5] became a domesticating force in the formation of artists. Schiller's old-fashioned Humanism helped dull the teaching of art-making into moralizing pictorial instruction, like the clear-headed Pre-Raphaelite pieces [#81] or the sweet Swiss idealizations of middle-class life [#82]. **European artists came to be conceived as the school-masterly ethical teachers in Beauty of humankind.**

What is so curious is that the concerted revolt against this scholastic sterilization of art [#83] into an academic drawing exercise within a walled studio, still busy copying plaster casts of ancient Greco-Roman torsos: the spirited reaction against beautiful artistic moralization minted the mentality of what is the mainstream avant garde conception of artists to this day. Whether it was early Romantic *Sturm und Drang* Herder, outdoor cloud-painting Constable and the so-called "Impressionists," or Whistler's [*NA* #68] lawsuit against Ruskin who unwisely claimed Whistler was just throwing paint at a canvas, artists said and acted out that "we artists are not here to testify for Church doctrine, to promote the status

---

5 *Über die Ästhetische Erziehung des Menschen in einer Reihe von Briefen* (1794–1795), especially the concluding letters 25–27.

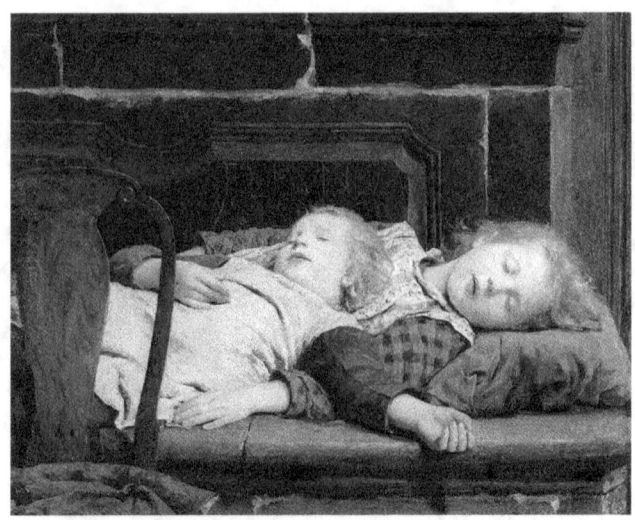

[#82] Albert S. Anker, *Two Sleeping Girls
on the Bench by the Stove*, 1895

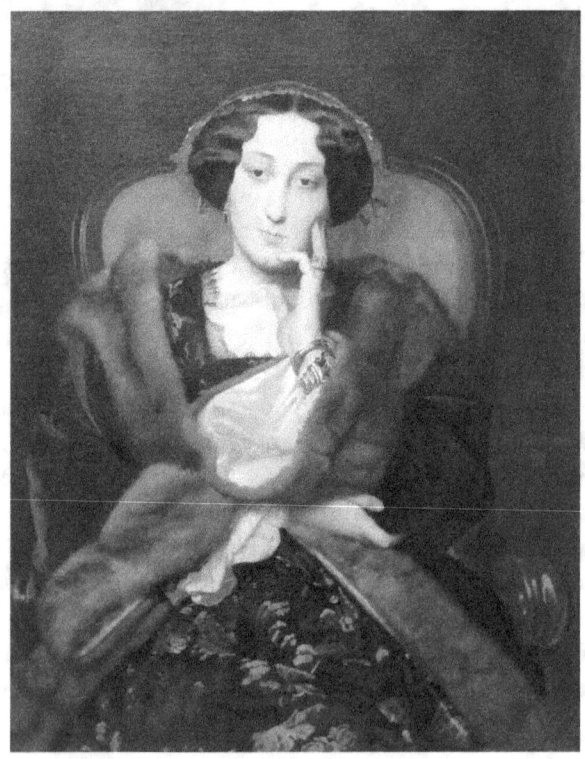

[#83] Jean-Léon Gérôme, *Portrait of a Woman*, 1851

of the royal highnesses and chauvinistic rulers of nations; we categorically reject being lackeys of the rich Robber Barons building libraries to salve their greedy consciences; we artists do not need to teach bourgeois morality. **Our genius is to make art for the sake of art alone!** Give us a break and some breathing room! We artists have the right to create art as we intensely feel it! Mind your own business, people, and watch our smoke—"

Inspired by the Romantic belief that a "creative individual" is sacrosanct, from Walter Pater in England, Mallarmé in France, to the Dada escapades in 1917 Zurich, one avant garde fashion after the other—Futurists, Surrealist, Minimalists, Punk—followed each other in the last several generations. **The creed of autonomous artists who above all must to one's own self be true—damn the consequences!—is a principal conviction and spirit among many who aspire to be real artists today.**

Craft-with-art tied to commerce

Before I pull together this historical sketch to present the systematic controversial part of my analysis, I need to mention just one other significant event on the historical European record: the Bauhaus movement and its precursor, a man trying to "pick up Humpty-Dumpty" and get artists back into daily life employment.

William Morris (1834–1896), to be brief, was the strange concoction of a medieval-fascinated Utopian Socialist who wanted to counteract the havoc raised in English village life by the Industrial factories and their polluting mass production of soul-less appliances. **The Arts-and-Craft Movement, which Morris fathered in the 1880s, meant to restore the craft workshops of *artisans* who could take pride in the beauty of their handmade products.** Like a one-man evangelist team, Morris went around the country lecturing to lower-class laborers on how lovely wallpaper [#84] could ennoble their daily lives. William Morris—as a gentleman enamored by Icelandic sagas—failed to reform the role of art in people's lives because he refused to acknowledge the technical development of machines in the industrious **manufacturing** of household utensils and commercial enterprise.

But the Bauhaus begun by Walter Gropius (1883–1969), supported by the Grand Duke of Saxe-Weimar, c. 1919, was structured to **unite craft *and* artistic design in a schooling setup that was industrial machine-construction-friendly,** and would train persons to think together architecturally toward building art in a pragmatic world. Students at the *Staatliches Bauhaus* complex were first introduced to materials and tools for six months; then they spent three years under a single master-

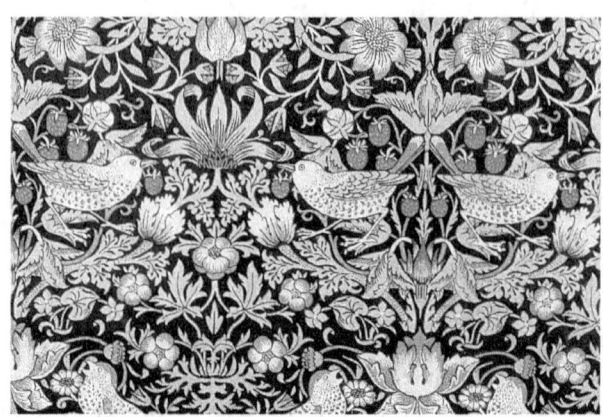

[#84] William Morris, *Strawberry Thief*, chintz, 1883

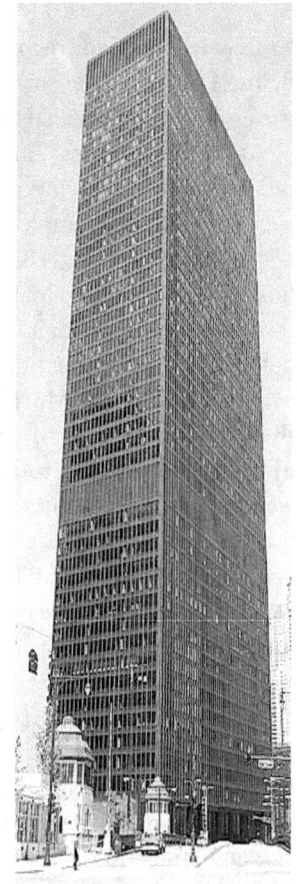

craftsman in practical design-study, model-making, co-operative construction projects, until they earned a certificate as journeyman in a trade; and then they joined in actual experimental Bauhaus building projects. Instructors included Moholy-Nagy, painters Kandinsky, Feininger, and Paul Klee, Breuer who invented tubular furniture, and others, including Mies van der Rohe (1886–1969) [#85] whose severe no-nonsense steel-&-glass buildings around the world typify **the vision and spirit of Bauhaus**, which **was geared to form artistic crafts persons, "cultural workers," who can earn a living in our hi-tech cultured world** . . . if you are trained in this style and will be part of a team. (The Bauhaus closed down in 1933.)

I rehearsed this European historical route in sketchy form to show and tell in answer to Anselm Kiefer's trenchant, painterly question that **artists are *not* alone** under a heavenly dome of protection in a wasteland, **but have been and are now surrounded by institutional frameworks** like Church, the Wealthy, Nation States, Schools, the Art-world, Industrial Commerce and others; it is arrogant narcissism for artists to act as if "I

[#85] Mies van der Rohe, Chicago

can do my art thing by myself," as if I alone am god.

I told the story in roughly chronological order, suggesting that different institutions took the lead at times in offering artisans and artists a living wage. I did it with a selection of graphic artworks for illustration, but one could do it with literature, music, and song. For example, in order for a singer to receive room and board from the medieval Church (c. 500–1300 AD) you became a monk or nun to chant mass in monophonic unison. For Renaissance courtiers (c. 1300–1600 AD) you composed madrigals, became a *castrati* counter-tenor, or as an enterprising roving troubadour sang for your supper and lodging like a visiting court jester. At Madame Pompadour's state dinners (c. 1600–1800 AD) as dancing master you arranged for the mincing minuet until around 1760 the flamboyant waltz became *au courant*. Heavy German symphonies by Beethoven, Brahms, and Mahler (1800s AD) gave work to accomplished instrumentalists. Twelve-tone music entered the European scene (1922) after Stravinsky shook up the music world in 1912 with the riotous *Rite of Spring*. And today post Elvis (1935–1977) and the Beatles (1960s–1970) there are The Three Tenors (1994–2004), the Mediæval Bæbes (1996–), the Commerce of myriad bands vying for gold or platinum sales and burn-your-own CDs—?

Systematic thesis regarding artisans and artists in the European Union countries today

My basic thesis for discussion if we are to take a step toward integrating artists as normal workers with regular income in contemporary society is this: **you cannot correctly encapsulate artwork for institutional service until both artists and the various institutions understand the nature and glory of making art-as-such, and the interactive tasks and responsibilities of the different institutions in God's world**.

That's a large project, which I shall scratch at by describing the nature and task of artistry as I christianly understand it, which holds, I think, for artists of any or no faith persuasion. I'll try to do that while distilling from the historical sketch I gave what could be missteps or openings for us to remember. Then to close I'll complicate the societal mesh we artists inhabit once more with attention to the public cultural sector to bring us messily up-to-date on how art is integral to human well-being and how we shall live.

The nature of artistry and the artistic task

Artistry is skilled human imaginative construction of a medium into

an artifact or an event that embodies certain nuances of meaning, and presents them to people with a suggestion-rich, allusive quality.[6] Because artwork is made by humans, the artistic product normally discloses, however faintly, the perspectival vision of the world and history, and a certain spirited dynamic to which the artist is presently committed. Artworks may be weak or strong, fairly simple or richly complicated, run-of-the-mill or idiosyncratic, forgettable or memorable, but art is always a particular dated/located offering by some person(s), as I understand it, usually with assistance from others, a free-will offering called to be thanks to God and a harbinger of steadying hope to one's neighbor.

Both the medieval guild and the subsequent art academy correctly assumed that artistry is based on skill. A bona fide artist cannot be an unskilled worker. And the guild had the master craftsman with apprentice at beck-and-call, with salaried journeymen around, to insure quality of performance in goldsmithing or painting in foliage around the figures. The Academy rightly wanted to make artisans literate, historically and culturally informed, because art-making involves more than its skill foundation. Art-makers count on imaginativity, brimming over like a reservoir filled with random images, percolating ideas, stories and strange memories, to spark associations that the artist fuses into the metaphor of a hauntingly sad song or an exuberant dance. Unfortunately when the Art Academy took on a secularizing Enlightenment spirit, the liberal arts education of prospective graphic artists was done in classes with lectures and rote instruction that lacked the invigorating on-the-job training received by learning personally offhand from a master artist. No wonder subsequent Romantic artists, trying to honor and save the defining imaginative quality of artwork from Rationalist dullness, claimed that genuine visionary art must be supra-rational and bear the mark of inspired genius. It later took the Bauhaus conception, with its severe penchant for architecture, to reintroduce the master artist with apprentice in a team setting, and to bring art out of the exotic stratosphere back to earth for practical use.

The fact that artistry evolved out of artisan craftsmanship as a vocation with its own special independent task is normal. The long historical clash regarding status between artist and craftsperson, however,

---

6 Cf. my earlier definition: "If you have law-abiding allusive symbolical objectification of meaning you have art. . . ." in [1962] *A Christian Critique of Art and Literature* (Toronto: Tuppence Press, rev. ed., 1995), 46, 42–47.

is misbegotten in my judgment. A surgeon is not **better** than a nurse, and a learned Ph.D. is not **better** than a good teacher: their different gifts serve different related needs in an other person's healing or intellectual development. And whether one be an amateur or become a professional is a still different cup-of-tea, since you can be a professional cabinet maker and an amateur painterly artist (or obscurantic scholar). Amateurs do things simply for the love of it: professionals are practitioners who willingly have been disciplined in their occupation by peers to meet certain standards of performance, also on off-days. Every professional artist begins as an amateur. **But it is wrong, I believe, to think craftspersons who can design a good toaster are necessarily more usefully integrated with daily life than artists who make what I call** *art-as-such*—**a novel, a sculpture, a poem, an engraving, a song. A skilled aesthetically qualified artifact or performance—***art-as-such***—that brings relief or wonderment to a tired person and puts a smile on somebody's face is a good trade for a person to cultivate and is of a piece with ordinary societal existence, deeply serviceable to one's neighbor.**

So, no matter whether you worship Allah, God revealed in Jesus Christ, Human Rights, or Moneyed Success, no matter Who or What you live for: **as artist you are bound skillfully to elicit, lead, heal, gently provoke the imaginative activity of human nature so people become gratefully nuance-aware, and allow such an imaginative sensitivity to filter into all the other ways one acts**—thinks, talks, eats, buys, prays, feels, whatever.

And it is important for me to posit that art-making (and art reception, art-comment and theory) is **a modest undertaking.** To be busy with art is not as necessary as to have food and drink, health, safety, shelter, clothing, breathing room, and employment with a living wage. However, artistry is almost as important in society, I dare say, as garbage collecting and waste disposal, because **imaginative activity acts like taking a deep breath in one's ordinary pursuits; it refreshes like sleep**, in a way like taking a power nap. To have the leisure to sleep is not a luxury, but is normal, activates a creatural norm. And to have your imaginativity primed and triggered by artwork is normal and is meant to be a blessing, opening up a person to the rich subtleties nearby in God's world. The artwork can be Shakespeare's *King Lear*, Fats Waller's rendition of *Limehouse Blues* (1978), a Russian Cossack folk dance, or your child's drawing up on the refrigerator [#86]. We need a more humble understanding of the artistry of artwork: its defining imaginative (not-rational) nature is not a supra-rational, pivotal, and apocalyptic gnostic illumination of the Numinous but is a pre-theoretic, sub-analytic, infrastructural contribution to human well-being. If we artists could have a more humble estimation of our task in society—closely aligned with the instrumental service of artisans, folk "cultural workers"— and "dare to respond to the cries of the world" (Gablik, 100) with a skillful compassionate imaginativity, there might be much less defensive posturing by artists and a more ready acceptance of our fruitful place in society.

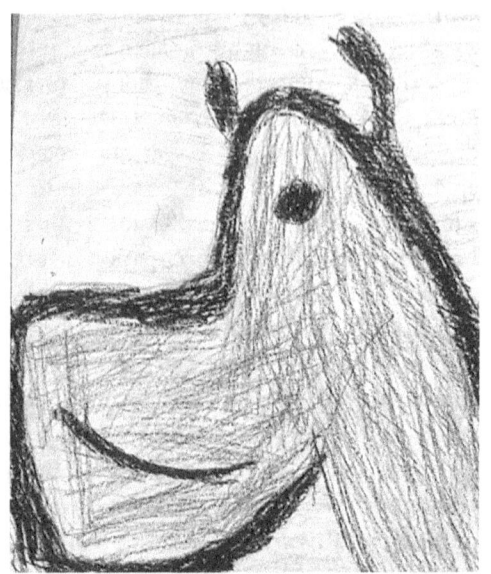

[#86] Lucas, *The Jaw*

The interactive institutional setting of the society we humans inhabit

Once this particular service of artists—somewhat as I have delineated— has been granted as a legitimate, bona fide task integral to societal shalom, then one may explore how to make professional artistry a viable, life-sustaining activity in society. Must artists enter the so-called "free enterprise" Darwinian stock market, hire an agent, join a labor union, and engage the competition? The 1600s Dutch guild barter marketplace precedent (before Adam Smith) worked fairly well, although many artists back then had to take a second part-time job. To have a wealthy patron behind you as artist, one who guarantees you a livelihood, even provides a few perks, can be quite liberating from a hand-to-mouth existence, so long as the support is really at arm's length and is not a gift with strings attached that you produce only music or pictures soothing to the sponsor. The enabling finances of rich patrons can become patronizing and patriarchal; it can even result in giving money to mediocre artists. In my judgment, however, the wealthy are ethically bound to share their surplus with those less well-off, and a not-for-profit foundation to which artists can apply for time-bound grants is perhaps not a bad way to keep the bonding relation between the Wealthy Few and artists at large to be a relation of willing ethical trust.

When the political government of a country steps up to implement its responsibility to support the presence of its artistic citizens in the land and to engage the contribution of art for the populace at large, artists need to be responsive and wary because national governments can be chauvinistic and dictatorial rather than be executives of restorative justice. We artists do not want to lend imaginative clout as Leni Riefensthal's cinematic extravaganzas did for Hitler's *Dritte Reich*, nor be Siberianized by Stalin's cultural minister Zhdanov because of a Solzhenitsyn-like novel. The fierce debate in the United States government on how to make a memorial of the Vietnam War exemplifies what is at stake for artists: a contingent of US lawmakers wanted Frederick E. Hart's (1943–1999) bronze statue [#87] eulogizing the rugged, determined multi-ethnic US army combat troops still ready to fight and kill, while Maya Ying Lin's (1959–) black granite slabs sunk into the earth inscribed with more than 58,000 names [#88] of only the American dead presents an imaginative stifled cry at the incredible wastefulness of that war. It may be a touchy subject, but I find it very instructive as a Canadian citizen to contrast the confrontational *Marseillaise* (1792) and the clarion *Deutschlandlied*

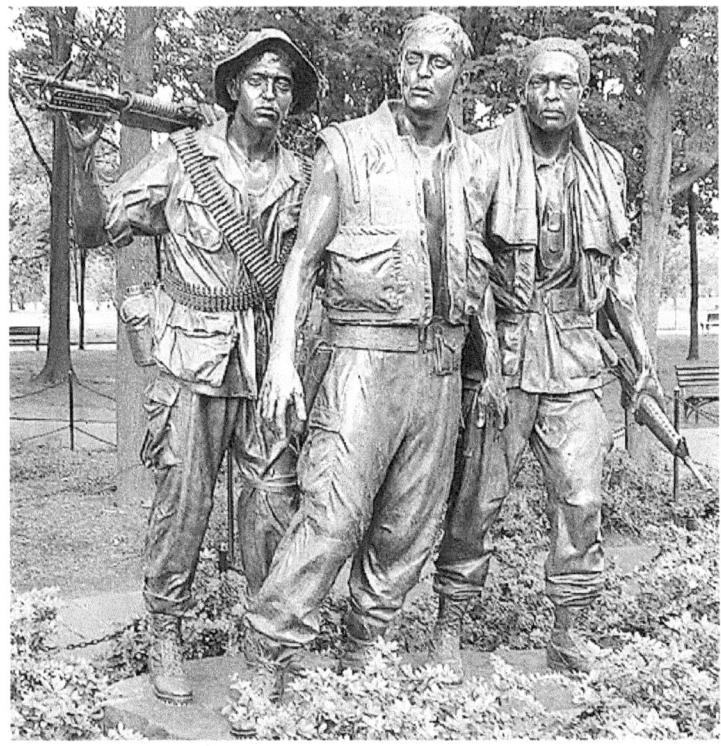

[#87] Frederick Hart, *The Three Soldiers*, 1984, commemorating the Vietnam War

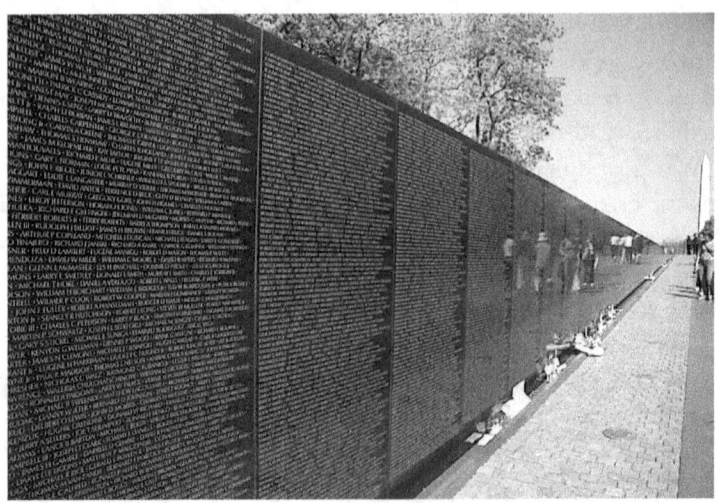

[#88] Maya Lin, *Vietnam Veterans Memorial Wall*, 1982

(1841/1922) with the stately, moving national anthem of Hungary, *Him-nusz* (1823/1844), which devoutly pleads with God for protection—"We Hungarians have suffered enough for all our past **and** future sins." That's in the Hungarian national anthem.

The artistry can be sound or poor, and the political government's action to which the art is hinged can be right or wrongheaded: politically engaged artistry has a double duty to mind in order to do the task justice. But the legal political rulers—national, regional, municipal—need to find ways to fund artistic projects, at arm's length, so that the populace comes to realize that a cultural setting conducive to art education can be an enrichment of the commonwealth. **To have artworks encapsulated** (voluntarily "integrated") **with societal life by institutional support can be for good or for evil, depending upon how the institution and the artists both enact each of their different responsibilities.** So too with the organized Church, the *ulama*, or the Humanist Enlightenment cathedral [#89]: artists who may determine the symbolic form of their artwork and voluntarily make it liturgical, giving public voice to the creed of an organized group of believers, perform a good deed. There are a few dangers connected with outright confessional art: Mannerist art celebrated the overwhelming power, honor, glory, and mystery of the Ecclesial hierarchy at the expense of most of earthly life; Evangelical Christians today sometimes go non-representationally "abstract," so their words can tell you what you should be seeing—such "spirituality" seems cheapened to me because it requires neither graphic aesthetic effort nor

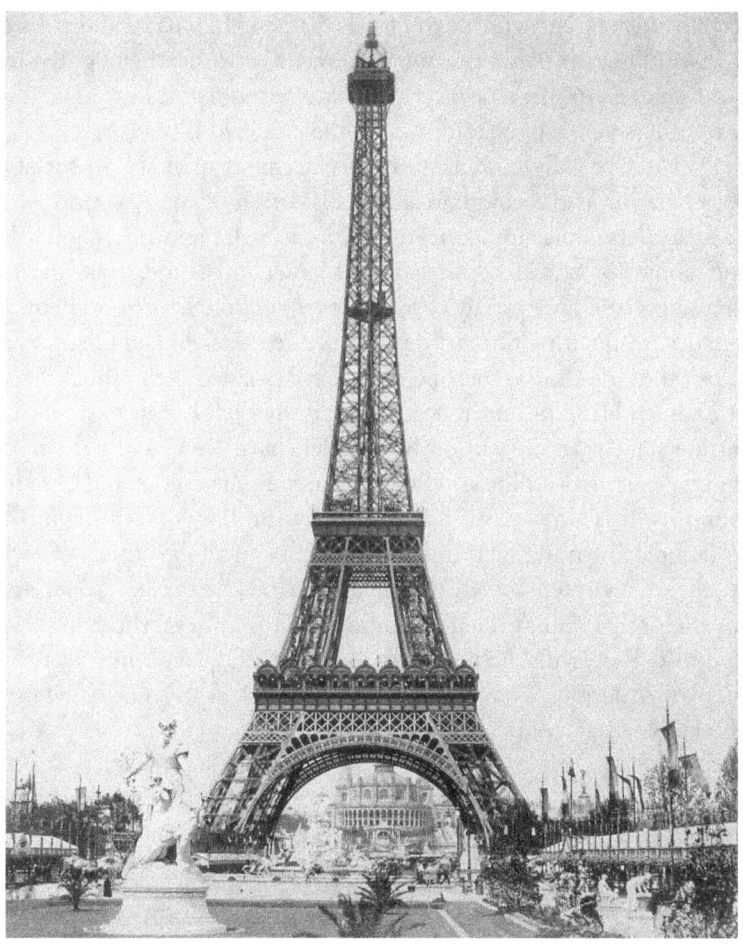

[#89] Eiffel tower

any suffering for following the Way of obedience.

And **it is a mistak**e, I think, **for Christians to take liturgical Church art as the pattern for redemptive christian artistry in society.** I am with Hans Rookmaaker on this point, who wanted to show Billy Graham around the Rijksmuseum in Amsterdam, he told me, and tell Graham that the "still life" [*NA* #4] by Willem Claeszoon Heda (1633) is the most "christian" painting in the museum: it discloses the glories in the creatural texture of God's fruit, wood, and pewter, and softly reminds us, *memento mori*, of our mortality, our lives are as transient as a dried yellow lemon peel or a broken walnut. You don't need to have a "Jesus" hit in your song to make it a song of thankfulness to God. Wim Botha's hanging Christ composed of Bibles is probably too strong in critique of our hypocrisy to be right for the nave of a church; what could a sermon say, except *miserere nobis?* But it is a powerful artwork when lighted in an art museum environs, especially when it is exposited to let you be a voyeur of others viewing the sculpture of the crucified Bible-Christ [#47].

What especially complicates the placement of artists in society in our generation is the commercialized distortion of the Artworld which, like art gallery, museum, concert hall, and media network, should be a good home for makers of artworks. Market forces today are decidedly monopolistic and greedy. Brand name auction houses Sotheby and Christies, who with global art dealers like Leo Castelli and Charles Saatchi run the Artworld as their fiefdom, have paraded their "shock" troops like Damien Hirst and the preemptive kitsch of Jeff Koons to set the tone for superstar Art in the world: these leaders have been a curse on making art that generates kindliness [#90] or awareness of wonder and of sadness around us. It is almost as if Schiller's moralism has gone through Adorno's jaundiced requirement that art must, first of all, be critical of society and then, corrupted by MONEY, allow a few sacrosanct Super-artists vent their self-righteous, hateful putdowns toward everybody else, with impunity. The media helps others like Chris Ofili become sensational too, by mentioning, as if it be important, the elephant dung used on his "The Holy Virgin Mary" (1996).

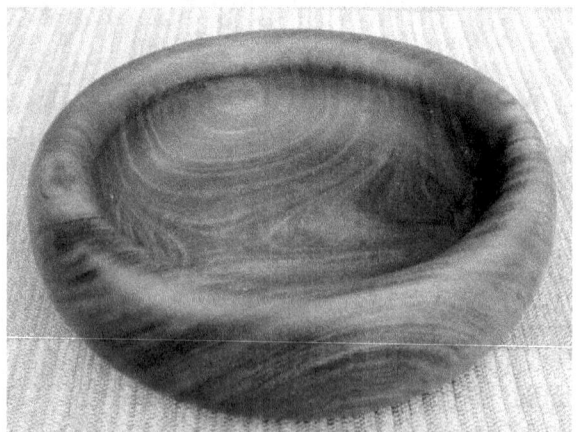

[#90] Julian Di Stefano, bowl lathed from the Black Wattle tree

The Music Industry and Pop Art Entertainment World often follow suit: Madonna's brilliant adverteasing mix of sexual solicitation and refusal that generates seduction is a formula much pop music attempts to imitate. That presents a basic problem: if you want to crash the ruling fashionable Art Scene, you are almost forced to adopt its formulaic mantra and become derivative, yet with some kind of novel wrinkle. Museums, feeling guilty about their past Eurocentric bias and uncertain of how to include non-European art objects, have jettisoned the chronological compass and, like the Tate Modern, opted to organize expositions around themes. I do not deny that Anselm Kiefer, however unlikely a candidate, may even be a Cyrus bestriding the world's art galleries today, whose massive *High Priestess/Zweistromland* [#1] (1985–1989) facsimile of library carrels with books made of lead foil sheets so heavy you cannot lift one off the shelves—Western cultural history is no longer available as "cultural capital" to our amnesiac generation. Or his *Palmsonntag* (2007) [#91] piece of a huge helpless, uprooted fiber-glass palm tree surrounded by multiple panels of fragile grasses encased in dead lead frames—an ironic memento of Jesus' triumphal entry into Jerusalem: Kiefer is an odd but thought-provoking Cassandra in the current Artworld. But in my judgment, the Museumworld and especially the Artworld today by and large borders on being a self-centered, quite hermetic corporate commercial organization,[7] —which Power world U2 has breached with integ-

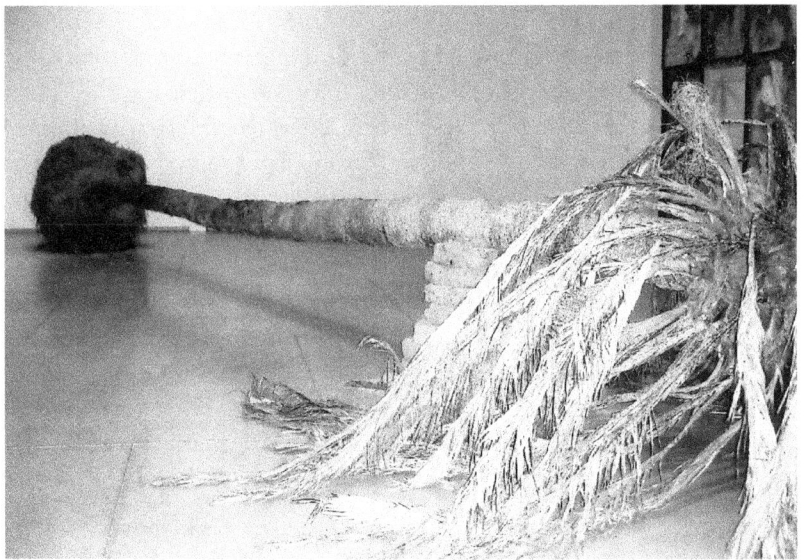

[#91] Anselm Kiefer, *Palmsonntag*

---

7   Sander Griffioen pinpoints the idolatrous yeast within the Artworld too in his 1981 writing, *Facing the New Corporatism*: "If there is no determination to assume responsibility for what it is and what it does, a company will become a self-seeking, self-centered organization, one that is only intent upon survival and growth" (6).

rity—and lesser artists might best look for alternatives to ply our trade.

The public social realm as channel for artistic service

The public civic sphere of societal life may be a more accessible institutional opening for artists to consider serving because it comes closest to letting one be a "free" cultural artistic agent with a home base and local opportunities. By a "public" realm today I mean **the legal fiction where private persons voluntarily meet openly with strangers for a common good**, although they may disagree on what and precisely how the matters should be accomplished. Frescoes were public on medieval church walls, although the confessor in his darkened booth might be looking over your shoulder. The Renaissance piazzas in cities of Italy were public places where even Jews could move about freely, although they may have needed a special license to live there. London England coffee houses in the 1700s were building a bourgeois public where, if you had the price of a coffee and enough education, you could meet to discuss articles in *The Tatler* and *The Spectator* papers. French Revolutionaries opened the king's art treasures for the *sans-culottes* and made the Louvre "public." That is, there are different "publics" over time—**free-willing associations of people assembled** not as citizens, not as believers, not as business persons, not necessarily as friends, but as neighbors and strangers to discuss something and to circulate opinions or at least agree to be somewhere together. Pick-up educational gatherings, rallies for "causes" where interactive communication is person-to-person and easy, are auxiliary sources conducive to an awareness of being "public."[8] Such predominantly voluntary social gatherings are publics, and many such placements today like reading libraries, hospitals, farmer markets, even precincts of cities, are threatened with privatization (at least in North America)—malls and cemeteries are land under private exclusionary entrepreneurial control.[9] So the public social sphere as well as the artworld and governments are susceptible to the destructive tidal wave of global Capitalistic Finance.

But I am suggesting that **we artists explore making public artworks and events in order to develop global networks where our ar-**

---

8   The crucial importance of civil society for the cultural development, along with schooling and media and art, for the well-being of the European Union is signaled in Bruno Machiels' article, "EZA and its Contacts with the Civil Society in Central and Eastern Europe," in *EZA Jahrbericht* 2001–2002, pp. 14–16.

9   We need to stretch "public" beyond Habermas's conditional requirement of rationality for an assembly to be "public," to include "irrational" outcasts. I agree there are problems: if destitute persons use the **public** city streets for **home** sleeping quarters instead of for walking and traveling, how do we work for civil public well-being instead of going punitive?

tistic gifts can find a voice. Peter S. Smith, as prize-winning member of the British Wood Engraving Society, can, in the line of Willem Claes-zoon, quietly engrave a massive tree only God could make that when felled in the Kew Gardens near his home by a whirlwind act of God had to be neatly sliced in pieces for men to be able to lay it to rest [*NA* #81]. It is a significant accomplishment that Britt Wikström's *Caritas* [#92] will soon be placed in the open market square of the Dutch village Deurne to honor the beloved, famed psy-chiatrist Anna Terruwe. I was glad to hear Jason Carter, rov-ing artistic ambassador for the British embassy to Near Eastern sites, ask on the internet, "How about doing a household con-cert in your neighborhood?" **It is crucial for artists to work with and in and for a commu-nity of sorts, lest one hang out alone to dry.**

That is, I suggest we chris-tian artists need to participate in professional art (guild) societies, search out civic commissions, stoop to serving NGO's and NPO's (Not-for-profit organiza-tions)—which still pay wages to persons for services rendered—we need to explore occasional paying gigs, as **an independent community** of composers, performers, or graphic artists, especially in urban settings. I know independent bookstores are in trouble, threatened with extinction by blockbuster global Amazon-ic corporate giants. And the instantaneous internet media and the allure of mass production/mass consumption

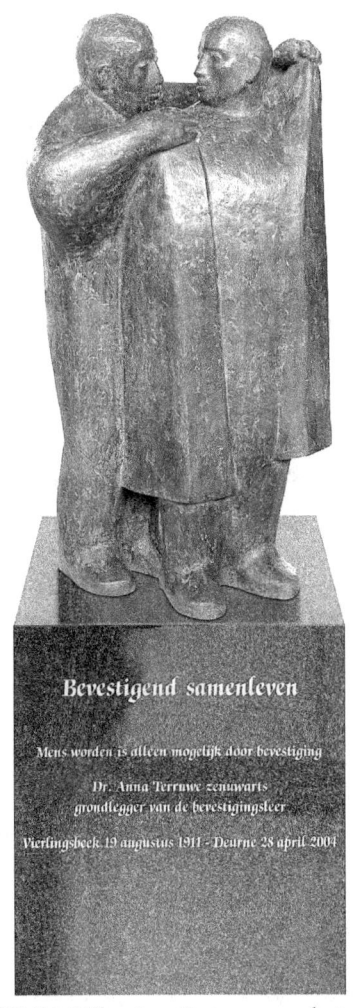

[#92] Brit Wikström, *Caritas, remembering in the village of Deurne, The Netherlands*

militates against **our remembering and cherishing that imaginative**

artistry-as-such is rooted in some kind of personal human manual dexterity. Actual manual/corporeal artistry will always remain in tension with the drive by TV and Facebook developments to be only **virtually** present. Just as the blessing of a caress by a loving human hand is unmatched by machines, so an artistic deed—like live theatre or being serenaded in song—that comforts an other fellow human going through rough times face-to-face is often worth more in its tangible presence than help delivered by check. We should not try to live nostalgically in times long past, but we may need to revalue our fantastic current instruments of screened interpersonal contact and structurally recoup the blessings of homespun, handmade artful gifts tuned actually and personally to the **imaginative bodily *needs* of our neighbors** (rather than on tending to distance desires imposed on them by the unseen powers in the air [cf. Ephesians 2:1–3]).

We may need to be wary, I think, of the phrase "cultural capital," lest it be a Trojan horse proffered by the all-absorbing Capitalist principality, which wants to **embed** artists like monetary digits in its global enterprises to make Big Profits, the way news reporters are now sometimes embedded in military armed conflicts, subtly confusing independent observers and fellow combatants. Yes, **it makes christian sense to encapsulate your professional art-making with appropriate institutional service**: hymns and banners and liturgical dances for Church worship services; anthems and monuments for the nation state; photographic portraits and videos for the family and friends; smart advertising art for businesses; lecturing-writing-doing installation art on site as artists or novelist-in-residence at a university; poster and logo production for media outlets; engaged in designing the style of clothing and formatting websites; inventing curious toys and convivial fascinations for city parks: there are multiple opportunities for a persevering artist to be true to artistic gifts and be institutionally employed—"cultural workers" indeed—even if the artist does not become poet laureate.

The cultural resources ("capital") that Christian Artists International represents is the kind of envisioning art community that, as resource, rightly but unusually includes clowns, philosophical aestheticians like myself whom performing artists will try to listen to, and critics, labor leaders, political representatives, potential patrons, a dance troupe, singers, designers, church observers, teachers—we are all in this matter of artistry and its societal task together! This "cultural capital" is meant to bring mustard seed, fruit-bearing interest. We christian artists are in a cosmic fracas beset by powers and principalities bigger than individual persons and roadblocks. There is systemic violence hidden in the societal complex we are living in that would idolize or bagatellize the modest task of making art-as-such. The brief but annual intense meetings of Christian Artists (Europe) International is quite unusual in taking a stand to say that **artistry-as-such is to be given its societal due in God's world**.

My hope is that Christian Artists International has spawned **communities** of christian artisans and artists throughout the European Union to develop from the ground up, in a myriad of ways, wholesome communal movements with diaconal art comparable to the way the Blues developed from its transplanted African troubles: artistry that will surround those who are hurting with an embrace of love rather than with a request for identification, and offering the laughter of hope fulfilled [*NA* #87] by the biblical Sarah (Genesis 18:9–15, 21:1–7) and known by sinful artistic saints who follow Jesus Christ and have heard God's promise of everlasting life (Revelation 19).[10] Each generation is only called upon to provide as faithfully as possible for the next generation an historical setting a little more redemptive for the tasks than the societal setting we have inherited. That lifelong calling requires patience but is a joyful adventure. Believe it or not, the broken Humpty-Dumpty of working artists in society will be put back together again someday as a blessing upon faithful imaginative serving, thank God!

Bibliography

Altet, Xavier Barral I., ed. *Artistes, Artisans et Production Artistique au Moyen Âge: Colloque international 1983*. Volume 1, *Les Hommes* (Paris: Picard, 1986).

Baldry, Harold. *The Case for the Arts* (London: Secker & Warburg, 1981).

Berengo, Marino. *L'Europa delle Città: Il volto della società urbana europea tra Medioevo ed Età moderna* (Turin: Einaudi, 1999).

Berlin, Michael. "Guilds in Decline? London livery companies and the rise of a liberal economy, 1600–1800," in *Guilds, Innovation, and the European Economy, 1400–1800,* eds. S.R. Epstein and M. Prak (Cambridge University Press, 2008), 316–341.

Campbell, Lorne. "The Art Market in the Southern Netherlands in the Fifteenth Century," in *Burlington Magazine* 188 (April 1976), 188–198.

Cayley, David. "The Origins of the Modern Public," 14-part series on *Ideas* hosted by Paul Kennedy on CBC radio, 26–30 April 26–30, 4, 12, 19, 26 May,

---

10 May I be so bold as to recommend that you christian artists become active with the hypocrites of a local church congregation, hard as that may be, so you will know who you are too as a member of Christ's worldwide body. You will find, I believe, once you get past the "praise God!" veneer that they too will respond to the "Blues" art you glocally provide for persons who are hurting and need hope.

2, 9, 16, 23, 30 June 2010.

Cohen, Jean L. and Andrew Arato. *Civil Society and Political Theory* (Cambridge: MIT Press, 1992).

Crouch, David J.F. *Piety, Fraternity and Power: Religious gilds in late medieval Yorkshire 1389–1547* (University of York Press, 2000).

Debray, Régis. "The Three Ages of Looking," trans. Eric Raulth, *Critical Inquiry* 21 (September 1955): 529–555.

Degrassi, Donata "Organizzazione di mestiere, corpi professionali e istituzioni alla fine del medioevo nell'Italia centro settentrionale," in *Le Regole dei Mestieri e delle Professioni, Secoli XV–XIX*, eds. Marco Meriggi and Alessandro Pastore (Milano: Franco Angeli, 2000), 17–35.

Epstein, S.R. "Craft Guilds, Apprenticeship and Technological Change in Pre-industrial Europe" (1998), in *Guilds, Innovation, and the European Economy 1400–1800*, eds. S.R. Epstein and Maarten Prak (Cambridge University Press, 2008), 52–80.

Eyck, F. Gunther. *The Voice of Nations: European national anthems and their authors* (London: Greenwood Press, 1995).

Floor, Willem. *Guilds, Merchants, and Ulama in Nineteenth-Century Iran* (Washington, DC: Mage, 2009).

Gablik, Suzi. *The Reenchantment of Art* (New York: Thames & Hudson, 1991).

Gauchet, Marcel. *The Disenchantment of the World: A political history of religion*, trans. Oscar Burge (Princeton University Press, 1997).

Griffioen, Sander. *Facing the New Corporatism* (Toronto: Christian Labour Association of Canada, 1981).

Habermas, Jürgen. "Öffentlichkeit," *Fischer-Lexikon*, eds. W.H. Friedrich and W. Killy (Frankfurt: Fischer Bücherei, 1964).

Hedgehog Review: Critical reflections on contemporary culture. "The Fate of the Arts," 6:2 (2004): 5–6.

Hobsbawn, E.J. *Labouring Men: Studies in the history of labour* (London: Weidenfeld and Nicolson, 1964).

Jeantet, Thierry. *L'économie Sociale: Une alternative au capitalisme* (Paris: Economica, 2008).

Kaufhold, Karl Heinrich. "Stadt und Handwerk. Zusammenfassung der wesentlichen Arbeitsergebnisse," in *Stadt und Handwerk im Mittelalter und Früher Neuzeit*, eds. Karl Heinrich Kaufhold und Wilfried Reininghaus (Köln: Böhlau, 2000).

Keat, Russell. *Cultural Goods and the Limits of the Market* (London: Macmillan, 2000).

Laurie, Bruce. *Artisans into Workers: Labor in nineteenth-century America* (New York: Noonday, 1989).

Little, Lester K. *Religious Poverty and the Profit Economy in Medieval Europe* (London: Paul Elek, 1978).

Loughman, John and John Michael Montias. *Public and Private Spaces: Works of art in seventeenth-century Dutch houses* (Zwolle: Waanders, 2000).

Malatesta, Maria. "Introduction: The Italian professions from a comparative perspective," in *Society and the Professions in Italy, 1860–1914*, ed. Maria Malatesta, trans. Adrian Belton (Cambridge University Press, 1995), 1–23.

Najemy, John M. "Guild Republicanism in Trecento Florence: The successes and ultimate failure of corporate politics," in *The American Historical Review*, 84:1 (1979): 53–71.

———.*Corporation and Consensus in Florentine Electoral Politics, 1280–1400* (Chapel Hill: University of North Carolina Press, 1982).

Northcote, Sydney. *Byrd to Britten: A survey of English song* (London: John Baker, 1966).

Our Creative Diversity: Report of the World Commission on Culture and Development, 2nd ed. (Paris: UNESCO, 1995).

Petersen, Nils Holger, Claus Cliver, and Nicolas Bel, eds. *Signs of Change: Transformations of Christian traditions and their representation in the arts, 1000–2000* (Amsterdam: Rodopi, 2000).

Pevsner, Nikolaus. *Academies of Art Past and Present* (Cambridge University Press, 1940).

Prak, Maarten. "Painters, Guilds, and the Art Market during the Dutch Golden Age," in *Guilds, Innovation, and the European Economy, 1400–1800,* eds. S.R. Epstein and M. Prak (Cambridge University Press, 2008), 143–171.

Preziosi, Donald. "Museology and Museography," in *The Art Bulletin* 77:1 (1995): 13–15.

———."The Art of Art History," in *The Art of Art History*, ed. D. Preziosi (New York: Oxford University Press, 1998), 507–525, 565–568.

Rifkin, Jeremy. *The End of Work: The decline of the global labor force and the dawn of the post-market era* (New York: G.P. Putnam's Sons, 1995).

Robbins, Bruce, ed. *The Phantom Public Sphere* (Minneapolis: University of Minnesota Press, 1993).

Roeck, Bernd. "Kunstpatronage in der Frühen Neuzeit," in *Kunstpatronage in der Frühen Neuzeit: Studien zu Kunstmarkt, Künstlern und ihren Auftraggebern in Italien und im Heiligen Römischen Reich (15.–17. Jahrhundert)* (Göttingen: Vandenhoeck & Ruprecht, 1999), 11–34.

———."Kunst und Öffentlichkeit in der Frühneuzeitlichen Stadt," in *Stadt und Region: Internationale Forschungen und Perspektiven*, eds. Heinz Duchhardt and Wilfried Reininghaus (Köln: Böhlau, 2005), 73–82.

Sachs, Albie. *Spring is Rebellious: Arguments about cultural freedom by Albie Sachs and respondents*, eds. Ingrid de Kok and Karen Press (Capetown: Buchu Books, 1990).

Scitovsky, Tibor. *Human Desire and Economic Satisfaction: Essays on the frontiers of economics* (Brighton: Wheatsheaf, 1986).

Schwartz, David T. *Art, Education, and the Democratic Commitment: A defense of state support for the arts* (Dordrecht: Kluwer, 2000).

Taylor, Mark C. *Nots* (University of Chicago Press, 1993).

Theroux, Paul. "Money and Art: The paradox of patronage," in *Harpers*

(September 1981): 31–40.

Thompson, Don. *The $12 Million Stuffed Shark: The curious economics of contemporary art* (Canada, Doubleday, 2008).

Thrupp, Sylvia L. "The Gilds," in *The Cambridge Economic History of Europe*, eds. M. M. Postan, E. E. Rich and Edward Miller (Cambridge University Press, 1963), 3:230–280.

Van Til, John. *Growing Civil Society: From nonprofit sector to third space* (Bloomington: Indiana University Press, 2000).

Vigiano, Valentina. "I 'mezzani' nella Palermo della prima metà del cinquecento: norme, pratiche, modelli aggregativi e reti fiduciarie," in *Le Regole dei Mestieri e delle Professioni, Secoli XV–XIX*, eds. Marco Meriggi and Alessandro Pastore (Milano: Franco Angeli, 2000), 346–363.

Wessels, Antonie. *Secularized Europe: Who will carry off its soul?* (Geneva: World Council of Churches, 1996).

Williams, Hwyn A. *Artisans and Sans-Culottes: Popular movements in France and Britain during the French Revolution* (London: Edward Arnold, 1968).

Williams, Raymond. *Culture and Society 1780–1950* (New York: Harper & Row, 1958).

Žižek, Slavoj. *The Fragile Absolute or, Why is the Christian Legacy worth fighting for?* (London: Verso, 2000).

List of illustrations■

© – copyright granted or purchased
AP – reproduced with the artist's permission
CS – photograph by Calvin Seerveld
CSU – © status unknown
PD – in the public domain

1   Anselm Kiefer, *Zweistromland, or The High Priestess* (1989), 200 lead
    books in 2 steel bookcases, with glass and copper wire, Astrup Fearnley
    Museet, Oslo. © Anselm Kiefer

2   Anselm Kiefer, *Nero Malt* (1974), oil on canvas, 220 x 300 cm,
    Staatsgalerie Moderner Kunst, München. © Anselm Kiefer

3   David Ruben Piqtoukun, *Death of a Tradition* (1992), Brazilian soapstone,
    African wonderstone, ivory. 21.3 x 45.5 x 15.2 cm. Private collection. AP

4   Henny van Hartingsveldt, *Mourning* (1992), stoneware 1200°, 50 x 50 x
    70 cm. Photo by Ben Vulkers. AP

5   Britt Wikström, *Jacob and the Angel* (1996), bronze, 60 x 80 cm,
    Psychiatric Hospital Wolfheze, Netherlands. AP

6   Julian Di Stefano, *Ornamental Hope* (1966), egg tempera on wood. AP

7   Julian Di Stefano, *Community of Saints* (1998), oil on canvas, 70 x 70 cm.
    AP

8   Henk (Senggih) Krijger, *Estranged* (1963), final painting in Anna Blaman
    series of 8, 17¼ x 23½ in. CS

9   James Ensor, *Christ's Entry into Brussels in 1889* (1888), oil on canvas,
    252.5 x 430.5 cm, Paul Getty Museum. PD

10 Warren Breninger, *Gates of Prayer* (1993–2008) [detail]. AP

11 Nicolas Poussin, *The Exposition of Moses* (1654), oil on canvas, 150 x 204
    cm, Ashmolean Museum, Oxford. PD

12 Johannes Vermeer, *Woman Holding a Balance* (c. 1664), 42 x 35.5 cm,
    Washington, D.C. National Gallery of Art. PD

13 Joan Cots (1927–2004), *Stele*. CS taken in 1995 in the artist's workshop/
    studio in Torrelles de Llobregat, Province of Barcelona, Spain. AP

14 Joyce Recker, *Shadows Crossing* (1992), torn paper. AP

15 Britt Wikström, *Wim de Mol* gravestone (1983), chiseled granite, Essenhof
    Cemetery, Dordrecht, The Netherlands. AP

■   Links to many of these illustrations in full color can be easily accessed at
    www.dordt.edu/DCPimagesSeerveld

16 Ernst Barlach, *Das Wiedersehen* (1926), walnut wood, 103 x 40 x 26 cm, Ernst Barlach House, Hamburg. Photo by Rufus46. CC

17 Anselm Kiefer, *Kranke Kunst* [Sick Art] (1974), watercolor, gouache, and ball point pen on paper, 20 x 23.8 cm, Metropolitan Museum of Art. © Anselm Kiefer

18 Peter S. Smith, *Working Late* (1986), wood engraving, 76 x 102 mm. AP

19 Emile Nolde, *Heilige Nacht* (1912). © Nolde Stiftung Seebüll

20 Emile Nolde, *Verlorenes Paradies* (1921). © Nolde Stiftung Seebüll

21 Sunday school card for memorizing texts (1930s), USA. CS

22 Emile Nolde, *Christus und die Kinder* (1910), oil on canvas, 86.7 x 106.4 cm, Museum of Modern Art. © Nolde Stiftung Seebüll

23 Anselm Kiefer, *Jeder Mensch steht unter seiner Himmelskugel* [Everyone Stands Under His Own Dome of Heaven] (1970), watercolor, gouache, and graphite pencil on joined paper, 15.75 x 18.88 in, Metropolitan Museum of Art, Denise and Andrew Saul Fund, 1995. © Anselm Kiefer

24 Friedensreich Hundertwasser, ⟨151⟩, *Bleeding Houses* (1952), mixed media. © 2013 Hundertwasser Archive, Vienna

25 Friedensreich Hundertwasser, ⟨166⟩, *On the Sunny side of the Street* (1953), oil on plywood. © 2013 Hundertwasser Archive, Vienna

26 Friedensreich Hundertwasser, ⟨763⟩, *Rainbowhouse* (1977), mixed media. © 2013 Hundertwasser Archive, Vienna

27 Britt Wikström, *Jacob and the Angel* (1996), bronze cast, 60 x 80 cm, Psychiatric Hospital, Wolfheze. AP

28 Papua New Guinea missionaries teaching Jesus to the nations (1960s). Photo by Peter S. Smith.

29 Watanabe Sadao, *Kiku* [*Listening*] (1960), momigami, 21½ x 15 in. CSU

30 David Ruben Piqtoukun, *Drawing Out Evils* (1995), Brazilian soapstone, African wonderstone, and sinew, 25.2 x 34.7 x 19.5. Private collection. AP

31 Stanley Peters, *Totem Cross* (1975), poplar wood, 9½ x 6½ foot. CSU

32–36 Duane Michals, *The Return of the Prodigal Son* (1982), 5 gelatin silver prints, 13 x 18 cm, Henry L. Hillman Fund. CSU

37 Traditional Ankle Bracelet/Fetter, Niger, Africa (1970). Gift from Dr. Philip Westra to Inès and Calvin Seerveld. CS

38 Henry Moore, *Reclining Figure,* outside UNESCO Building in Paris (1957–58). Reproduced by permission of The Henry Moore Foundation

39 Johannes Vermeer, *Melkmeisje* (c. 1658–61), oil on canvas, 45.5 x 41 cm, Rijksmuseum, Amsterdam. PD

62 Temple of Poseidon ruins at Cape Sounion, Greece (1990). CS

63 Köln Cathedral. CS (1954)

64 Swabian Master carver, *Maria expecting* (1500s), wood, Liebieghaus, Frankfurt am Main, Germany. PD

65 Middle Rhineland carver, *Vesperbild, Mary mourning over the dead Christ* (c.1390), Liebieghaus, Frankfurt am Main, Germany. PD

66 Gargoyle high up on Notre Dame Cathedral, Paris (c. 1200). CS

67 Middle Rhineland Master carver, *Holy Augustine (?)* (1489–96), wood, Liebieghaus, Frankfurt am Main, Germany. PD

68 Luca della Robbia, panel decorating the *Cantoria* [singers' gallery] (1431–1438), which is actually a balcony for the 1438 organ of the Duomo, marble, Museo dell'Opera del Duomo, Florence, Italy. PD

69 Leonardo da Vinci, *Studies of Embryos* (1510–1513), pen over red chalk. PD

70 Bernini, Baldachino over the main altar (1633), bronze, 30 feet, St. Peter's Cathedral. CS

71 Titian, *Venus and the Organ Player* (c. 1550), oil on canvas, 115 x 210 cm, Gemaldegalerie, Berlin. PD

72 Philippe de Champaigne, *Cardinal de Richelieu* (c. 1640), oil on canvas, 260 x 178 cm. PD

73 Nicolas Poussin, *The Adoration of the Golden Calf* (1633–1634), oil on canvas, 154 x 214 cm, The National Gallery, U.K. PD

74 Gardens of Versailles, France, conceived by André Le Nôtre (beginning in 1661). PD

75 Jean-Baptiste-Simeon Chardin, *Pipe and Jug* (1737), 32.5 x 40 cm, Louvre Museum, Paris. PD

76 Antoine Watteau, *Pèlerinage à l'île de Cythère* (1717), oil on canvas, 129 x 194 cm, Louvre Museum, Paris. PD

77 Joshua Reynolds, *General Eliott, Baron Heathfield of Gibraltar* (1787), oil on canvas, National Gallery, London. PD

78 William Hogarth, *The Graham Children* (1737), oil on canvas, National Gallery, U.K. PD

79 Jacques-Louis David, *Oath of the Horatii* (1786), oil on canvas, Toledo Museum of Art. PD

80 Lamp and lampshade made of Tiffany glass, 1890–1900. Louis Comfort Tiffany / The Duffner and Kimberly Company. Photo by Yelkrokoyade. CC

The image on page 117 was prepared by Ana Feliciano.

Index

Brief Biography

Although Dr. Seerveld is born American and has become a Canadian citizen, he is husband to Dutch born Inès Cecile Naudin ten Cate, and spent five formative years as a graduate student in Europe (1953–1958). His research sabbaticals have been spent at Heidelberg Universität studying with Gerhard von Rad, Claus Westermann, and Hans Georg Gadamer (1966–1967), in the musea of München (1981), in the archives of the Bibliothèque Nationale in Paris working on Watteau (1986), and until recently he has been a frequent summer reader every couple years at the Warburg Institute, University of London, since 1973. So Seerveld has a European penchant for multiple languages and the history of Western culture.

He was privileged to be a recurrent plenary speaker at the Christian Artists International conferences held annually in the Netherlands, organized by Leen la Riviere, and sponsored by the European Union through its various labor affiliates, such as the Dutch Christelijk Nationaal Vakverbond and the German Europäischen Zentrum fur Arbeitnehmerfragen. The ferment of different European nations, with various national cultures, struggling to discover what economic, and possibly political, integration might entail for artist unions in the different countries is practically a mandala for the troubles and opportunities facing working, professional artists in Western society. This series of lectures by Seerveld was given from 1997–2010. www.seerveld.com/tuppence.html

www.ingramcontent.com/pod-product-compliance
Lightning Source LLC
Chambersburg PA
CBHW071258220526
45468CB00001B/186